AMIEL'S JOURNAL

AMIEL'S JOURNAL

THE JOURNAL INTIME

OF

HENRI-FRÉDÉRIC AMIEL

TRANSLATED

WITH AN INTRODUCTION AND NOTES

BY

MRS. HUMPHRY WARD

Author of "The History of David Grieve," etc.

WITH A PORTRAIT

VOL. II.

NEW YORK
THE MACMILLAN COMPANY
LONDON: MACMILLAN & CO., LTD.
1900

All rights reserved

COPYRIGHT, 1893,

By MACMILLAN AND CO.

First Edition (2 Vols. Globe 8vo) 1885. Second Edition (1 Vol. Crown 8vo) 1888. Reprinted 1889; January and October, 1890; March and September, 1891, 1892; January and April, 1893; January, August, 1894; August, 1895; February, 1896; October, 1897; March, 1899; July, 1900.

Norwood Press:
J. S. Cushing & Co. — Berwick & Smith.
Boston, Mass., U.S.A.

AMIEL'S JOURNAL.

VOL. II.

[Where no other name is mentioned, Geneva is to be understood as the author's place of residence.]

11th April 1868 (*Mornex sur Salève*).— I left town in a great storm of wind, which was raising clouds of dust along the suburban roads, and two hours later I found myself safely installed among the mountains, just like last year. I think of staying a week here. . . . The sounds of the village are wafted to my open window, barkings of distant dogs, voices of women at the fountain, the songs of birds in the lower orchards. The green carpet of the plain is dappled by passing shadows thrown upon it by the clouds; the landscape has the charm of delicate tint and a sort of languid grace. Already I am full of a sense of wellbeing, I am tasting the joys of that contemplative state in which the soul, issuing from itself, becomes as it were the soul of a country or a landscape, and feels living within it a multitude of lives. Here is no more resistance, negation, blame; everything is affirmative; I feel myself in harmony with nature and with surroundings, of which I seem to myself the expression. The heart opens to the immensity of things. This is what I love! *Nam mihi res, non me rebus submittere conor.*

12th April 1868 (*Easter Day*), *Mornex, Eight* A.M. — The day has opened solemnly and religiously. There is a tinkling of bells from the valley : even the fields seem to be breathing forth a canticle of praise. — Humanity must have a worship, and, all things considered, is not the Christian worship the best amongst those which have existed on a large scale? The religion of sin, of repentance, and reconciliation — the religion of the new birth and of eternal life — is not a religion to be ashamed of. In spite of all the aberrations of fanaticism, all the superstitions of formalism, all the ugly superstructures of hypocrisy, all the fantastic puerilities of theology, the Gospel has modified the world and consoled mankind. Christian humanity is not much better than Pagan humanity, but it would be much worse without a religion, and without this religion. Every religion proposes an ideal and a model; the Christian ideal is sublime, and its model of a divine beauty. We may hold aloof from the churches, and yet bow ourselves before Jesus. We may be suspicious of the clergy, and refuse to have anything to do with catechisms, and yet love the Holy and the Just, who came to save and not to curse. Jesus will always supply us with the best criticism of Christianity, and when Christianity has passed away the religion of Jesus will in all probability survive. After Jesus as God we shall come back to faith in the God of Jesus.

Five o'clock P.M. — I have been for a long walk through Cézargues, Eseri, and the Yves woods, returning by the Pont du Loup. The weather was cold and gray. — A great popular merrymaking of some sort, with its multitude of blouses, and its drums and fifes, has been going on riotously for an hour under my window. The crowd has sung a number of songs, drinking songs, ballads, romances, but all more or less heavy and ugly. The muse has never touched our country people, and the Swiss race is not graceful even in its gaiety. A bear in high spirits — this is what one thinks of. The poetry it produces too is desperately vulgar and commonplace. Why? In the first place, because, in spite of the pretences of our democratic philosophies, the classes whose backs are bent with manual labour are æsthetically inferior to the others. In the next place, because our old rustic peasant poetry is dead, and the peasant, when he tries to share the music or the poetry of the cultivated classes, only succeeds in caricaturing it, and not in copying it. Democracy, by laying it down that there is but one class for all men, has in fact done a wrong to everything that is not first-rate. As we can no longer without offence judge men according to a certain recognised order, we can only compare them to the best that exists, and then they naturally seem to us more mediocre, more ugly, more deformed than before. If the passion for equality potentially raises the average, it *really* degrades nineteen-twentieths of individuals below their former place. There is a progress in the domain of law and a falling back in the domain of art. And meanwhile the artists see multiplying before them their *bête-noire*, the *bourgeois*, the Philistine, the presumptuous ignoramus, the quack who plays at science, and the feather-brain who thinks himself the equal of the intelligent.

'Commonness will prevail,' as De Candolle said in speaking of the graminaceous plants. The era of equality means the triumph of mediocrity. It is disappointing, but inevitable; for it is one of time's revenges. Humanity, after having organised itself on the basis of the dissimilarity of individuals, is now organising itself on the basis of their similarity, and the one exclusive principle is about as true as the other. Art no doubt will lose, but justice will gain. Is not universal levelling-down the law of nature, and when all has been levelled will not all have been destroyed? So that the world is striving with all its force for the destruction of what it has itself brought forth! Life is the blind pursuit of its own negation; as has been said of the wicked, nature also works for her own disappointment, she labours at what she hates, she weaves her own shroud, and piles up the stones of her own tomb. God may well forgive us, for 'we know not what we do.'

Just as the sum of force is always identical in the material universe, and presents a spectacle not of diminution nor of augmentation but simply of constant metamorphosis, so it is not impossible that the sum of good is in reality always the same, and that therefore all progress on one side is compensated inversely on another side. If this were so we ought never to say that period or a people is absolutely and as a whole superior to another time or another people, but only that there is superiority in certain points. The great difference between man and man would, on these principles, consist in the art of transforming vitality into spirituality, and latent power into useful energy. The same difference would hold good between nation and nation, so that the object of the simultaneous or successive competition of mankind in history would be the extraction of the maximum of humanity from a given amount of animality. Education, morals, and politics would be only variations of the same art, the art of living — that is to say, of disengaging the pure form and subtlest essence of our individual being.

26th April 1868 (*Sunday, Mid-day*). — A gloomy morning. On all sides a depressing outlook, and within, disgust with self.

Ten P.M. — Visits and a walk. I have spent the evening alone. Many things to-day have taught me lessons of wisdom. I have seen the hawthorns covering themselves with blossom, and the whole valley springing up afresh under the breath of the spring. I have been the spectator of faults of conduct on the part of old men who will not grow old, and whose heart is in rebellion against the natural law. I have watched the working of marriage in its frivolous and commonplace forms, and listened to trivial preaching. I have been a witness of griefs without hope, of loneliness that claimed one's pity. I have listened to pleasantries on the subject of madness, and to the merry songs of the birds. And everything has had the same message for me : 'Place yourself once more in harmony with the universal law; accept the will of God; make a religious use of life; work while it is yet day ; be at once serious and cheerful; know how to repeat with the Apostle, "I have learned in whatsoever state I am therewith to be content."'

26th August 1868. — After all the storms of feeling within and the organic disturbances without, which during these latter months have pinned me so closely to my own individual existence, shall I ever be able to reascend into the region of pure intelligence, to enter again upon the disinterested and impersonal life, to recover my old indifference towards subjective miseries, and regain a purely scientific and contemplative state of mind? Shall I ever succeed in forgetting all the needs which bind me to earth and to humanity? Shall I ever become pure spirit? Alas! I cannot persuade myself to believe it possible for an instant. I see infirmity and weakness close upon me, I feel I cannot do without affection, and I know that I have no ambition, and that my faculties are declining. I remember that I am forty-seven years old, and that all my brood of youthful hopes has flown away. So that there is no deceiving myself as to the fate which awaits me: — increasing loneliness, mortification of spirit, long-continued regret, melancholy neither to be consoled nor confessed, a mournful old age, a slow decay, a death in the desert!

Terrible dilemma! Whatever is still possible to me has lost its savour, while all that I could still desire escapes me, and will always escape me. Every impulse ends in weariness and disappointment. Discouragement, depression, weakness, apathy: there is the dismal series which must be for ever begun and re-begun, while we are still rolling up the Sisyphean rock of life. Is it not simpler and shorter to plunge head-foremost into the gulf?

No, rebel as we may, there is but one solution — to submit to the general order, to accept, to resign ourselves, and to do still what we can. It is our self-will, our aspirations, our dreams, that must be sacrificed. We must give up the hope of happiness once for all! Immolation of the self — death to self, — this is the only suicide which is either useful or permitted. In my present mood of indifference and disinterestedness, there is some secret ill-humour, some wounded pride, a little rancour; there is selfishness in short, since a premature claim for rest is implied in it. Absolute disinterestedness is only reached in that perfect humility which tramples the self under foot for the glory of God.

I have no more strength left, I wish for nothing; but that is not what is wanted. I must wish what God wishes; I must pass from indifference to sacrifice, and from sacrifice to self-devotion. The cup which I would fain put away from me is the misery of living, the shame of existing and suffering as a common creature who has missed his vocation; it is the bitter and increasing humiliation of declining power, of growing old under the weight of one's own disapproval, and the disappointment of one's friends! 'Wilt thou be healed?' was the text of last Sunday's sermon. 'Come to me, all ye who are weary and heavy laden, and I will give you rest.' — 'And if our heart condemn us, God is greater than our heart.'

27th August 1868. — To-day I took up the *Penseroso*[1] again. I have often violated its maxims and forgotten its lessons. Still, this volume is a true son of my soul, and breathes the true spirit of the inner life. Whenever I wish to revive my consciousness of my own tradition, it is pleasant to me to read over this little gnomic collection which has had such scant justice done to it, and which, were it another's, I should often quote. I like to feel that in it I have attained to that relative truth which may be defined as consistency with self, the harmony of appearance with reality, of thought with expression, — in other words, sincerity, ingenuousness, inwardness. It is personal experience in the strictest sense of the word.

21st September 1868 (*Villars*).—A lovely autumn effect. Everything was veiled in gloom this morning, and a gray mist of rain floated between us and the whole circle of mountains. Now the strip of blue sky which made its appearance at first behind the distant peaks has grown larger, has mounted to the zenith, and the dome of heaven, swept almost clear of cloud, sends streaming down upon us the pale rays of a convalescent sun. The day now promises kindly, and all is well that ends well.

Thus after a season of tears a sober and softened joy may return to us. Say to yourself that you are entering upon the autumn of your life ; that the graces of spring and the splendours of summer are irrevocably gone, but that autumn too has its beauties. The autumn weather is often darkened by rain, cloud, and mist, but the air is still soft, and the sun still delights the eyes, and touches the yellowing leaves caressingly : it is the time for fruit, for harvest, for the vintage, the moment for making provision for the winter. — Here

After belief comes judgment; but a believer is not a judge. A fish lives in the ocean, but it cannot see all round it; it cannot take a view of the whole: therefore it cannot judge what the ocean is. In order to understand Christianity we must put it in its historical place in its proper framework; we must regard it as a part of the religious development of humanity, and so judge it, not from a Christian point of view, but from a human point of view, *sine ira nec studio.*

16*th December* 1868. — I am in the most painful state of anxiety as to my poor kind friend, Charles Heim. . . . Since the 30th November I have had no letter from the dear invalid, who then said his last farewell to me. How long these two weeks have seemed to me, — and how keenly I have realised that strong craving which many feel for the last words, the last looks, of those they love! Such words and looks are a kind of testament. They have a solemn and sacred character which is not merely an effect of our imagination. For that which is on the brink of death already participates to some extent in eternity. A dying man seems to speak to us from beyond the tomb; what he says has the effect upon us of a sentence, an oracle, an injunction; we look upon him as one endowed with second sight. Serious and solemn words come naturally to the man who feels life escaping him, and the grave opening before him. The depths of his nature are then revealed; the Divine within him need no longer hide itself. Oh! do not let us wait to be just or pitiful or demonstrative towards those we love until they or we are struck down by illness or threatened with death! Life is short, and we have never too much time for gladdening the hearts of those who are travelling the dark journey with us. Oh, be swift to love, make haste to be kind!

26th December 1868. — My dear friend died this morning at Hyères. A beautiful soul has returned to heaven. So he has ceased to suffer! Is he happy now?

. . . . . .

If men are always more or less deceived on the subject of women, it is because they forget that they and women do not speak altogether the same language, and that words have not the same weight or the same meaning for them, especially in questions of feeling. Whether from shyness or precaution or artifice, a woman never speaks out her whole thought, and moreover what she herself knows of it is but a part of what it really is. Complete frankness seems to be impossible to her, and complete self-knowledge seems to be forbidden her. If she is a sphinx to us, it is because she is a riddle of doubtful meaning even to herself. She has no need of perfidy, for she is mystery itself. A woman is something fugitive, irrational, indeterminable, illogical, and contradictory. A great deal of forbearance ought to be shown her, and a good deal of prudence exercised with regard to her, for she may bring about innumerable evils without knowing it. Capable of all kinds of devotion, and of all kinds of treason, '*monstre incompréhensible*,' raised to the second power, she is at once the delight and the terror of man.

• • • • •

The more a man loves, the more he suffers. The sum of possible grief for each soul is in proportion to its degree of perfection.

• • • • •

He who is too much afraid of being duped has lost the power of being magnanimous.

• • • • •

Doubt of the reality of love ends by making us doubt everything. The final result of all deceptions and disappointments is atheism, which may not always yield up its name and secret, but which lurks, a masked spectre, within the depths of thought, as the last supreme explainer. 'Man is what his love is,' and follows the fortunes of his love.

. . . .

The beautiful souls of the world have an art of saintly alchemy, by which bitterness is converted into kindness, the gall of human experience into gentleness, ingratitude into benefits, insults into pardon. And the transformation ought to become so easy and habitual that the lookers-on may think it spontaneous, and nobody give us credit for it.

27th January 1869. — What, then, is the service rendered to the world by Christianity? The proclamation of 'good news.' And what is this 'good news'? The pardon of sin. The God of holiness loving the world and reconciling it to Himself by Jesus, in order to establish the kingdom of God, the city of souls, the life of heaven upon earth, — here you have the whole of it; but in this is a revolution. 'Love ye one another, as I have loved you;' 'Be ye one with me, as I am one with the Father:' for this is life eternal, here is perfection, salvation, joy. Faith in the fatherly love of God, who punishes and pardons for our good, and who desires not the death of the sinner, but his conversion and his life, — here is the motive power of the redeemed.

What we call Christianity is a vast ocean, into which flow a number of spiritual currents of distant and various origin; certain religions, that is to say, of Asia and of Europe, the great ideas of Greek wisdom, and especially those of Platonism. Neither its doctrine nor its morality, as they have been historically developed, are new or spontaneous. What is essential and original in it is the practical demonstration that the human and the divine nature may co-exist, may become fused into one sublime flame; that holiness and pity, justice and mercy, may meet together and become one, in man and in God. What is specific in Christianity is Jesus — the religious consciousness of Jesus. The sacred sense of his absolute union with God through perfect love and self-surrender, this profound, invincible, and tranquil faith of his, has become a religion; the faith of Jesus has become the faith of millions and millions of men. From this torch has sprung a vast conflagration. And such has been the brilliancy and the radiance both of revealer and revelation, that the astonished world has forgotten its justice in its admiration, and has referred to one single benefactor the whole of those benefits which are its heritage from the past.

The conversion of ecclesiastical and confessional Christianity into historical Christianity is the work of Biblical science. The conversion of historical Christianity into philosophical Christianity is an attempt which is to some extent an illusion, since faith cannot be entirely resolved into science. The transference, however, of Christianity from the region of history to the region of psychology is the great craving of our time. What we are trying to arrive at is the *eternal* Gospel. But before we can reach it, the comparative history and philosophy of religions must assign to Christianity its true place, and must judge it. The religion too which Jesus professed must be disentangled from the religion which has taken Jesus for its object. And when at last we are able to point out the state of consciousness which is the primitive cell, the principle of the eternal Gospel, we shall have reached our goal, for in it is the *punctum saliens* of pure religion.

Perhaps the extraordinary will take the place of the supernatural, and the great geniuses of the world will come to be regarded as the messengers of God in history, as the providential revealers through whom the spirit of God works upon the human mass. What is perishing is not the admirable and the adorable; it is simply the arbitrary, the accidental, the miraculous. Just as the poor illuminations of a village *fête*, or the tapers of a procession, are put out by the great marvel of the sun, so the small local miracles, with their meanness and doubtfulness, will sink into insignificance beside the law of the world of spirits, the incomparable spectacle of human history, led by that all-powerful Dramaturgus whom we call God. — *Utinam!*

1st March 1869. — Impartiality and objectivity are as rare as justice, of which they are but two special forms. Self-interest is an inexhaustible source of convenient illusions. The number of beings who wish to see truly is extraordinarily small. What governs men is the fear of truth, unless truth is useful to them, which is as much as to say that self-interest is the principle of the common philosophy, or that truth is made for us but not we for truth. — As this fact is humiliating, the majority of people will neither recognise nor admit it. And thus a prejudice of self-love protects all the prejudices of the understanding, which are themselves the result of a stratagem of the *ego*. Humanity has always slain or persecuted those who have disturbed this selfish repose of hers. She only improves in spite of herself. The only progress which she desires is an increase of enjoyments. All advances in justice, in morality, in holiness, have been imposed upon or forced from her by some noble violence. Sacrifice, which is the passion of great souls, has never been the law of societies. It is too often by employing one vice against another, — for example, vanity against cupidity, greed against idleness, — that the great agitators have broken through routine. In a word, the human world is almost entirely directed by the law of nature, and the law of the spirit, which is the leaven of its coarse paste, has but rarely succeeded in raising it into generous expansion.

From the point of view of the ideal, humanity is *triste* and ugly. But if we compare it with its probable origins, we see that the human race has not altogether wasted its time. Hence there are three possible views of history: the view of the pessimist, who starts from the ideal; the view of the optimist, who compares the past with the present; and the view of the hero-worshipper, who sees that all progress whatever has cost oceans of blood and tears.

European hypocrisy veils its face before the voluntary suicide of those Indian fanatics who throw themselves under the wheels of their goddess's triumphal car. And yet these sacrifices are but the symbol of what goes on in Europe as elsewhere, of that offering of their life which is made by the martyrs of all great causes. We may even say that the fierce and sanguinary goddess is humanity itself, which is only spurred to progress by remorse, and repents only when the measure of its crimes runs over. The fanatics who sacrifice themselves are an eternal protest against the universal selfishness. We have only overthrown those idols which are tangible and visible, but perpetual sacrifice still exists everywhere, and everywhere the *élite* of each generation suffers for the salvation of the multitude. It is the austere, bitter, and mysterious law of solidarity. Perdition and redemption in and through each other is the destiny of men.

18*th March* 1869 (*Thursday*). — Whenever I come back from a walk outside the town I am disgusted and repelled by this cell of mine. Out of doors sunshine, birds, spring, beauty, and life ; in here, ugliness, piles of paper, melancholy, and death. — And yet my walk was one of the saddest possible. I wandered along the Rhone and the Arve, and all the memories of the past, all the disappointments of the present, and all the anxieties of the future, laid siege to my heart like a whirlwind of phantoms. I took account of my faults, and they ranged themselves in battle against me. The vulture of regret gnawed at my heart, and the sense of the irreparable choked me like the iron collar of the pillory. It seemed to me that I had failed in the task of life, and that now life was failing me. — Ah ! how terrible spring is to the lonely ! All the needs which had been lulled to sleep start into life again, all the sorrows which had disappeared are reborn, and the old man which had been gagged and conquered rises once more and makes his groans heard. It is as though all the old wounds opened and bewailed themselves afresh. Just when one had ceased to think, when one had succeeded in deadening feeling by work or by amusement, all of a sudden the heart, solitary captive that it is, sends a cry from its prison depths, a cry which shakes to its foundations the whole surrounding edifice.

Even supposing that one had freed oneself from all other fatalities, there is still one yoke left from which it is impossible to escape — that of Time. I have succeeded in avoiding all other servitudes, but I had reckoned without the last — the servitude of age. Age comes, and its weight is equal to that of all other oppressions taken together. Man, under his mortal aspect, is but a species of ephemera. As I looked at the banks of the Rhone, which have seen the river flowing past them some ten or twenty thousand years, or at the trees forming the avenue of the cemetery, which, for two centuries, have been the witnesses of so many funeral processions; as I recognised the walls, the dykes, the paths, which saw me playing as a child, and watched other children running over that grassy plain of Plain Palais which bore my own childish steps, — I had the sharpest sense of the emptiness of life and the flight of things. I felt the shadow of the upas tree darkening over me. I gazed into the great implacable abyss in which are swallowed up all those phantoms which call themselves living beings. I saw that the living are but apparitions hovering for a moment over the earth, made out of the ashes of the dead, and swiftly re-absorbed by eternal night, as the will-o'-the-wisp sinks into the marsh. The nothingness of our joys, the emptiness of our existence, and the futility of our ambitions, filled me with a quiet disgust. From regret to disenchantment I floated on to Buddhism, to universal weariness. — Ah, the hope of a blessed immortality would be better worth having!

With what different eyes one looks at life at ten, at twenty, at thirty, at sixty! Those who live alone are specially conscious of this psychological metamorphosis. Another thing, too, astonishes them; it is the universal conspiracy which exists for hiding the sadness of the world, for making men forget suffering, sickness, and death, for smothering the wails and sobs which issue from every house, for painting and beautifying the hideous face of reality. Is it out of tenderness for childhood and youth, or is it simply from fear, that we are thus careful to veil the sinister truth? Or is it from a sense of equity? and does life contain as much good as evil — perhaps more? However it may be, men feed themselves rather upon illusion than upon truth. Each one unwinds his own special reel of hope, and as soon as he has come to the end of it he sits him down to die, and lets his sons and his grandsons begin the same experience over again. We all pursue happiness, and happiness escapes the pursuit of all.

The only *viaticum* which can help us in the journey of life is that furnished by a great duty and some serious affections. And even affections die, or at least their objects are mortal; a friend, a wife, a child, a country, a church, may precede us in the tomb; duty alone lasts as long as we.

This maxim exorcises the spirits of revolt, of anger, discouragement, vengeance, indignation, and ambition, which rise one after another to tempt and trouble the heart, swelling with the sap of the spring. — O all ye saints of the East, of antiquity, of Christianity, phalanx of heroes! — Ye too drank deep of weariness and agony of soul, but ye triumphed over both. Ye who have come forth victors from the strife, shelter us under your palms, fortify us by your example!

6th April 1869. — Magnificent weather. The Alps are dazzling under their silver haze. Sensations of all kinds have been crowding upon me; the delights of a walk under the rising sun, the charms of a wonderful view, longing for travel, and thirst for joy, hunger for work, for emotion, for life, dreams of happiness and of love. A passionate wish to live, to feel, to express, stirred the depths of my heart. It was a sudden re-awakening of youth, a flash of poetry, a renewing of the soul, a fresh growth of the wings of desire. I was overpowered by a host of conquering, vagabond, adventurous aspirations. I forgot my age, my obligations, my duties, my vexations, and youth leapt within me as though life were beginning again. It was as though something explosive had caught fire, and one's soul were scattered to the four winds; in such a mood one would fain devour the whole world, experience everything, see everything. Faust's ambition enters into one, universal desire, — a horror of one's own prison cell. One throws off one's hair shirt, and one would fain gather the whole of nature into one's arms and heart. O ye passions, a ray of sunshine is enough to rekindle you all! The cold black mountain is a volcano once more, and melts its snowy crown with one single gust of flaming breath. It is the spring which brings about these sudden and improbable resurrections, the spring which, sending a thrill and tumult of life through all that lives, is the parent of impetuous desires, of overpowering inclinations, of unforeseen and inextinguishable outbursts of passion. It breaks through the rigid bark of the trees, and rends the mask on the face of asceticism; it makes the monk tremble in the shadow of his convent, the maiden behind the curtains of her room, the child sitting on his school bench, the old man bowed under his rheumatism.

'O Hymen, Hymenæe!'

24th April 1869. — Is Nemesis indeed more real than Providence, the jealous God more true than the good God? — grief more certain than joy? — darkness more secure of victory than light? Is it pessimism or optimism which is nearest the truth, and which — Leibnitz or Schopenhauer — has best understood the universe? Is it the healthy man or the sick man who sees best to the bottom of things? which is in the right?

Ah! the problem of grief and evil is and will be always the greatest enigma of being, only second to the existence of being itself. The common faith of humanity has assumed the victory of good over evil. But if good consists not in the result of victory, but in victory itself, then good implies an incessant and infinite contest, interminable struggle, and a success for ever threatened. And if this is life, is not Buddha right in regarding life as synonymous with evil, since it means perpetual restlessness and endless war? Repose according to the Buddhist is only to be found in annihilation. The art of self-annihilation, of escaping the world's vast machinery of suffering, and the misery of renewed existence, — the art of reaching Nirvâna, is to him the supreme art, the only means of deliverance. The Christian says to God: Deliver us from evil. The Buddhist adds: And to that end deliver us from finite existence, give us back to nothingness! The first believes that when he is enfranchised from the body he will enter upon eternal happiness; the second believes that individuality is the obstacle to all repose, and he longs for the dissolution of the soul itself. The dread of the first is the Paradise of the second.

One thing only is necessary, — the committal of the soul to God. Look that thou thyself art in order, and leave to God the task of unravelling the skein of the world and of destiny. What do annihilation or immortality matter? What is to be, will be. And what will be, will be for the best. Faith in good, — perhaps the individual wants nothing more for his passage through life. Only he must have taken sides with Socrates, Plato, Aristotle, and Zeno, against materialism, against the religion of accident and pessimism. Perhaps also he must make up his mind against the Buddhist nihilism, because a man's system of conduct is diametrically opposite according as he labours to increase his life or to lessen it, according as he aims at cultivating his faculties or at systematically deadening them.

To employ one's individual efforts for

the increase of good in the world, — this modest ideal is enough for us. To help forward the victory of good has been the common aim of saints and sages. *Socii Dei sumus* was the word of Seneca, who had it from Cleanthus.

30th April 1869. — I have just finished Vacherot's [3] book (*La Religion*, 1869), and it has set me thinking. I have a feeling that his notion of religion is not rigorous and exact, and that therefore his logic is subject to correction. If religion is a psychological stage, anterior to that of reason, it is clear that it will disappear in man, but if, on the contrary, it is a mode of the inner life, it may and must last, as long as the need of feeling, and alongside the need of thinking. The question is between theism and non-theism. If God is only the category of the ideal, religion will vanish, of course, like the illusions of youth. But if Universal Being can be felt and loved at the same time as conceived, the philosopher may be a religious man just as he may be an artist, an orator, or a citizen. He may attach himself to a worship or ritual without derogation. I myself incline to this solution. To me religion is life before God and in God.

And even if God were defined as the universal life, so long as this life is positive and not negative, the soul penetrated with the sense of the infinite is in the religious state. Religion differs from philosophy as the simple and spontaneous self differs from the reflecting self, as synthetic intuition differs from intellectual analysis. We are initiated into the religious state by a sense of voluntary dependence on and joyful submission to the principle of order and of goodness. Religious emotion makes man conscious of himself; he finds his own place within the infinite unity, and it is this perception which is sacred.

But in spite of these reservations I am much impressed by the book, which is a fine piece of work, ripe and serious in all respects.

13th May 1869. — A break in the clouds, and through the blue interstices a bright sun throws flickering and uncertain rays. Storms, smiles, whims, anger, tears, — it is May, and nature is in its feminine phase! She pleases our fancy, stirs our heart, and wears out our reason by the endless succession of her caprices and the unexpected violence of her whims.

This recalls to me the 213th verse of the second book of the Laws of Manou. 'It is in the nature of the feminine sex to seek here below to corrupt men, and therefore wise men never abandon themselves to the seductions of women.' The same code, however, says: 'Wherever women are honoured the gods are satisfied.' And again: 'In every family where the husband takes pleasure in his wife, and the wife in her husband, happiness is ensured.' And again: 'One mother is more venerable than a thousand fathers.' But knowing what stormy and irrational elements there are in this fragile and delightful creature, Manou concludes: 'At no age ought a woman to be allowed to govern herself as she pleases.'

Up to the present day, in several contemporary and neighbouring codes, a woman is a minor all her life. Why? Because of her dependence upon nature, and of her subjection to passions which are the diminutives of madness; in other words, because the soul of a woman has something obscure and mysterious in it, which lends itself to all superstitions and weakens the energies of man. To man belong law, justice, science, and philosophy, all that is disinterested, universal, and rational.

Women, on the contrary, introduce into everything favour, exception, and personal prejudice. As soon as a man, a people, a literature, an epoch, become feminine in type, they sink in the scale of things. As soon as a woman quits the state of subordination in which her merits have free play, we see a rapid increase in her natural defects. Complete equality with man makes her quarrelsome; a position of supremacy makes her tyrannical. To honour her and to govern her will be for a long time yet the best solution. When education has formed strong, noble, and serious women in whom conscience and reason hold sway over the effervescence of fancy and sentimentality, then we shall be able not only to honour woman, but to make a serious end of gaining her consent and adhesion. Then she will be truly an equal, a work-fellow, a companion. At present she is so only in theory. The moderns are at work upon the problem, and have not solved it yet.

15th June 1869. — The great defect of liberal Christianity [4] is that its conception of holiness is a frivolous one, or, what comes to the same thing, its conception of sin is a superficial one. The defects of the baser sort of political liberalism recur in liberal Christianity; it is only half serious, and its theology is too much mixed with worldliness. The sincerely pious folk look upon the liberals as persons whose talk is rather profane, and who offend religious feelings by making sacred subjects a theme for rhetorical display. They shock the *convenances* of sentiment, and affront the delicacy of conscience by the indiscreet familiarities they take with the great mysteries of the inner life. They seem to be mere clever special pleaders, religious rhetoricians like the Greek sophists, rather than guides in the narrow road which leads to salvation.

It is not to the clever folk, nor even to the scientific folk, that the empire over souls belongs, but to those who impress us as having conquered nature by grace, as having passed through the burning bush, and as speaking, not the language of human wisdom, but that of the divine will. In religious matters it is holiness which gives authority; it is love, or the power of devotion and sacrifice, which goes to the heart, which moves and persuades.

What all religious, poetical, pure, and tender souls are least able to pardon is the diminution or degradation of their ideal. We must never rouse an ideal against us; our business is to point men to another ideal, purer, higher, more spiritual than the old, and so to raise behind a lofty summit one more lofty still. In this way no one is despoiled; we gain men's confidence, while at the same time forcing them to think, and enabling those minds which are already tending towards change to perceive new objects and goals for thought. Only that which is replaced is destroyed, and an ideal is only replaced by satisfying the conditions of the old with some advantages over.

Let the liberal Protestants offer us a spectacle of Christian virtue of a holier, intenser, and more intimate kind than before; let us see it active in their persons and in their influence, and they will have furnished the proof demanded by the Master: the tree will be judged by its fruits.

. . . . .

22d June 1869 (*Nine* A.M.) — Gray and lowering weather. — A fly lies dead of cold on the page of my book, in full summer! What is life? I said to myself, as I looked at the tiny dead creature. It is a loan, as movement is. The universal life is a sum total, of which the units are visible here, there, and everywhere, just as an electric wheel throws off sparks along its whole surface. Life passes through us; we do not possess it. Hirn admits three ultimate principles:[5] the atom, the force, the soul; the force which acts upon atoms, the soul which acts upon force. Probably he distinguishes between anonymous souls and personal souls. Then my fly would be an anonymous soul.

(*Same day.*) — The national churches are all up in arms against so-called Liberal Christianity; Basle and Zurich began the fight, and now Geneva has entered the lists too. Gradually it is becoming plain that historical Protestantism has no longer a *raison d'être* between pure liberty and pure authority. It is, in fact, a provisional stage, founded on the worship of the Bible — that is to say, on the idea of a written revelation, and of a book divinely inspired, and therefore authoritative. When once this thesis has been relegated to the rank of a fiction Protestantism crumbles away. There is nothing for it but to retire upon natural religion, or the religion of the moral consciousness. MM. Réville, Coquerel, Fontanès, Buisson,[6] accept this logical outcome.

They are the advance-guard of Protestantism and the laggards of free thought.

Their mistake is in not seeing that all institutions rest upon a legal fiction, and that every living thing involves a logical absurdity. It may be logical to demand a church based on free examination and absolute sincerity; but to realise it is a different matter. A church lives by what is positive, and this positive element necessarily limits investigation. People confound the right of the individual, which is to be free, with the duty of the institution, which is to be something. They take the principle of Science to be the same as the principle of the Church, which is a mistake. They will not see that Religion is different from Philosophy, and that the one seeks union by faith, while the other upholds the solitary independence of thought. That the bread should be good it must have leaven; but the leaven is not the bread. Liberty is the means whereby we arrive at an enlightened faith — granted; but an assembly of people agreeing only upon this criterion and this method could not possibly found a church, for they might differ completely as to the results of the method. Suppose a newspaper the writers of which were of all possible parties, — it would no doubt be a curiosity in journalism, but it would have no opinions, no faith, no creed. A drawing-room filled with refined people, carrying on polite discussion, is not a church, and a dispute, however courteous, is not worship. It is a mere confusion of kinds.

13th July 1869. — Lamennais, Heine — the one the victim of a mistaken vocation, the other of a tormenting craving to astonish and mystify his kind. The first was wanting in common sense; the second was wanting in seriousness. The Frenchman was violent, arbitrary, domineering; the German was a jesting Mephistopheles, with a horror of Philistinism. The Breton was all passion and melancholy; the Hamburger all fancy and satire. Neither developed freely nor normally. Both of them, because of an initial mistake, threw themselves into an endless quarrel with the world. Both were revolutionists. They were not fighting for the good cause, for impersonal truth; both were rather the champions of their own pride. Both suffered greatly, and died isolated, repudiated, and reviled. Men of magnificent talents, both of them, but men of small wisdom, who did more harm than good to themselves and to others! — It is a lamentable existence which wears itself out in maintaining a first antagonism, or a first blunder. The greater a man's intellectual power, the more dangerous is it for him to make a false start and to begin life badly.

20th July 1869. — I have been reading over again five or six chapters, here and there, of Renan's *St. Paul*. Analysed to the bottom, the writer is a freethinker, but a freethinker whose flexible imagination still allows him the delicate epicurism of religious emotion. In his eyes the man who will not lend himself to these graceful fancies is vulgar, and the man who takes them seriously is prejudiced. He is entertained by the variations of conscience, but he is too clever to laugh at them. The true critic neither concludes nor excludes; his pleasure is to understand without believing, and to profit by the results of enthusiasm, while still maintaining a free mind, unembarrassed by illusion. Such a mode of proceeding has a look of dishonesty; it is nothing, however, but the good-tempered irony of a highly-cultivated mind, which will neither be ignorant of anything nor duped by anything. It is the dilettanteism of the Renaissance in its perfection. — At the same time what innumerable proofs of insight and of exultant scientific power !

14th August 1869. — In the name of Heaven, who art thou ? — what wilt thou — wavering inconstant creature ? What future lies before thee ? What duty or what hope appeals to thee ?

My longing, my search is for love, for peace, for something to fill my heart; an idea to defend ; a work to which I might devote the rest of my strength; an affection which might quench this inner thirst; a cause for which I might die with joy. But shall I ever find them ? I long for all that is impossible and inaccessible: for true religion, serious sympathy, the ideal life ; for paradise, immortality, holiness, faith, inspiration, and I know not what besides ! What I really want is to die and to be born again, transformed myself, and in a different world. And I can neither stifle these aspirations nor deceive myself as to the possibility of satisfying them. I seem condemned to roll for ever the rock of Sisyphus, and to feel that slow wearing away of the mind which befalls the man whose vocation and destiny are in perpetual conflict. 'A Christian heart and a pagan head,' like Jacobi; tenderness and pride; width of mind and feebleness of will; the two men of St. Paul; a seething chaos of contrasts, antinomies, and contradictions; humility and pride; childish simplicity and boundless mistrust; analysis and intuition; patience and irritability; kindness and dryness of heart; carelessness and anxiety; enthusiasm and languor; indifference and passion; altogether a being incomprehensible and intolerable to myself and to others!

Then from a state of conflict I fall back into the fluid, vague, indeterminate state, which feels all form to be a mere violence and disfigurement. All ideas, principles, acquirements, and habits are effaced in me like the ripples on a wave, like the convolutions of a cloud. My personality has the least possible admixture of individuality. I am to the great majority of men what the circle is to rectilinear figures; I am everywhere at home, because I have no particular and nominative self. — Perhaps, on the whole, this defect has good in it. Though I am less of *a* man, I am perhaps nearer to *the* man; perhaps rather more *man*. There is less of the individual, but more of the species, in me. My nature, which is absolutely unsuited for practical life, shows great aptitude for psychological study. It prevents me from taking sides, but it allows me to understand all sides. It is not only indolence which prevents me from drawing conclusions; it is a sort of a secret aversion to all *intellectual proscription.* I have a feeling that something of everything is wanted to make a world, that all citizens have a right in the State, and that if every opinion is equally insignificant in itself, all opinions have some hold upon truth. To live and let live, think and let think, are maxims which are equally dear to me. My tendency is always to the whole, to the totality, to the general balance of things. What is difficult to me is to exclude, to condemn, to say no; except, indeed, in the presence of the exclusive. I am always fighting for the absent, for the defeated cause, for that portion of truth which seems to me neglected; my aim is to complete every thesis, to see round every problem, to study a thing from all its possible sides. Is this scepticism? Yes, in its result, but not in its purpose. It is rather the sense of the absolute and the infinite reducing to their proper value and relegating to their proper place the finite and the relative.

But here, in the same way, my ambition is greater than my power; my philosophical perception is superior to my speculative gift. I have not the energy of my opinions; I have far greater width than inventiveness of thought, and, from timidity, I have allowed the critical intelligence in me to swallow up the creative genius. — Is it indeed from timidity?

Alas! with a little more ambition, or a little more good luck, a different man might have been made out of me, and such as my youth gave promise of.

16th August 1869. — I have been thinking over Schopenhauer. — It has struck me and almost terrified me to see how well I represent Schopenhauer's typical man, for whom 'happiness is a chimera and suffering a reality,' for whom 'the negation of will and of desire is the only road to deliverance,' and 'the individual life is a misfortune from which impersonal contemplation is the only enfranchisement,' etc. But the principle that life is an evil and annihilation a good lies at the root of the system, and this axiom I have never dared to enunciate in any general way, although I have admitted it here and there in individual cases. — What I still like in the misanthrope of Frankfort, is his antipathy to current prejudice, to European hobbies, to Western hypocrisies, to the successes of the day. Schopenhauer is a man of powerful mind, who has put away from him all illusions, who professes Buddhism in the full flow of modern Germany, and absolute detachment of mind in the very midst of the nineteenth-century orgie. His great defects are barrenness of soul, a proud and perfect selfishness, an adoration of genius which is combined with complete indifference to the rest of the world, in spite of all his teaching of resignation and sacrifice. He has no sympathy, no humanity, no love. And here I recognise the unlikeness between us. Pure intelligence and solitary labour might easily lead me to his point of view; but once appeal to the heart, and I feel the contemplative attitude untenable. Pity, goodness, charity, and devotion reclaim their rights, and insist even upon the first place.

29th August 1869. — Schopenhauer preaches impersonality, objectivity, pure contemplation, the negation of will, calmness, and disinterestedness, an æsthetic study of the world, detachment from life, the renunciation of all desire, solitary meditation, disdain of the crowd, and indifference to all that the vulgar covet. He approves all my defects, my childishness, my aversion to practical life, my antipathy to the utilitarians, my distrust of all desire. In a word, he flatters all my instincts; he caresses and justifies them.

This pre-established harmony between the theory of Schopenhauer and my own natural man causes me pleasure mingled with terror. I might indulge myself in the pleasure, but that I fear to delude and stifle conscience. Besides, I feel that goodness has no tolerance for this contemplative indifference, and that virtue consists in self-conquest.

30th August 1869.— Still some chapters of Schopenhauer. Schopenhauer believes in the unchangeableness of innate tendencies in the individual, and in the invariability of the primitive disposition. He refuses to believe in the new man, in any real progress towards perfection, or in any positive improvement in a human being. Only the appearances are refined; there is no change below the surface. Perhaps he confuses temperament, character, and individuality? I incline to think that individuality is fatal and primitive, that temperament reaches far back, but is alterable, and that character is more recent and susceptible of voluntary or involuntary modifications. Individuality is a matter of psychology, temperament, a matter of sensation or æsthetics; character alone is a matter of morals. Liberty and the use of it count for nothing in the first two elements of our being; character is a historical fruit, and the result of a man's biography. — For Schopenhauer, character is identified with temperament just as will with passion. In short, he simplifies too much, and looks at man from that more elementary point of view which is only sufficient in the case of the animal. That spontaneity which is vital or merely chemical he already calls will. Analogy is not equation; a comparison is not reason; similes and parables are not exact language. Many of Schopenhauer's originalities evaporate when we come to translate them into a more close and precise terminology.

Later. — One has merely to turn over the *Lichtstrahlen* of Herder to feel the difference between him and Schopenhauer. The latter is full of marked features and of observations which stand out from the page and leave a clear and vivid impression. Herder is much less of a writer; his ideas are entangled in his style, and he has no brilliant condensations, no jewels, no crystals. While he proceeds by streams and sheets of thought which have no definite or individual outline, Schopenhauer breaks the current of his speculation with islands, striking, original, and picturesque, which engrave themselves in the memory. It is the same difference as there is between Nicole and Pascal, between Bayle and Saint-Simon.

What is the faculty which gives relief, brilliancy, and incisiveness to thought? Imagination. Under its influence expression becomes concentrated, coloured, and strengthened, and by the power it has of individualising all it touches, it gives life and permanence to the material on which it works. A writer of genius changes sand into glass and glass into crystal, ore into iron and iron into steel; he marks with his own stamp every idea he gets hold of. He borrows much from the common stock, and gives back nothing; but even his robberies are willingly reckoned to him as private property. He has, as it were, *carte blanche*, and public opinion allows him to take what he will.

31st August 1869. — I have finished Schopenhauer. My mind has been a tumult of opposing systems — Stoicism, Quietism, Buddhism, Christianity. Shall I never be at peace with myself? If impersonality is a good, why am I not consistent in the pursuit of it? and if it is temptation, why return to it, after having judged and conquered it?

Is happiness anything more than a conventional fiction? The deepest reason for my state of doubt is that the supreme end and aim of life seems to me a mere lure and deception. The individual is an eternal dupe, who never obtains what he seeks, and who is for ever deceived by hope. My instinct is in harmony with the pessimism of Buddha and of Schopenhauer. It is a doubt which never leaves me even in my moments of religious fervour. Nature is indeed for me a Maïa; and I look at her, as it were, with the eyes of an artist. My intelligence remains sceptical. What, then, do I believe in? I do not know. And what is it I hope for? It would be difficult to say. — Folly! I believe in goodness, and I hope that good will prevail. Deep within this ironical and disappointed being of mine there is a child hidden — a frank, sad, simple creature, who believes in the ideal, in love, in holiness, and all heavenly superstitions. A whole millennium of idylls sleeps in my heart; I am a pseudo-sceptic, a pseudo-scoffer.

'Borné dans sa nature, infini dans ses vœux,
   L'homme est un dieu tombé qui se souvient des cieux.'

14th October 1869. — Yesterday, Wednesday, death of Sainte-Beuve. What a loss!

16th October 1869. — *Laboremus* seems to have been the motto of Sainte-Beuve, as it was that of Septimius Severus. He died in harness, and up to the evening before his last day he still wrote, overcoming the sufferings of the body by the energy of the mind. To-day, at this very moment, they are laying him in the bosom of Mother Earth. He refused the sacraments of the Church; he never belonged to any confession; he was one of the 'great diocese' — that of the independent seekers of truth, and he allowed himself no final moment of hypocrisy. He would have nothing to do with any one except God only — or rather the mysterious Isis beyond the veil. Being unmarried, he died in the arms of his secretary. He was sixty-five years old. His power of work and of memory was immense and intact. What is Scherer thinking about this life and this death?

19*th October* 1869. — An admirable article by Edmond Scherer on Sainte-Beuve in the *Temps*. He makes him the prince of French critics and the last representative of the epoch of literary taste, the future belonging to the bookmakers and the chatterers, to mediocrity and to violence. The article breathes a certain manly melancholy, befitting a funeral oration over one who was a master in the things of the mind. — The fact is, that Sainte-Beuve leaves a greater void behind him than either Béranger or Lamartine; their greatness was already distant, historical; he was still helping us to think. The true critic acts as a fulcrum for all the world. He represents the public judgment, that is to say the public reason, the touchstone, the scales, the refining rod, which tests the value of every one and the merit of every work. Infallibility of judgment is perhaps rarer than anything else, so fine a balance of qualities does it demand — qualities both natural and acquired, qualities of mind and heart. What years of labour, what study and comparison, are needed to bring the critical judgment to maturity! Like Plato's sage, it is only at fifty that the critic rises to the true height of his literary priesthood, or, to put it less pompously, of his social function. By then only can he hope for insight into all the modes of being, and for mastery of all possible shades of appreciation. And Sainte-Beuve joined to this infinitely refined culture a prodigious memory, and an incredible multitude of facts and anecdotes stored up for the service of his thought.

8th December 1869.—Everything has chilled me this morning: the cold of the season, the physical immobility around me, but, above all, Hartmann's *Philosophy of the Unconscious*. This book lays down the terrible thesis that creation is a mistake; being, such as it is, is not as good as non-being, and death is better than life.

I felt the same mournful impression that Obermann left upon me in my youth. The black melancholy of Buddhism encompassed and overshadowed me. If, in fact, it is only illusion which hides from us the horror of existence and makes life tolerable to us, then existence is a snare and life an evil. Like the Greek Annikeris, we ought to counsel suicide, or rather with Buddha and Schopenhauer, we ought to labour for the radical extirpation of hope and desire, — the causes of life and resurrection. *Not* to rise again; there is the point, and there is the difficulty. Death is simply a beginning again, whereas it is annihilation that we have to aim at. Personal consciousness being the root of all our troubles, we ought to avoid the temptation to it and the possibility of it as diabolical and abominable. — What blasphemy! And yet it is all logical; it is the philosophy of happiness carried to its farthest point. Epicurism must end in despair. The philosophy of duty is less depressing. But salvation lies in the conciliation of duty and happiness, in the union of the individual will with the divine will, and in the faith that this supreme will is directed by love.

. . . .

It is as true that real happiness is good, as that the good become better under the purification of trial. Those who have not suffered are still wanting in depth; but a man who has not got happiness cannot impart it. We can only give what we have. Happiness, grief, gaiety, sadness, are by nature contagious. Bring your health and your strength to the weak and sickly, and so you will be of use to them. Give them, not your weakness, but your energy, — so you will revive and lift them up. Life alone can rekindle life. What others claim from us is not our thirst and our hunger, but our bread and our gourd.

. . . . . .

The benefactors of Humanity are those who have thought great thoughts about her; but her masters and her idols are those who have flattered and despised her, those who have muzzled and massacred her, inflamed her with fanaticism or used her for selfish purposes. Her benefactors are the poets, the artists, the inventors, the apostles, and all pure hearts. Her masters are the Cæsars, the Constantines, the Gregory VII.'s, the Innocent III.'s, the Borgias, the Napoleons.

. . . . . .

Every civilisation is, as it were, a dream of a thousand years, in which heaven and earth, nature and history, appear to men illumined by fantastic light and representing a drama which is nothing but a projection of the soul itself, influenced by some intoxication — I was going to say hallucination — or other. Those who are widest awake still see the real world across the dominant illusion of their race or time. And the reason is that the deceiving light starts from our own mind: the light is our religion. Everything changes with it. It is religion which gives to our kaleidoscope, if not the material of the figures, at least their colour, their light and shade, and general aspect. Every religion makes men see the world and humanity under a special light; it is a mode of apperception, which can only be scientifically handled when we have cast it aside, and can only be judged when we have replaced it by a better.

. . . .

23d February 1870. — There is in man an instinct of revolt, an enemy of all law, a rebel which will stoop to no yoke, not even that of reason, duty, and wisdom. This element in us is the root of all sin — *das radicale Böse* of Kant. The independence which is the condition of individuality is at the same time the eternal temptation of the individual. That which makes us beings makes us also sinners.

Sin is, then, in our very marrow, it circulates in us like the blood in our veins, it is mingled with all our substance.[7] Or rather I am wrong: temptation is our natural state, but sin is not necessary. Sin consists in the voluntary confusion of the independence which is good with the independence which is bad; it is caused by the half-indulgence granted to a first sophism. We shut our eyes to the beginnings of evil because they are small, and in this weakness is contained the germ of our defeat. *Principiis obsta* — this maxim dutifully followed would preserve us from almost all our catastrophes.

We will have no other master but our caprice — that is to say, our evil self will have no God, and the foundation of our nature is seditious, impious, insolent, refractory, opposed to and contemptuous of all that tries to rule it, and therefore contrary to order, ungovernable and negative. It is this foundation which Christianity calls the natural man. But the savage which is within us, and constitutes the primitive stuff of us, must be disciplined and civilised in order to produce a man. And the man must be patiently cultivated to produce a wise man, and the wise man must be tested and tried if he is to become righteous. And the righteous man must have substituted the will of God for his individual will, if he is to become a saint. And this new man, this regenerate being, is the spiritual man, the heavenly man, of which the Vedas speak as well as the Gospel, and the Magi as well as the Neo-Platonists.

17th March 1870. — This morning the music of a brass band which had stopped under my windows moved me almost to tears. It exercised an indefinable, nostalgic power over me; it set me dreaming of another world, of infinite passion and supreme happiness. Such impressions are the echoes of Paradise in the soul; memories of ideal spheres, whose sad sweetness ravishes and intoxicates the heart. O Plato! O Pythagoras! ages ago you heard these harmonies, — surprised these moments of inward ecstasy, — knew these divine transports! If music thus carries us to heaven, it is because music is harmony, harmony is perfection, perfection is our dream, and our dream is heaven. This world of quarrels and of bitterness, of selfishness, ugliness, and misery, makes us long involuntarily for the eternal peace, for the adoration which has no limits, and the love which has no end. It is not so much the infinite as the beautiful that we yearn for. It is not being, or the limits of being, which weigh upon us; it is evil, in us and without us. It is not at all necessary to be great, so long as we are in harmony with the order of the universe. Moral ambition has no pride; it only desires to fill its place, and make its note duly heard in the universal concert of the God of love.

30th March 1870. — Certainly, Nature is unjust and shameless, without probity, and without faith. Her only alternatives are gratuitous favour or mad aversion, and her only way of redressing an injustice is to commit another. The happiness of the few is expiated by the misery of the greater number. — It is useless to accuse a blind force. —

The human conscience, however, revolts against this law of nature, and to satisfy its own instinct of justice it has imagined two hypotheses, out of which it has made for itself a religion, — the idea of an individual providence, and the hypothesis of another life.

In these we have a protest against nature, which is thus declared immoral and scandalous to the moral sense. Man believes in good, and that he may ground himself on justice he maintains that the injustice all around him is but an appearance, a mystery, a cheat, and that justice *will* be done. *Fiat justitia, pereat mundus!*

It is a great act of faith. And since humanity has not made itself, this protest has some chance of expressing a truth. If there is conflict between the natural world and the moral world, between reality and conscience, conscience must be right.

It is by no means necessary that the universe should exist, but it is necessary that justice should be done, and atheism is bound to explain the fixed obstinacy of conscience on this point. Nature is not just; we are the products of nature: why are we always claiming and prophesying justice? why does the effect rise up against its cause? It is a singular phenomenon. Does the protest come from any puerile blindness of human vanity? No, it is the deepest cry of our being, and it is for the honour of God that the cry is uttered. Heaven and earth may pass away, but good *ought* to be, and injustice ought *not* to be. Such is the creed of the human race. Nature will be conquered by spirit: the eternal will triumph over time.

1st April 1870. — I am inclined to believe that for a woman love is the supreme authority — that which judges the rest and decides what is good or evil. For a man, love is subordinate to right. It is a great passion, but it is not the source of order, the synonym of reason, the criterion of excellence. It would seem, then, that a woman places her ideal in the perfection of love, and a man in the perfection of justice. It was in this sense that St. Paul was able to say, 'The woman is the glory of the man, and the man is the glory of God.' Thus the woman who absorbs herself in the object of her love is, so to speak, in the line of nature: she is truly woman, she realises her fundamental type. On the contrary, the man who should make life consist in conjugal adoration, and who should imagine that he has lived sufficiently when he has made himself the priest of a beloved woman, such a one is but half a man; he is despised by the world, and perhaps secretly disdained by women themselves. The woman who loves truly seeks to merge her own individuality in that of the man she loves. She desires that her love should make him greater, stronger, more masculine, and more active. Thus each sex plays its appointed part: the woman is first destined for man, and man is destined for society. Woman owes herself to one, man owes himself to all; and each obtains peace and happiness only when he or she has recognised this law and accepted this balance of things. The same thing may be a good in the woman and an evil in the man, may be strength in her, weakness in him.

There is then a feminine and a masculine morality, — preparatory chapters, as it were, to a general human morality. Below the virtue which is evangelical and sexless, there is a virtue of sex. And this virtue of sex is the occasion of mutual teaching, for each of the two incarnations of virtue makes it its business to convert the other, the first preaching love in the ears of justice, the second justice in the ears of love. And so there is produced an oscillation and an average which represent a social state, an epoch, sometimes a whole civilisation.

Such at least is our European idea of the harmony of the sexes in a graduated order of functions. America is on the road to revolutionise this ideal by the introduction of the democratic principle of the equality of individuals in a general equality of functions. Only, when there is nothing left but a multitude of equal individualities, neither young nor old, neither men nor women, neither benefited nor benefactors, — all social difference will turn upon money. The whole hierarchy will rest upon the dollar, and the most brutal, the most hideous, the most inhuman of inequalities will be the fruit of the passion for equality. What a result! Plutolatry — the worship of wealth, the madness of gold — to it will be confided the task of chastising a false principle and its followers. And plutocracy will be in its turn executed by equality. It would be a strange end for it, if Anglo-Saxon individualism were ultimately swallowed up in Latin socialism.

It is my prayer that the discovery of an equilibrium between the two principles may be made in time, before the social war, with all its terror and ruin, overtakes us. But it is scarcely likely. The masses are always ignorant and limited, and only advance by a succession of contrary errors. They reach good only by the exhaustion of evil. They discover the way out, only after having run their heads against all other possible issues.

15th April 1870. — *Crucifixion!* That is

the word we have to meditate to-day. Is it not Good Friday?

To curse grief is easier than to bless it, but to do so is to fall back into the point of view of the earthly, the carnal, the natural man. By what has Christianity subdued the world if not by the apotheosis of grief, by its marvellous transmutation of suffering into triumph, of the crown of thorns into the crown of glory, and of a gibbet into a symbol of salvation? What does the apotheosis of the Cross mean, if not the death of death, the defeat of sin, the beatification of martyrdom, the raising to the skies of voluntary sacrifice, the defiance of pain? — 'O Death, where is thy sting? O Grave, where is thy victory?' — By long brooding over this theme — the agony of the just, peace in the midst of agony, and the heavenly beauty of such peace — humanity came to understand that a new religion was born, — a new mode, that is to say, of explaining life and of understanding suffering.

Suffering was a curse from which man fled; now it becomes a purification of the soul, a sacred trial sent by Eternal Love, a divine dispensation meant to sanctify and ennoble us, an acceptable aid to faith, a strange initiation into happiness. O power of belief! All remains the same, and yet all is changed. A new certitude arises to deny the apparent and the tangible; it pierces through the mystery of things, it places an invisible Father behind visible nature, it shows us joy shining through tears, and makes of pain the beginning of joy.

And so, for those who have believed, the tomb becomes heaven, and on the funeral pyre of life they sing the hosanna of immortality; a sacred madness has renewed the face of the world for them, and when they wish to explain what they feel, their ecstasy makes them incomprehensible; they speak with tongues. A wild intoxication of self-sacrifice, contempt for death, the thirst for eternity, the delirium of love, — these are what the unalterable gentleness of the Crucified has had power to bring forth. By his pardon of his executioners, and by that unconquerable sense in him of an indissoluble union with God, Jesus, on his cross, kindled an inextinguishable fire and revolutionised the world. He proclaimed and realised salvation by faith in the infinite mercy, and in the pardon granted to simple repentance. By his saying, 'There is more joy in heaven over one sinner that repenteth than over ninety and nine just persons who need no repentance,' he made humility the gate of entrance into Paradise.

Crucify the rebellious self, mortify yourself wholly, give up all to God, and the peace which is not of this world will descend upon you. For eighteen centuries no grander word has been spoken; and although humanity is for ever seeking after a more exact and complete application of justice, yet her secret faith is not in justice but in pardon, for pardon alone conciliates the spotless purity of perfection with the infinite pity due to weakness — that is to say, it alone preserves and defends the idea of holiness, while it allows full scope to that of love. The Gospel proclaims the ineffable consolation, the good news, which disarms all earthly griefs, and robs even death of its terrors — the news of irrevocable pardon, that is to say, of eternal life. The Cross is the guarantee of the Gospel. Therefore it has been its standard.

7th May 1870. — The faith which clings to its idols and resists all innovation is a retarding and conservative force; but it is the property of all religion to serve as a curb to our lawless passion for freedom, and to steady and quiet our restlessness of temper. Curiosity is the expansive force, which, if it were allowed an unchecked action upon us, would disperse and volatilise us; belief represents the force of gravitation and cohesion, which makes separate bodies and individuals of us. Society lives by faith, develops by science. Its basis, then, is the mysterious, the unknown, the intangible, — religion, — while the fermenting principle in it is the desire of knowledge. Its permanent substance is the uncomprehended or the divine; its changing form is the result of its intellectual labour. The unconscious adhesions, the confused intuitions, the obscure presentiments, which decide the first faith of a people, are then of capital importance in its history. All history moves between the religion which is the genial, instinctive, and fundamental philosophy of a race, and the philosophy which is the ultimate religion, — the clear perception, that is to say, of those principles which have engendered the whole spiritual development of humanity.

It is always the same thing which is, which was, and which will be; but this thing — the absolute — betrays with more or less transparency and profundity the law of its life and of its metamorphoses. In its fixed aspect it is called God; in its mobile aspect the world or nature. God is present in nature, but nature is not God; there is a nature in God, but it is not God Himself. I am neither for immanence nor for transcendence taken alone.

9th May 1870. — Disraeli, in his new novel, *Lothair,* shows that the two great forces of the present are Revolution and Catholicism, and that the free nations are lost if either of these two forces triumphs. It is exactly my own idea. Only, while in France, in Belgium, in Italy, and in all Catholic societies, it is only by checking one of these forces by the other that the State and civilisation can be maintained, the Protestant countries are better off; in them there is a third force, a middle faith between the two other idolatries, which enables them to regard liberty not as a neutralisation of two contraries, but as a moral reality, self-subsistent, and possessing its own centre of gravity and motive force. In the Catholic world religion and liberty exclude each other. In the Protestant world they accept each other, so that in the second case there is a smaller waste of force.

Liberty is the lay, the philosophical principle. It expresses the juridical and social aspiration of the race. But as there is no society possible without regulation, without control, without limitations on individual liberty, above all without moral limitations, the peoples which are legally the freest do well to take their religious consciousness for check and ballast. In mixed States, Catholic or freethinking, the limit of action, being a merely penal one, invites incessant contravention.

The puerility of the freethinkers consists in believing that a free society can maintain itself and keep itself together without a common faith, without a religious prejudice of some kind. Where lies the will of God? Is it the common reason which expresses it, or rather, are a clergy or a church the depositories of it? So long as the response is ambiguous and equivocal in the eyes of half or the majority of consciences — and this is the case in all Catholic States — public peace is impossible, and public law is insecure. If there is a God, we must have Him on our side, and if there is not a God, it would be necessary first of all to convert everybody to the same idea of the lawful and the useful, to reconstitute, that is to say, a lay religion, before anything politically solid could be built.

Liberalism is merely feeding upon abstractions, when it persuades itself that liberty is possible without free individuals, and when it will not recognise that liberty in the individual is the fruit of a foregoing education, a moral education, which presupposes a liberating religion. To preach liberalism to a population jesuitised by education, is to press the pleasures of dancing upon a man who has lost a leg. How is it possible for a child who has never been out of swaddling clothes to walk? How can the abdication of individual conscience lead to the government of individual conscience? To be free, is to guide oneself, to have attained one's majority, to be emancipated, master of one's actions, and judge of good and evil; but Ultramontane Catholicism never emancipates its disciples, who are bound to admit, to believe, and to obey, as they are told, because they are minors in perpetuity, and the clergy alone possess the law of right, the secret of justice, and the measure of truth. This is what men are landed in by the idea of an exterior revelation, cleverly made use of by a patient priesthood.

But what astonishes me is the short-sight of the statesmen of the south, who do not see that the question of questions is the religious question, and even now do not recognise that a liberal State is wholly incompatible with an anti-liberal religion, and almost equally incompatible with the absence of religion. They confound accidental conquests and precarious progress with lasting results.

There is some probability that all this noise which is made nowadays about liberty may end in the suppression of liberty; it is plain that the International, the irreconcilables, and the ultramontanes, are, all three of them, aiming at absolutism, at dictatorial omnipotence. Happily they are not one but many, and it will not be difficult to turn them against each other.

If liberty is to be saved, it will not be by the doubters, the men of science, or the materialists; it will be by religious conviction, by the faith of individuals who believe that God wills man to be free but also pure; it will be by the seekers after holiness, by those old-fashioned pious persons who speak of immortality and eternal life, and prefer the soul to the whole world; it will be by the enfranchised children of the ancient faith of the human race.

5th June 1870. — The efficacy of religion lies precisely in that which is not rational, philosophic, nor eternal; its efficacy lies in the unforeseen, the miraculous, the extraordinary. Thus religion attracts more devotion in proportion as it demands more faith — that is to say, as it becomes more incredible to the profane mind. The philosopher aspires to explain away all mysteries, to dissolve them into light. It is mystery, on the other hand, which the religious instinct demands and pursues: it is mystery which constitutes the essence of worship, the power of proselytism. When the cross became the 'foolishness' of the cross, it took possession of the masses. And in our own day, those who wish to get rid of the supernatural, to enlighten religion, to economise faith, find themselves deserted, like poets who should declaim against poetry, or women who should decry love. Faith consists in the acceptance of the incomprehensible, and even in the pursuit of the impossible, and is self-intoxicated with its own sacrifices, its own repeated extravagances.

It is the forgetfulness of this psychological law which stultifies the so-called liberal Christianity. It is the realisation of it which constitutes the strength of Catholicism.

Apparently no positive religion can survive the supernatural element which is the reason for its existence. Natural religion seems to be the tomb of all historic cults. All concrete religions die eventually in the pure air of philosophy. So long then as the life of nations is in need of religion as a motive and sanction of morality, as food for faith, hope, and charity, so long will the masses turn away from pure reason and naked truth, so long will they adore mystery, so long — and rightly so — will they rest in faith, the only region where the ideal presents itself to them in an attractive form.

9th June 1870. — At bottom, everything depends upon the presence or absence of one single element in the soul — hope. All the activity of man, all his efforts and all his enterprises, presuppose a hope in him of attaining an end. Once kill this hope and his movements become senseless, spasmodic, and convulsive, like those of some one falling from a height. To struggle with the inevitable has something childish in it. To implore the law of gravitation to suspend its action would no doubt be a grotesque prayer. Very well! but when a man loses faith in the efficacy of his efforts, when he says to himself, 'You are incapable of realising your ideal; happiness is a chimera, progress is an illusion, the passion for perfection is a snare; and supposing all your ambitions were gratified, everything would still be vanity,' then he comes to see that a little blindness is necessary if life is to be carried on, and that illusion is the universal spring of movement. Complete disillusion would mean absolute immobility. He who has deciphered the secret and read the riddle of finite life escapes from the great wheel of existence; he has left the world of the living — he is already dead. Is this the meaning of the old belief that to raise the veil of Isis or to behold God face to face brought destruction upon the rash mortal who attempted it? Egypt and Judæa had recorded the fact, Buddha gave the key to it; the individual life is a nothing ignorant of itself, and as soon as this nothing knows itself, individual life is abolished in principle. For as soon as the illusion vanishes, Nothingness resumes its eternal sway, the suffering of life is over, error has disappeared, time and form have ceased to be for this enfranchised individuality; the coloured air-bubble has burst in the infinite space, and the misery of thought has sunk to rest in the changeless repose of all-embracing Nothing. The absolute, if it were spirit, would still be activity, and it is activity, the daughter of desire, which is incompatible with the absolute. The absolute, then, must be the zero of all determination, and the only manner of being suited to it is Non-being.

2d July 1870. — One of the vices of France is the frivolity which substitutes public conventions for truth, and absolutely ignores personal dignity and the majesty of conscience. The French are ignorant of the A B C of individual liberty, and still show an essentially catholic intolerance towards the ideas which have not attained universality or the adhesion of the majority. The nation is an army which can bring to bear mass, number, and force, but not an assembly of free men in which each individual depends for his value on himself. The eminent Frenchman depends upon others for his value; if he possess stripe, cross, scarf, sword, or robe, — in a word, function and decoration, — then he is held to be something, and he feels himself somebody. It is the symbol which establishes his merit; it is the public which raises him from nothing, as the Sultan creates his viziers. These highly-trained and social races have an antipathy for individual independence; everything with them must be founded upon authority military, civil, or religious, and God Himself is non-existent until He has been established by decree. Their fundamental dogma is that social omnipotence which treats the pretension of truth to be true without any official stamp, as a mere usurpation and sacrilege, and scouts the claim of the individual to possess either a separate conviction or a personal value.

20*th July* 1870 (*Bellalpe*). — A marvellous day. The panorama before me is of a grandiose splendour; it is a symphony of mountains, a cantata of sunny Alps.

I am dazzled and oppressed by it. The feeling uppermost is one of delight in being able to admire, of joy, that is to say, in a recovered power of contemplation which is the result of physical relief, in being able at last to forget myself and surrender myself to things, as befits a man in my state of health. Gratitude is mingled with euthusiasm. I have just spent two hours of continuous delight at the foot of the Sparrenhorn, the peak behind us. A flood of sensations overpowered me. I could only look, feel, dream, and think.

Later. — Ascent of the Sparrenhorn. The peak of it is not very easy to climb, because of the masses of loose stones and the steepness of the path, which runs between two abysses. But how great is one's reward!

The view embraces the whole series of the Valais Alps from the Furka to the Combin; and even beyond the Furka one sees a few peaks of the Ticino and the Rhaetian Alps; while if you turn you see behind you a whole Polar world of snowfields and glaciers forming the southern side of the enormous Bernese group of the Finsteraarhorn, the Mönch, and the Jungfrau. The near representative of the group is the Aletschhorn, whence diverge like so many ribbons the different Aletsch glaciers which wind about the peak from which I saw them. I could study the different zones, one above another, — fields, woods, grassy Alps, bare rock and snow, and the principal types of mountain; the pagoda-shaped Mischabel, with its four *arêtes* as flying buttresses and its staff of nine clustered peaks; the cupola of the Fletschhorn, the dome of Monte Rosa, the pyramid of the Weisshorn, the obelisk of the Cervin.

Round me fluttered a multitude of butterflies and brilliant green-backed flies; but nothing grew except a few lichens. The deadness and emptiness of the upper Aletsch glacier, like some vast white street, called up the image of an icy Pompeii. All around boundless silence. On my way back I noticed some effects of sunshine, — the close elastic mountain grass, starred with gentian, forget-me-not, and anemones, the mountain cattle standing out against the sky, the rocks just piercing the soil, various circular dips in the mountain side, stone waves petrified thousands of thousands of years ago, the undulating ground, the tender quiet of the evening: and I invoked the soul of the mountains and the spirit of the heights!

22d *July* 1870 (*Bellalpe*). — The sky, which was misty and overcast this morning, has become perfectly blue again, and the giants of the Valais are bathed in tranquil light.

Whence this solemn melancholy which oppresses and pursues me? I have just read a series of scientific books (Bronn on the *Laws of Palæontology*, Karl Ritter on the *Law of Geographical Forms*). Are they the cause of this depression? or is it the majesty of this immense landscape, the splendour of this setting sun, which brings the tears to my eyes?

'Créature d'un jour qui t'agites une heure,'

what weighs upon thee — I know it well — is the sense of thine utter nothingness! ... The names of great men hover before my eyes like a secret reproach, and this grand impassive nature tells me that to-morrow I shall have disappeared, butterfly that I am, without having lived. Or perhaps it is the breath of eternal things which stirs in me the shudder of Job. What is man — this weed which a sunbeam withers? What is our life in the infinite abyss? I feel a sort of sacred terror, not only for myself, but for my race, for all that is mortal. Like Buddha, I feel the great wheel turning, — the wheel of universal illusion, — and the dumb stupor which enwraps me is full of anguish. Isis lifts the corner of her veil, and he who perceives the great mystery beneath is struck with giddiness. I can scarcely breathe. It seems to me that I am hanging by a thread above the fathomless abyss of destiny. Is this the Infinite face to face, an intuition of the last great death?

'Créature d'un jour qui t'agites une heure,
  Ton âme est immortelle et tes pleurs vont finir.'

Finir? When depths of ineffable desire are opening in the heart, as vast, as yawning as the immensity which surrounds us? Genius, self-devotion, love, — all these cravings quicken into life and torture me at once. Like the shipwrecked sailor about to sink under the waves, I am conscious of a mad clinging to life, and at the same time of a rush of despair and repentance, which forces from me a cry for pardon. And then all this hidden agony dissolves in wearied submission. 'Resign yourself to the inevitable! Shroud away out of sight the flattering delusions of youth! Live and die in the shade! Like the insects humming in the darkness, offer up your evening prayer. Be content to fade out of life without a murmur whenever the Master of life shall breathe upon your tiny flame! It is out of myriads of unknown lives that every clod of earth is built up.

The infusoria do not count until they are millions upon millions. Accept your nothingness.' Amen!

But there is no peace except in order, in law. Am I in order? Alas, no! My changeable and restless nature will torment me to the end. I shall never see plainly what I ought to do. The love of the better will have stood between me and the good. Yearning for the ideal will have lost me reality. Vague aspiration and undefined desire will have been enough to make my talents useless, and to neutralise my powers. Unproductive nature that I am, tortured by the belief that production was required of me, may not my very remorse be a mistake and a superfluity?

Scherer's phrase comes back to me, 'We must accept ourselves as we are.'

8th September 1870 (*Zurich*).— All the exiles are returning to Paris — Edgar Quinet, Louis Blanc, Victor Hugo. By the help of their united experience will they succeed in maintaining the Republic? It is to be hoped so. But the past makes it lawful to doubt. While the Republic is in reality a fruit, the French look upon it as a seed-sowing. Elsewhere such a form of government presupposes free men; in France it is and must be an instrument of instruction and protection. France has once more placed sovereignty in the hands of universal suffrage, as though the multitude were already enlightened, judicious, and reasonable, and now her task is to train and discipline the force which, by a fiction, is master.

The ambition of France is set upon self-government, but her capacity for it has still to be proved. For eighty years she has confounded revolution with liberty; will she now give proof of amendment and of wisdom? Such a change is not impossible. Let us wait for it with sympathy, but also with caution.

12th September 1870 (*Basle*). — The old Rhine is murmuring under my window. The wide gray stream rolls its great waves along and breaks against the arches of the bridge, just as it did ten years or twenty years ago; the red cathedral shoots its arrow-like spires towards heaven; the ivy on the terraces which fringe the left bank of the Rhine hangs over the walls like a green mantle; the indefatigable ferry-boat goes and comes as it did of yore; in a word, things seem to be eternal, while man's hair turns gray and his heart grows old. I came here first as a student, then as a professor. Now I return to it at the downward turn of middle age, and nothing in the landscape has changed except myself.

The melancholy of memory may be commonplace and puerile, — all the same it is true, it is inexhaustible, and the poets of all times have been open to its attacks.

At bottom, what is individual life? A variation of an eternal theme — to be born, to live, to feel, to hope, to love, to suffer, to weep, to die. Some would add to these, to grow rich, to think, to conquer; but in fact, whatever frantic efforts one may make, however one may strain and excite oneself, one can but cause a greater or slighter undulation in the line of one's destiny. Supposing a man renders the series of fundamental phenomena a little more evident to others or a little more distinct to himself, what does it matter? The whole is still nothing but a fluttering of the infinitely little, the insignificant repetition of an invariable theme. In truth, whether the individual exists or no, the difference is so absolutely imperceptible in the whole of things that every complaint and every desire is ridiculous. Humanity in its entirety is but a flash in the duration of the planet, and the planet may return to the gaseous state without the sun's feeling it even for a second. The individual is the infinitesimal of nothing.

What, then, is nature? Nature is Maïa — that is to say, an incessant, fugitive, indifferent series of phenomena, the manifestation of all possibilities, the inexhaustible play of all combinations.

And is Maïa all the while performing for the amusement of somebody, of some spectator — Brahma? Or is Brahma working out some serious and unselfish end? From the theistic point of view, is it the purpose of God to make souls, to augment the sum of good and wisdom by the multiplication of Himself in free beings — facets which may flash back to Him His own holiness and beauty? This conception is far more attractive to the heart. But is it more true? The moral consciousness affirms it. If man is capable of conceiving goodness, the general principle of things, which cannot be inferior to man, must be good. The philosophy of labour, of duty, of effort, is surely superior to that of phenomena, chance, and universal indifference. If so, the whimsical Maïa would be subordinate to Brahma, the eternal thought, and Brahma would be in his turn subordinate to a holy God.

25th October 1870 *(Geneva).* — 'Each function to the most worthy :' this maxim governs all constitutions, and serves to test them. Democracy is not forbidden to apply it, but democracy rarely does apply it, because she holds, for example, that the most worthy man is the man who pleases her, whereas he who pleases her is not always the most worthy, and because she supposes that reason guides the masses, whereas in reality they are most commonly led by passion. And in the end every falsehood has to be expiated, for truth always takes its revenge.

Alas, whatever one may say or do, wisdom, justice, reason, and goodness will never be anything more than special cases and the heritage of a few elect souls. Moral and intellectual harmony, excellence in all its forms, will always be a rarity of great price, an isolated *chef d'œuvre*. All that can be expected from the most perfect institutions is that they should make it possible for individual excellence to develop itself, not that they should produce the excellent individual. Virtue and genius, grace and beauty, will always constitute a *noblesse* such as no form of government can manufacture. It is of no use, therefore, to excite oneself for or against revolutions which have only an importance of the second order — an importance which I do not wish either to diminish or to ignore, but an importance which, after all, is mostly negative. The political life is but the means of the true life.

26th October 1870. — Sirocco. A bluish sky. The leafy crowns of the trees have dropped at their feet; the finger of winter has touched them. The errand-woman has just brought me my letters. Poor little woman, what a life! She spends her nights in going backwards and forwards from her invalid husband to her sister, who is scarcely less helpless, and her days are passed in labour. Resigned and indefatigable, she goes on without complaining, till she drops.

Lives such as hers prove something: that the true ignorance is moral ignorance, that labour and suffering are the lot of all men, and that classification according to a greater or less degree of folly is inferior to that which proceeds according to a greater or less degree of virtue. The kingdom of God belongs not to the most enlightened but to the best; and the best man is the most unselfish man. Humble, constant, voluntary self-sacrifice, — this is what constitutes the true dignity of man. And therefore is it written, 'The last shall be first.' Society rests upon conscience and not upon science. Civilisation is first and foremost a moral thing. Without honesty, without respect for law, without the worship of duty, without the love of one's neighbour, — in a word, without virtue, — the whole is menaced and falls into decay, and neither letters nor art, neither luxury nor industry, nor rhetoric, nor the policeman, nor the custom-house officer, can maintain erect and whole an edifice of which the foundations are unsound.

A State founded upon interest alone and cemented by fear is an ignoble and unsafe construction. The ultimate ground upon which every civilisation rests is the average morality of the masses, and a sufficient amount of practical righteousness. Duty is what upholds all. So that those who humbly and unobtrusively fulfil it, and set a good example thereby, are the salvation and the sustenance of this brilliant world, which knows nothing about them. Ten righteous men would have saved Sodom, but thousands and thousands of good homely folk are needed to preserve a people from corruption and decay.

If ignorance and passion are the foes of popular morality, it must be confessed that moral indifference is the malady of the cultivated classes. The modern separation of enlightenment and virtue, of thought and conscience, of the intellectual aristocracy from the honest and vulgar crowd, is the greatest danger that can threaten liberty. When any society produces an increasing number of literary exquisites, of satirists, sceptics, and *beaux esprits*, some chemical disorganisation of fabric may be inferred. Take, for example, the century of Augustus and that of Louis XV. Our cynics and railers are mere egotists, who stand aloof from the common duty, and in their indolent remoteness are of no service to society against any ill which may attack it. Their cultivation consists in having got rid of feeling. And thus they fall farther and farther away from true humanity, and approach nearer to the demoniacal nature. What was it that Mephistopheles lacked? Not intelligence certainly, but goodness.

28th October 1870. — It is strange to see how completely justice is forgotten in the presence of great international struggles. Even the great majority of the spectators are no longer capable of judging except as their own personal tastes, dislikes, fears, desires, interests, or passions may dictate, — that is to say, their judgment is not a judgment at all. How many people are capable of delivering a fair verdict on the struggle now going on? Very few! This horror of equity, this antipathy to justice, this rage against a merciful neutrality, represents a kind of eruption of animal passion in man, a blind fierce passion, which is absurd enough to call itself a reason, whereas it is nothing but a force.

16th November 1870. — We are struck by something bewildering and ineffable when we look down into the depths of an abyss; and every soul is an abyss, a mystery of love and pity. A sort of sacred emotion descends upon me whenever I penetrate the recesses of this sanctuary of man, and hear the gentle murmur of the prayers, hymns, and supplications which rise from the hidden depths of the heart. These involuntary confidences fill me with a tender piety and a religious awe and shyness. The whole experience seems to me as wonderful as poetry, and divine with the divineness of birth and dawn. Speech fails me, I bow myself and adore. And, whenever I am able, I strive also to console and fortify.

6th December 1870. — *Dauer im Wechsel* — 'Persistence in change.' This title of a poem by Goethe is the summing up of nature. Everything changes, but with such unequal rapidity that one existence appears eternal to another. A geological age, for instance, compared to the duration of any living being, the duration of a planet compared to a geological age, appear eternities, — our life, too, compared to the thousand impressions which pass across us in an hour. Wherever one looks, one feels oneself overwhelmed by the infinity of infinites. The universe, seriously studied, rouses one's terror. Everything seems so relative that it is scarcely possible to distinguish whether anything has a real value.

Where is the fixed point in this boundless and bottomless gulf? Must it not be that which perceives the relations of things, — in other words, thought, infinite thought?

The perception of ourselves within the infinite thought, the realisation of ourselves in God, self-acceptance in Him, the harmony of our will with His, — in a word, religion, — here alone is firm ground. Whether this thought be free or necessary, happiness lies in identifying oneself with it. Both the Stoic and the Christian surrender themselves to the Being of beings, which the one calls sovereign wisdom and the other sovereign goodness. St. John says, 'God is Light,' 'God is Love.' The Brahmin says, 'God is the inexhaustible fount of poetry.' Let us say, 'God is Perfection.' And man? Man, for all his inexpressible insignificance and frailty, may still apprehend the idea of perfection, may help forward the supreme will, and die with Hosanna on his lips!

. . . . . .

All teaching depends upon a certain presentiment and preparation in the taught; we can only teach others profitably what they already virtually know; we can only give them what they had already. This principle of education is also a law of history. Nations can only be developed on the lines of their tendencies and aptitudes. Try them on any other and they are rebellious and incapable of improvement.

* * * * * *

By despising himself too much a man comes to be worthy of his own contempt.

* * * * * *

Its way of suffering is the witness which a soul bears to itself.

* * * * * *

The beautiful is superior to the sublime because it lasts and does not satiate, while the sublime is relative, temporary, and violent.

* * * * * *

4th February 1871. — Perpetual effort is the characteristic of modern morality. A painful process has taken the place of the old harmony, the old equilibrium, the old joy and fulness of being. We are all so many fauns, satyrs, or Silenuses, aspiring to become angels; so many deformities labouring for our own embellishment; so many clumsy chrysalises each working painfully towards the development of the butterfly within him. Our ideal is no longer a serene beauty of soul; it is the agony of Laocoon struggling with the hydra of evil. The lot is cast irrevocably. There are no more happy whole-natured men among us, nothing but so many candidates for heaven, galley-slaves on earth.

'Nous ramons notre vie en attendant le port.'

Molière said that reasoning banished reason. It is possible also that the progress towards perfection we are so proud of is only a pretentious imperfection. Duty seems now to be more negative than positive; it means lessening evil rather than actual good; it is a generous discontent, but not happiness; it is an incessant pursuit of an unattainable goal, a noble madness, but not reason; it is home-sickness for the impossible, — pathetic and pitiful, but still not wisdom.

The being which has attained harmony, and every being may attain it, has found its place in the order of the universe, and represents the divine thought at least as clearly as a flower or a solar system. Harmony seeks nothing outside itself. It is what it ought to be; it is the expression of right, order, law, and truth; it is greater than time, and represents eternity.

6th February 1871. — I am reading Juste Olivier's *Chansons du Soir* over again, and all the melancholy of the poet seems to pass into my veins. It is the revelation of a complete existence, and of a whole world of melancholy reverie.

How much character there is in *Musette*,

the *Chanson de l'Alouette*, the *Chant du Retour*, and the *Gaîté*, and how much freshness in *Lina*, and '*À ma fille!*' But the best pieces of all are *Au delà*, *Homunculus*, *La Trompeuse*, and especially *Frère Jacques*, its author's masterpiece. To these may be added the *Marionettes* and the national song, *Helvétie*. Serious purpose and intention disguised in gentle gaiety and childlike badinage, feeling hiding itself under a smile of satire, a resigned and pensive wisdom expressing itself in rustic round or ballad, the power of suggesting everything in a nothing, — these are the points in which the Vaudois poet triumphs. On the reader's side there is emotion and surprise, and on the author's a sort of pleasant slyness which seems to delight in playing tricks upon you, only tricks of the most dainty and brilliant kind. Juste Olivier has the passion we might imagine a fairy to have for delicate mystification. He hides his gifts. He promises nothing and gives a great deal. His generosity, which is prodigal, has a surly air; his simplicity is really subtlety; his malice pure tenderness; and his whole talent is, as it were, the fine flower of the Vaudois mind in its sweetest and dreamiest form.

10th February 1871. — My reading for this morning has been some vigorous chapters of Taine's *History of English Literature*. Taine is a writer whose work always produces a disagreeable impression upon me, as though of a creaking of pulleys and a clicking of machinery; there is a smell of the laboratory about it. His style is the style of chemistry and technology. The science of it is inexorable; it is dry and forcible, penetrating and hard, strong and harsh, but altogether lacking in charm, humanity, nobility, and grace. The disagreeable effect which it makes on one's taste, ear, and heart, depends probably upon two things: upon the moral philosophy of the author and upon his literary principles. The profound contempt for humanity which characterises the physiological school, and the intrusion of technology into literature inaugurated by Balzac and Stendhal, explain the underlying aridity of which one is sensible in these pages, and which seems to choke one like the gases from a manufactory of mineral products. The book is instructive in the highest degree, but instead of animating and stirring, it parches, corrodes, and saddens its reader. It excites no feeling whatever; it is simply a means of information. — I imagine this kind of thing will be the literature of the future — a literature *à l'Américaine*, as different as possible from Greek art, giving us algebra instead of life, the formula instead of the image, the exhalations of the crucible instead of the divine madness of Apollo. Cold vision will replace the joys of thought, and we shall see the death of poetry, flayed and dissected by science.

15th February 1871. — Without intending it, nations educate each other, while having apparently nothing in view but their own selfish interests. It was France who made the Germany of the present, by attempting its destruction during ten generations; it is Germany who will regenerate contemporary France, by the effort to crush her. Revolutionary France will teach equality to the Germans, who are by nature hierarchical. Germany will teach the French that rhetoric is not science, and that appearance is not as valuable as reality. The worship of prestige — that is to say, of falsehood; the passion for vainglory — that is to say, for smoke and noise; — these are what must die in the interests of the world. It is a false religion which is being destroyed. I hope sincerely that this war will issue in a new balance of things better than any which has gone before — a new Europe, in which the government of the individual by himself will be the cardinal principle of society, in opposition to the Latin principle, which regards the individual as a thing, a means to an end, an instrument of the Church or of the State.

In the order and harmony which would result from free adhesion and voluntary submission to a common ideal, we should see the rise of a new moral world. It would be an equivalent, expressed in lay terms, to the idea of a universal priesthood. The model state ought to resemble a great musical society in which every one submits to be organised, subordinated, and disciplined for the sake of art, and for the sake of producing a masterpiece. Nobody is coerced, nobody is made use of for selfish purposes, nobody plays a hypocritical or selfish part. All bring their talent to the common stock, and contribute knowingly and gladly to the common wealth. Even self-love itself is obliged to help on the general action, under pain of rebuff should it make itself apparent.

18th February 1871. — It is in the novel that the average vulgarity of German society, and its inferiority to the societies of France and England, are most clearly visible. The notion of 'bad taste' seems to have no place in German æsthetics. Their elegance has no grace in it; and they cannot understand the enormous difference there is between distinction (what is *gentlemanly*, *ladylike*), and their stiff *vornehmlichkeit*. Their imagination lacks style, training, education, and knowledge of the world; it has an ill-bred air even in its Sunday dress. The race is poetical and intelligent, but common and ill-mannered. Pliancy and gentleness, manners, wit, vivacity, taste, dignity, and charm, are qualities which belong to others.

Will that inner freedom of soul, that profound harmony of all the faculties which I have so often observed among the best Germans, ever come to the surface? Will the conquerors of to-day ever learn to civilise and soften their forms of life? It is by their future novels that we shall be able to judge. As soon as they are capable of the novel of 'good society' they will have excelled all rivals. Till then, finish, polish, the maturity of social culture, are beyond them; they may have humanity of feeling, but the delicacies, the little perfections of life, are unknown to them. They may be honest and well-meaning, but they are utterly without *savoir vivre*.

22d February 1871. — *Soirée* at the M——. About thirty people representing our best society were there, a happy mixture of sexes and ages. There were gray heads, young girls, bright faces, — the whole framed in some Aubusson tapestries which made a charming background, and gave a soft air of distance to the brilliantly-dressed groups.

In society people are expected to behave as if they lived on ambrosia and concerned themselves with nothing but the loftiest interests. Anxiety, need, passion, have no existence. All realism is suppressed as brutal. In a word, what we call 'society' proceeds for the moment on the flattering illusory assumption that it is moving in an ethereal atmosphere and breathing the air of the gods. All vehemence, all natural expression, all real suffering, all careless familiarity, or any frank sign of passion, are startling and distasteful in this delicate *milieu*; they at once destroy the common work, the cloud palace, the magical architectural whole, which has been raised by the general consent and effort. It is like the sharp cock-crow which breaks the spell of all enchantments, and puts the fairies to flight. These select gatherings produce, without knowing it, a sort of concert for eyes and ears, an improvised work of art. By the instinctive collaboration of everybody concerned, intellect and taste hold festival, and the associations of reality are exchanged for the associations of imagination. So understood, society is a form of poetry; the cultivated classes deliberately recompose the idyll of the past and the buried world of Astrea. Paradox or no, I believe that these fugitive attempts to reconstruct a dream whose only end is beauty represent confused reminiscences of an age of gold haunting the human heart, or rather aspirations towards a harmony of things which everyday reality denies to us, and of which art alone gives us a glimpse.

28th April 1871. — For a psychologist it is extremely interesting to be readily and directly conscious of the complications of one's own organism and the play of its several parts. It seems to me that the sutures of my being are becoming just loose enough to allow me at once a clear perception of myself as a whole and a distinct sense of my own brittleness. A feeling like this makes personal existence a perpetual astonishment and curiosity. Instead of only seeing the world which surrounds me, I analyse myself. Instead of being single, all of a piece, I become legion, multitude, a whirlwind — a very cosmos. Instead of living on the surface, I take possession of my inmost self, I apprehend myself, if not in my cells and atoms, at least so far as my groups of organs, almost my tissues, are concerned. In other words, the central monad isolates itself from all the subordinate monads, that it may consider them, and finds its harmony again in itself.

Health is the perfect balance between our organism, with all its component parts, and the outer world; it serves us especially for acquiring a knowledge of that world. Organic disturbance obliges us to set up a fresh and more spiritual equilibrium, to withdraw within the soul. Thereupon our bodily constitution itself becomes the object of thought. It is no longer we, although it may belong to us; it is nothing more than the vessel in which we make the passage of life, a vessel of which we study the weak points and the structure without identifying it with our own individuality.

Where is the ultimate residence of the self? In thought, or rather in consciousness. But below consciousness there is its germ, the *punctum saliens* of spontaneity; for consciousness is not primitive, it *becomes*. The question is, can the thinking monad return into its envelope, that is to say, into pure spontaneity, or even into the dark abyss of virtuality? I hope not. The kingdom passes; the king remains; or rather is it the royalty alone which subsists, — that is to say, the idea, — the personality being in its turn merely the passing vesture of the permanent idea? Is Leibnitz or Hegel right? Is the individual immortal under the form of the spiritual body? Is he eternal under the form of the individual idea? Who saw most clearly, St. Paul or Plato? The theory of Leibnitz attracts me most because it opens to us an infinite of duration, of multitude, and evolution. For a monad, which is the virtual universe, a whole infinite of time is not too much to develop the infinite within it. Only one must admit exterior actions and influences which affect the evolution of the monad. Its independence must be a mobile and increasing quantity between zero and the infinite, without ever reaching either completeness or nullity, for the monad can be neither absolutely passive nor entirely free.

21st June 1871. — The international socialism of the *ouvriers*, ineffectually put down in Paris, is beginning to celebrate its approaching victory. For it there is neither country, nor memories, nor property, nor religion. There is nothing and nobody but itself. Its dogma is equality, its prophet is Mably, and Babœuf is its god.[8]

How is the conflict to be solved, since there is no longer one single common principle between the partisans and the enemies of the existing form of society, between liberalism and the worship of equality? Their respective notions of man, duty, happiness, — that is to say, of life and its end, — differ radically. I suspect that the communism of the *Internationale* is merely the pioneer of Russian nihilism, which will be the common grave of the old races and the servile races, the Latins and the Slavs. If so, the salvation of humanity will depend upon individualism of the brutal American sort. I believe that the nations of the present are rather tempting chastisement than learning wisdom. Wisdom, which means balance and harmony, is only met with in individuals. Democracy, which means the rule of the masses, gives preponderance to instinct, to nature, to the passions, — that is to say, to blind impulse, to elemental gravitation, to generic fatality. Perpetual vacillation between contraries becomes its only mode of progress, because it represents that childish form of prejudice which falls in love and cools, adores and curses, with the same haste and unreason. A succession of opposing follies gives an impression of change which the people readily identify with improvement, as though Enceladus was more at ease on his left side than on his right, the weight of the volcano remaining the same. The stupidity of Demos is only equalled by its presumption. It is like a youth with all his animal and none of his reasoning powers developed.

Luther's comparison of humanity to a drunken peasant, always ready to fall from his horse on one side or the other, has always struck me as a particularly happy one. It is not that I deny the right of the democracy, but I have no sort of illusion as to the use it will make of its right, so long, at any rate, as wisdom is the exception and conceit the rule. Numbers make law, but goodness has nothing to do with figures. Every fiction is self-expiating, and democracy rests upon this legal fiction, that the majority has not only force but reason on its side — that it possesses not only the right to act but the wisdom necessary for action. The fiction is dangerous because of its flattery; the demagogues have always flattered the private feelings of the masses. The masses will always be below the average. Besides, the age of majority will be lowered, the barriers of sex will be swept away, and democracy will finally make itself absurd by handing over the decision of all that is greatest to all that is most incapable. Such an end will be the punishment of its abstract principle of equality, which dispenses the ignorant man from the necessity of self-training, the foolish man from that of self-judgment, and tells the child that there is no need for him to become a man, and the good-for-nothing that self-improvement is of no account. Public law, founded upon virtual equality, will destroy itself by its consequences. It will not recognise the inequalities of worth, of merit, and of experience; in a word, it ignores individual labour, and it will end in the triumph of platitude and the residuum. The *régime* of the Parisian Commune has shown us what kind of material comes to the top in these days of frantic vanity and universal suspicion.

Still, humanity is tough, and survives all catastrophes. Only it makes one impatient to see the race always taking the longest road to an end, and exhausting all possible faults before it is able to accomplish one definite step towards improvement. These innumerable follies, that are to be and must be, have an irritating effect upon me. The more majestic is the history of science, the more intolerable is the history of politics and religion. The mode of progress in the moral world seems an abuse of the patience of God.

Enough! There is no help in misanthropy and pessimism. If our race vexes us, let us keep a decent silence on the matter. We are imprisoned on the same ship, and we shall sink with it. Pay your own debt, and leave the rest to God. Sharer, as you inevitably are, in the sufferings of your kind, set a good example: that is all which is asked of you. Do all the good you can, and say all the truth you know or believe; and for the rest be patient, resigned, submissive. God does His business, do yours.

29th July 1871.—So long as a man is capable of self-renewal he is a living being. Goethe, Schleiermacher and Humboldt, were masters of the art. If we are to remain among the living there must be a perpetual revival of youth within us, brought about by inward change and by love of the Platonic sort. The soul must be for ever recreating itself, trying all its various modes, vibrating in all its fibres, raising up new interests for itself. . . .

The *Epistles* and the *Epigrams* of Goethe which I have been reading to-day do not make one love him. Why? Because he has so little soul. His way of understanding love, religion, duty, and patriotism has something mean and repulsive in it. There is no ardour, no generosity, in him. A secret barrenness, an ill-concealed egotism, makes itself felt through all the wealth and flexibility of his talent. It is true that the egotism of Goethe has at least this much that is excellent in it, that it respects the liberty of the individual, and is favourable to all originality. But it will go out of its way to help nobody; it will give itself no trouble for anybody; it will lighten nobody else's burden; — in a word, it does away with charity, the great Christian virtue. Perfection for Goethe consists in personal nobility, not in love; his standard is æsthetic, not moral. He ignores holiness, and has never allowed himself to reflect on the dark problem of evil. A Spinozist to the core, he believes in individual luck, not in liberty nor in responsibility. He is a Greek of the great time, to whom the inward crises of the religious consciousness are unknown. He represents, then, a state of soul earlier than or subsequent to Christianity, what the prudent critics of our time call the 'modern spirit;' and only one tendency of the modern spirit — the worship of nature. For Goethe stands outside all the social and political aspirations of the generality of mankind; he takes no more interest than Nature herself in the disinherited, the feeble, and the oppressed. . . .

The restlessness of our time does not exist for Goethe and his school. It is explicable enough. The deaf have no sense of dissonance. The man who knows nothing of the voice of conscience, the voice of regret or remorse, cannot even guess at the troubles of those who live under two masters and two laws, and belong to two worlds, — that of Nature and that of Liberty. For himself, his choice is made. But humanity cannot choose and exclude. All needs are vocal at once in the cry of her suffering. She hears the men of science, but she listens to those who talk to her of religion; pleasure attracts her, but sacrifice moves her; and she hardly knows whether she hates or whether she adores the crucifix.

Later. — Still re-reading the sonnets and the miscellaneous poems of Goethe. — The impression left by this part of the *Gedichte* is much more favourable than that made upon me by the *Elegies* and the *Epigrams*. The *Water Spirits* and *The Divine* are especially noble in feeling. One must never be too hasty in judging these complex natures. Completely lacking as he is in the sense of obligation and of sin, Goethe nevertheless finds his way to seriousness through dignity. Greek sculpture has been his school of virtue.

15*th August* 1871. — Re-read, for the second time, Renan's *Vie de Jésus*, in the sixteenth popular edition. The most characteristic feature of this analysis of Christianity is that sin plays no part at all in it. Now, if anything explains the success of the Gospel among men, it is that it brought them deliverance from sin — in a word, salvation. A man, however, is bound to explain a religion seriously, and not to shirk the very centre of his subject. This white-marble Christ is not the Christ who inspired the martyrs and has dried so many tears. The author lacks moral seriousness, and confounds nobility of character with holiness. He speaks as an artist conscious of a pathetic subject, but his moral sense is not interested in the question. It is not possible to mistake the epicureanism of the imagination, delighting itself in an æsthetic spectacle, for the struggles of a soul passionately in search of truth. In Renan there are still some remains of priestly *ruse;* he strangles with sacred cords. His tone of contemptuous indulgence towards a more or less captious clergy might be tolerated, but he should have shown a more respectful sincerity in dealing with the sincere and the spiritual. Laugh at Pharisaism as you will, but speak simply and plainly to honest folk.[9]

Later. — To understand is to be conscious of the fundamental unity of the thing to be explained — that is to say, to conceive it in its entirety both of life and development, to be able to remake it by a mental process without making a mistake, without adding or omitting anything. It means, first, complete identification of the object, and then the power of making it clear to others by a full and just interpretation. To understand is more difficult than to judge, for understanding is the transference of the mind into the conditions of the object, whereas judgment is simply the enunciation of the individual opinion.

25th August 1871 (*Charnex-sur-Montreux*). — Magnificent weather. The morning seems bathed in happy peace, and a heavenly fragrance rises from mountain and shore; it is as though a benediction were laid upon us. No vulgar intrusive noise disturbs the religious quiet of the scene. One might believe oneself in a church — a vast temple in which every being and every natural beauty has its place. I dare not breathe for fear of putting the dream to flight, — a dream traversed by angels.

'Comme autrefois j'entends dans l'éther infini
　La musique du temps et l'hosanna des
　mondes.'

In these heavenly moments the cry of
Pauline rises to one's lips.[10] 'I feel! I
believe! I see!' All the miseries, the
cares, the vexations of life, are forgotten;
the universal joy absorbs us; we enter into
the divine order, and into the blessedness
of the Lord. Labour and tears, sin, pain,
and death have passed away. To exist is
to bless; life is happiness. In this sublime
pause of things all dissonances have disappeared. It is as though creation were but
one vast symphony, glorifying the God of
goodness with an inexhaustible wealth of
praise and harmony. We question no
longer whether it is so or not. We have
ourselves become notes in the great concert; and the soul breaks the silence of
ecstasy only to vibrate in unison with the
eternal joy.

22d September 1871 (*Charnex*). — Gray
sky — a melancholy day. A friend has
left me, the sun is unkind and capricious.
Everything passes away, everything forsakes us. And in place of all we have
lost, age and gray hairs!

... After dinner I walked to Chailly between two showers. A rainy landscape has a great charm for me; the dark tints become more velvety, the softer tones more ethereal. The country in rain is like a face with traces of tears upon it,—less beautiful no doubt, but more expressive.

Behind the beauty which is superficial, gladsome, radiant, and palpable, the æsthetic sense discovers another order of beauty altogether, hidden, veiled, secret, and mysterious, akin to moral beauty. This sort of beauty only reveals itself to the initiated, and is all the more exquisite for that. It is a little like the refined joy of sacrifice, like the madness of faith, like the luxury of grief; it is not within the reach of all the world. Its attraction is peculiar, and affects one like some strange perfume, or bizarre melody. When once the taste for it is set up the mind takes a special and keen delight in it, for one finds in it

'Son bien premièrement, puis le dédain d'autrui,'

and it is pleasant to one's vanity not to be of the same opinion as the common herd. This, however, is not possible with things which are evident, and beauty which is incontestable. Charm, perhaps, is a better name for the esoteric and paradoxical beauty, which escapes the vulgar, and appeals to our dreamy meditative side. Classical beauty belongs, so to speak, to all eyes; it has ceased to belong to itself. Esoteric beauty is shy and retiring. It only unveils itself to unsealed eyes, and bestows its favours only upon love.

This is why my friend ——, who places herself immediately in relation with the souls of those she meets, does not see the ugliness of people when once she is interested in them. She likes and dislikes, and those she likes are beautiful, those she dislikes are ugly. There is nothing more complicated in it than that. For her, æsthetic considerations are lost in moral sympathy; she looks with her heart only; she passes by the chapter of the beautiful, and goes on to the chapter of charm. I can do the same; only it is by reflection and on second thoughts; my friend does it involuntarily and at once; she has not the artistic fibre. The craving for a perfect correspondence between the inside and the outside of things — between matter and form — is not in her nature. She does not suffer from ugliness, she scarcely perceives it. As for me, I can only forget what shocks me, I cannot help being shocked. All corporal defects irritate me, and the want of beauty in women, being something which ought not to exist, shocks me like a tear, a solecism, a dissonance, a spot of ink,—in a word, like something out of order. On the other hand, beauty restores and fortifies me like some miraculous food, like Olympian ambrosia.

'Que le bon soit toujours camarade du beau
  Dès demain je chercherai femme.
Mais comme le divorce entre eux n'est pas nouveau,
Et que peu de beaux corps, hôtes d'une belle âme,
  Assemblent l'un et l'autre point——'

I will not finish, for after all one must resign oneself. A beautiful soul in a healthy body is already a rare and blessed thing; and if one finds heart, common sense, intellect, and courage into the bargain, one may well do without that ravishing dainty which we call beauty, and almost without that delicious seasoning which we call grace. We do without— with a sigh, as one does without a luxury. Happy we, to possess what is necessary.

29th December 1871. — I have been reading Bahnsen (*Critique de l'évolutionisme de Hegel-Hartmann, au nom des principes de Schopenhauer*). What a writer! Like a cuttle-fish in water, every movement produces a cloud of ink which shrouds his thought in darkness. And what a doctrine! A thoroughgoing pessimism, which regards the world as absurd, 'absolutely idiotic,' and reproaches Hartmann for having allowed the evolution of the universe some little remains of logic, while, on the contrary, this evolution is eminently contradictory, and there is no reason anywhere except in the poor brain of the reasoner. Of all possible worlds that which exists is the worst. Its only excuse is that it tends of itself to destruction. The hope of the philosopher is that reasonable beings will shorten their agony and hasten the return of everything to nothing. It is the philosophy of a desperate Satanism, which has not even the resigned perspectives of Buddhism to offer to the disappointed and disillusioned soul. The individual can but protest and curse. This frantic Sivaism is developed from the conception which makes the world the product of blind will, the principle of everything.

The acrid blasphemy of the doctrine

naturally leads the writer to indulgence in epithets of bad taste which prevent our regarding his work as the mere challenge of a paradoxical theorist. We have really to do with a theophobist, whom faith in goodness rouses to a fury of contempt. In order to hasten the deliverance of the world, he kills all consolation, all hope, and all illusion in the germ, and substitutes for the love of humanity which inspired Çakyamouni, that Mephistophelian gall which defiles, withers, and corrodes everything it touches.

Evolutionism, fatalism, pessimism, nihilism — how strange it is to see this desolate and terrible doctrine growing and expanding at the very moment when the German nation is celebrating its greatness and its triumphs! The contrast is so startling that it sets one thinking.

This orgie of philosophic thought, identifying error with existence itself, and developing the axiom of Proudhon, — 'Evil is God,' will bring back the mass of mankind to the Christian theodicy, which is neither optimist nor pessimist, but simply declares that the felicity which Christianity calls eternal life is accessible to man.

Self-mockery, starting from a horror of

stupidity and hypocrisy, and standing in the way of all wholeness of mind and all true seriousness, — this is the goal to which intellect brings us at last, unless conscience cries out. The mind must have for ballast the clear conception of duty, if it is not to fluctuate between levity and despair.

* * * * *

Before giving advice we must have secured its acceptance, or rather, have made it desired.

* * * * *

If we begin by overrating the being we love, we shall end by treating it with wholesale injustice.

* * * * *

It is dangerous to abandon oneself to the luxury of grief; it deprives one of courage, and even of the wish for recovery.

* * * * *

We learn to recognise a mere blunting of the conscience in that incapacity for indignation which is not to be confounded with the gentleness of charity, or the reserve of humility.

* * * * *

7th February 1872. — Without faith a man can do nothing. But faith can stifle all science.

What, then, is this Proteus, and whence?

Faith is a certitude without proofs. Being a certitude, it is an energetic principle of action. Being without proof, it is the contrary of science. Hence its two aspects and its two effects. Is its point of departure intelligence? No. Thought may shake or strengthen faith; it cannot produce it. Is its origin in the will? No: good-will may favour it, ill-will may hinder it, but no one believes by will, and faith is not a duty. Faith is a sentiment, for it is a hope; it is an instinct, for it precedes all outward instruction. Faith is the heritage of the individual at birth; it is that which binds him to the whole of being. The individual only detaches himself with difficulty from the maternal breast; he only isolates himself by an effort from the nature around him, from the love which enwraps him, the ideas in which he floats, the cradle in which he lies. He is born in union with humanity, with the world, and with God. The trace of this original union is faith. Faith is the reminiscence of that vague Eden whence our individuality issued, but which it inhabited in the somnambulist state anterior to the personal life

Our individual life consists in separating

ourselves from our *milieu;* in so reacting upon it that we apprehend it consciously, and make ourselves spiritual personalities — that is to say, intelligent and free. Our primitive faith is nothing more than the neutral matter which our experience of life and things works up afresh, and which may be so affected by our studies of every kind as to perish completely in its original form. We ourselves may die before we have been able to recover the harmony of a personal faith which may satisfy our mind and conscience as well as our hearts. But the need of faith never leaves us. It is the postulate of a higher truth which is to bring all things into harmony. It is the stimulus of research ; it holds out to us the reward, it points us to the goal. Such at least is the true, the excellent faith. That which is a mere prejudice of childhood, which has never known doubt, which ignores science, which cannot respect or understand or tolerate different convictions — such a faith is a stupidity and a hatred, the mother of all fanaticisms. We may then repeat of faith what Æsop said of the tongue —

' Quid melius linguâ, linguâ quid pejus eâdem ?'

To draw the poison-fangs of faith in ourselves, we must subordinate it to the love of truth. The supreme worship of the true is the only means of purification for all religions, all confessions, all sects. Faith should only be allowed the second place, for faith has a judge — in truth. When she exalts herself to the position of supreme judge the world is enslaved: Christianity, from the fourth to the seventeenth century, is the proof it. . . . Will the enlightened faith ever conquer the vulgar faith? We must look forward in trust to a better future.

The difficulty, however, is this. A narrow faith has much more energy than an enlightened faith; the world belongs to will much more than to wisdom. It is not then certain that liberty will triumph over fanaticism; and besides, independent thought will never have the force of prejudice. The solution is to be found in a division of labour. After those whose business it will have been to hold up to the world the ideal of a pure and free faith, will come the men of violence, who will bring the new creed within the circle of recognised interests, prejudices, and institutions. Is not this just what happened to

Christianity? After the gentle Master, the impetuous Paul and the bitter Councils. It is true that this is what corrupted the Gospel. But still Christianity has done more good than harm to humanity, and so the world advances, by the successive decay of gradually improved ideals.

19*th June* 1872. — The wrangle in the Paris Synod still goes on.[11] The supernatural is the stone of stumbling. — It might be possible to agree on the idea of the Divine; but no, that is not the question — the chaff must be separated from the good grain. The supernatural is miracle, and miracle is an objective phenomenon independent of all preceding causality. Now, miracle thus understood cannot be proved experimentally; and besides, the subjective phenomena, far more important than all the rest, are left out of account in the definition. Men will not see that miracle is a perception of the soul; a vision of the Divine behind nature; a psychical crisis, analogous to that of Æneas on the last day of Troy, which reveals to us the heavenly powers prompting and directing human action. For the indifferent there are no miracles. It is only the religious souls who sincerity; he must explain to me how the matter lies, point out to me the questions involved in it, their origin, their difficulties, the different solutions attempted, and their degree of probability. He must respect my reason, my conscience, and my liberty. All scholasticism is an attempt to take by storm; the authority pretends to explain itself, but only pretends, and its deference is merely illusory. The dice are loaded and the premisses are prejudged. The unknown is taken as known, and all the rest is deduced from it.

Philosophy means the complete liberty of the mind, and therefore independence of all social, political, or religious prejudice. It is to begin with neither Christian nor pagan, neither monarchical nor democratic, neither socialist nor individualist; it is critical and impartial; it loves one thing only — truth. If it disturbs the ready-made opinions of the Church or the State — of the historical medium — in which the philosopher happens to have been born, so much the worse, but there is no help for it.

'Est ut est aut non est.'

Philosophy means, first, doubt; and afterwards the consciousness of what knowledge means, the consciousness of uncertainty and of ignorance, the consciousness of limit, shade, degree, possibility. The ordinary man doubts nothing and suspects nothing. The philosopher is more cautious, but he is thereby unfitted for action, because, although he sees the goal less dimly than others, he sees his own weakness too clearly, and has no illusions as to his chances of reaching it.

The philosopher is like a man fasting in the midst of universal intoxication. He alone perceives the illusion of which all creatures are the willing playthings; he is less duped than his neighbour by his own nature. He judges more sanely, he sees things as they are. It is in this that his liberty consists — in the ability to see clearly and soberly, in the power of mental record. Philosophy has for its foundation critical lucidity. The end and climax of it would be the intuition of the universal law, of the first principle and the final aim of the universe. Not to be deceived is its first desire: to understand, its second. Emancipation from error is the condition of real knowledge. The philosopher is a sceptic seeking a plausible hypothesis, which may explain to him the whole of his experiences.

When ne imagines that he has found such a key to life he offers it to, but does not force it on, his fellow-men.

9th October 1872. — I have been taking tea at the M.'s. These English homes are very attractive. They are the recompense and the result of a long-lived civilisation, and of an ideal untiringly pursued. What ideal? That of a moral order, founded on respect for self and for others, and on reverence for duty — in a word, upon personal worth and dignity. The master shows consideration to his guests, the children are deferential to their parents, and every one and everything has its place. They understand both how to command and how to obey. The little world is well governed, and seems to go of itself; duty is the *genius loci* — but duty tinged with a reserve and self-control which is the English characteristic. The children are the great test of this domestic system: they are happy, smiling, trustful, and yet no trouble. One feels that they know themselves to be loved, but that they know also that they must obey. *Our* children behave like masters of the house, and when any definite order comes to limit their encroachments they see in it an abuse of power, an arbitrary act. Why? Because it is their principle to believe that everything turns round them. Our children may be gentle and affectionate, but they are not grateful, and they know nothing of self-control.

How do English mothers attain this result? By a rule which is impersonal, invariable, and firm; in other words, by law, which forms man for liberty, while arbitrary decree only leads to rebellion and attempts at emancipation. This method has the immense advantage of forming characters which are restive under arbitrary authority, and yet amenable to justice, conscious of what is due to them and what they owe to others, watchful over conscience, and practised in self-government. In every English child one feels something of the national motto — 'God and my right,' and in every English household one has a sense that the home is a citadel, or better still, a ship in which every one has his place. Naturally in such a world the value set on family life corresponds with the cost of producing it; it is sweet to those whose efforts maintain it.

14th October 1872. — The man who gives

himself to contemplation looks on at rather than directs his life, is rather a spectator than an actor, seeks rather to understand than to achieve. Is this mode of existence illegitimate, immoral? Is one bound to act? Is such detachment an idiosyncrasy to be respected or a sin to be fought against? I have always hesitated on this point, and I have wasted years in futile self-reproach and useless fits of activity. My western conscience, penetrated as it is with Christian morality, has always persecuted my Oriental quietism and Buddhist tendencies. I have not dared to approve myself, I have not known how to correct myself. In this, as in all else, I have remained divided and perplexed, wavering between two extremes. So equilibrium is somehow preserved, but the crystallisation of action or thought becomes impossible.

Having early caught a glimpse of the absolute, I have never had the indiscreet effrontery of individualism. What right have I to make a merit of a defect? I have never been able to see any necessity for imposing myself upon others, nor for succeeding. I have seen nothing clearly except my own deficiencies and the superiority of others. That is not the way to make a career. With varied aptitudes and a fair intelligence, I had no dominant tendency, no imperious faculty, so that while by virtue of capacity I felt myself free, yet when free I could not discover what was best. Equilibrium produced indecision, and indecision has rendered all my faculties barren.

8th November 1872 (*Friday*). — I have been turning over the *Stoics* again. Poor Louisa Siefert![12] Ah! we play the Stoic, and all the while the poisoned arrow in the side pierces and wounds, *lethalis arundo*. What is it that, like all passionate souls, she really craves for? Two things which are contradictory — glory and happiness. She adores two incompatibles — the Reformation and the Revolution, France and the contrary of France: her talent itself is a combination of two opposing qualities, inwardness and brilliancy, noisy display and lyrical charm. She dislocates the rhythm of her verse, while at the same time she has a sensitive ear for rhyme. She is always wavering between Valmore and Baudelaire, between Leconte de Lisle and Sainte-Beuve — that is to say, her taste is a bringing together of extremes. She herself has described it: —

> 'Toujours extrême en mes désirs,
> Jadis, enfant joyeuse et folle,
> Souvent une seule parole
> Bouleversait tous mes plaisirs.'

But what a fine instrument she possesses! what strength of soul! what wealth of imagination!

3d December 1872. — What a strange dream! I was under an illusion and yet not under it; I was playing a comedy to myself, deceiving my imagination without being able to deceive my consciousness. This power which dreams have of fusing incompatibles together, of uniting what is exclusive, of identifying yes and no, is what is most wonderful and most symbolical in them. In a dream our individuality is not shut up within itself; it envelops, so to speak, its surroundings; it is the landscape, and all that it contains, ourselves included. But if our imagination is not our own, if it is impersonal, then personality is but a special and limited case of its general functions. *A fortiori* it would be the same for thought. And if so, thought might exist without possessing itself individually, without embodying itself in an *ego*. In other words, dreams lead us to the idea of an imagination enfranchised from the limits of personality, and even of a thought which should be no longer conscious. The individual who dreams is on the way to become dissolved in the universal phantasmagoria of Maïa. Dreams are excursions into the limbo of things, a semi-deliverance from the human prison. The man who dreams is but the *locale* of various phenomena, of which he is the spectator in spite of himself; he is passive and impersonal; he is the plaything of unknown vibrations and invisible sprites.

The man who should never issue from the state of dream would have never attained humanity, properly so called, but the man who had never dreamed would only know the mind in its completed or manufactured state, and would not be able to understand the genesis of personality; he would be like a crystal, incapable of guessing what crystallisation means. So that the waking life issues from the dream life, as dreams are an emanation from the nervous life, and this again is the fine flower of organic life. Thought is the highest point of a series of ascending metamorphoses, which is called nature. Personality by means of thought recovers in inward profundity what it has lost in extension, and makes up for the rich accumulations of receptive passivity by the enormous privilege of that empire over self which is called liberty. Dreams, by confusing and suppressing all limits, make us feel, indeed, the severity of the conditions attached to the higher existence; but conscious and voluntary thought alone brings knowledge and allows us to act — that is to say, is alone capable of science and of perfection. Let us then take pleasure in dreaming for reasons of psychological curiosity and mental recreation; but let us never speak ill of thought, which is our strength and our dignity. Let us begin as Orientals, and end as Westerns, for these are the two halves of wisdom.

11th December 1872. — A deep and dreamless sleep; and now I wake up to the gray, lowering, rainy sky, which has kept us company for so long. The air is mild, the general outlook depressing. I think that it is partly the fault of my windows, which are not very clean, and contribute by their dimness to this gloomy aspect of the outer world. Rain and smoke have besmeared them.

Between us and things how many screens there are! Mood, health, the tissues of the eye, the window-panes of our cell, mist, smoke, rain, dust, and light itself — and all infinitely variable! Heraclitus said: No man bathes twice in the same river. I feel inclined to say: No one sees the same landscape twice over, for a window is one kaleidoscope, and the spectator another.

What is madness? Illusion, raised to the second power. A sound mind establishes regular relations, a *modus vivendi*, between things, men, and itself, and it is under the delusion that it has got hold of stable truth and eternal fact. Madness does not even see what sanity sees, deceiving itself all the while by the belief that it sees better than sanity. The sane mind or common sense confounds the fact of experience with necessary fact, and assumes in good faith that what is, is the measure of what may be; while madness cannot perceive any difference between what is and what it imagines — it confounds its dreams with reality.

Wisdom consists in rising superior both to madness and to common sense, and in lending oneself to the universal illusion without becoming its dupe. It is best, on the whole, for a man of taste who knows how to be gay with the gay, and serious with the serious, to enter into the game of Maïa, and to play his part with a good grace in the fantastic tragi-comedy which is called the Universe. It seems to me that here intellectualism reaches its limit.[13] The mind, in its intellectual capacity, arrives at the intuition that all reality is but the dream of a dream. What delivers us from the palace of dreams is pain, personal pain; it is also the sense of obligation, or that which combines the two, the pain of sin; and again it is love; in short, the moral order. What saves us from the sorceries of Maïa is conscience; conscience dissipates the narcotic vapours, the opium-like hallucinations, the placid stupor of contemplative indifference. It drives us into contact with the terrible wheels within wheels of human suffering and human responsibility; it is the bugle-call, the cock-crow, which puts the phantoms to flight; it is the armed archangel who chases man from an artificial paradise. Intellectualism may be described as an intoxication conscious of itself; the moral energy which replaces it, on the other hand, represents a state of fast, a famine and a sleepless thirst. Alas! Alas!

. . . . . .

Those who have the most frivolous idea of sin are just those who suppose that there is a fixed gulf between good people and others.

. . . . . .

The ideal which the wife and mother makes for herself, the manner in which she understands duty and life, contain the fate of the community. Her faith becomes the star of the conjugal ship, and her love the animating principle that fashions the future of all belonging to her. Woman is the salvation or destruction of the family. She carries its destinies in the folds of her mantle.

. . . . . .

Perhaps it is not desirable that a woman should be free in mind; she would immediately abuse her freedom. She cannot become philosophical without losing her special gift, which is the worship of all that is individual, the defence of usage, manners, beliefs, traditions. Her *rôle* is to slacken the combustion of thought. It is analogous to that of azote in vital air.

. . . . . .

In every loving woman there is a priestess of the past — a pious guardian of some affection, of which the object has disappeared.

6th January 1873. — I have been reading the seven tragedies of Æschylus, in the translation of Leconte de Lisle. The *Prometheus* and the *Eumenides* are greatest where all is great; they have the sublimity of the old prophets. Both depict a religious revolution — a profound crisis in the life of humanity. In *Prometheus* it is civilisation wrenched from the jealous hands of the gods; in the *Eumenides* it is the transformation of the idea of justice, and the substitution of atonement and pardon for the law of implacable revenge. *Prometheus* shows us the martyrdom which waits for all the saviours of men; the *Eumenides* is the glorification of Athens and the Areopagus — that is to say, of a truly human civilisation. How magnificent it is as poetry, and how small the adventures of individual passion seem beside this colossal type of tragedy, of which the theme is the destinies of nations!

31st March 1873 (4 P.M.) —

'En quel songe
  Se plonge
Mon cœur, et que veut-il?'

For an hour past I have been the prey of a vague anxiety; I recognise my old enemy.

. . . It is a sense of void and anguish; a sense of something lacking: what? Love, peace — God perhaps. The feeling is one of pure want unmixed with hope, and there is anguish in it because I can clearly distinguish neither the evil nor its remedy.

'O printemps sans pitié, dans l'âme endolorie,
Avec tes chants d'oiseaux, tes brises, ton azur,
Tu creuses sourdement, conspirateur obscur,
Le gouffre des langueurs et de la rêverie.'

Of all the hours of the day, in fine weather, the afternoon, about three o'clock, is the time which to me is most difficult to bear. I never feel more strongly than I do then, '*le vide effrayant de la vie*,' the stress of mental anxiety, or the painful thirst for happiness. This torture born of the sunlight is a strange phenomenon. Is it that the sun, just as it brings out the stain upon a garment, the wrinkles in a face, or the discoloration of the hair, so also it illumines with inexorable distinctness the scars and rents of the heart? Does it rouse in us a sort of shame of existence? In any case the bright hours of the day are capable of flooding the whole soul with melancholy, of kindling in us the passion for death, or suicide, or annihilation, or of driving us to that which is next akin to death, the deadening of the senses by the pursuit of pleasure. They rouse in the lonely man a horror of himself; they make him long to escape from his own misery and solitude, —

'Le cœur trempé sept fois dans le néant divin.'

People talk of the temptations to crime connected with darkness, but the dumb sense of desolation which is often the product of the most brilliant moment of daylight must not be forgotten either. From the one, as from the other, God is absent; but in the first case a man follows his senses and the cry of his passion; in the second, he feels himself lost and bewildered, a creature forsaken by all the world.

'En nous sont deux instincts qui bravent la raison,
 C'est l'effroi du bonheur et la soif du poison.
 Cœur solitaire, à toi prends garde!'

3d April 1873. — I have been to see my friends ——. Their niece has just arrived with two of her children, and the conversation turned on Father Hyacinthe's lecture.

Women of an enthusiastic temperament have a curious way of speaking of extempore preachers and orators. They imagine that inspiration radiates from a crowd as such, and that inspiration is all that is wanted. Could there be a more *naïf* and childish explanation of what is really a lecture in which nothing has been left to accident, neither the plan, nor the metaphors, nor even the length of the whole, and where everything has been prepared with the greatest care! But women, in their love of what is marvellous and miraculous, prefer to ignore all this. The meditation, the labour, the calculation of effects, the art, in a word, which have gone to the making of it, diminishes for them the value of the thing, and they prefer to believe it fallen from Heaven, or sent down from on high. They ask for bread, but cannot bear the idea of a baker. The sex is superstitious, and hates to understand what it wishes to admire. It would vex it to be forced to give the smaller share to feeling, and the larger share to thought. It wishes to believe that imagination can do the work of reason, and feeling the work of science, and it never asks itself how it is that women, so rich in heart and imagination, have never distinguished themselves as orators,—that is to say, have never known how to combine a multitude of facts, ideas, and impulses, into one complex unity. Enthusiastic women never even suspect the difference that there is between the excitement of a popular harangue, which is nothing but a mere passionate outburst, and the unfolding of a didactic process, the aim of which is to prove something and to convince its hearers. Therefore, for them, study, reflection, technique, count as nothing; the improvisatore mounts upon the tripod, Pallas all armed issues from his lips, and conquers the applause of the dazzled assembly.

Evidently women divide orators into two groups; the artizans of speech, who manufacture their laborious discourses by the aid of the midnight lamp, and the inspired souls, who simply give themselves the trouble to be born. They will never understand the saying of Quintilian, 'Fit orator, nascitur poeta.'

The enthusiasm which acts is perhaps an enlightening force, but the enthusiasm which accepts is very like blindness. For this latter enthusiasm confuses the value of things, ignores their shades of difference, and is an obstacle to all sensible criticism and all calm judgment. The 'Ewig-Weibliche' favours exaggeration, mysticism, sentimentalism, — all that excites and startles.

It is the enemy of clearness, of a calm and rational view of things, the antipodes of criticism and of science. I have had only too much sympathy and weakness for the feminine nature. The very excess of my former indulgence towards it makes me now more conscious of its infirmity. Justice and science, law and reason, are virile things, and they come before imagination, feeling, reverie, and fancy. When one reflects that Catholic superstition is maintained by women, one feels how needful it is not to hand over the reins to the 'Eternal Womanly.'

23d May 1873. — The fundamental error of France lies in her psychology. France has always believed that to say a thing is the same as to do it, as though speech were action, as though rhetoric were capable of modifying the tendencies, habits, and character of real beings, and as though verbiage were an efficient substitute for will, conscience, and education.

France proceeds by bursts of eloquence, of cannonading, or of law-making: she thinks that so she can change the nature of things; and she produces only phrases and ruins. She has never understood the first line of Montesquieu: 'Laws are necessary relations, derived from the nature of things.' She will not see that her incapacity to organise liberty comes from her own nature; from the notions which she has of the individual, of society, of religion, of law, of duty — from the manner in which she brings up children. Her way is to plant trees downwards, and then she is astonished at the result! Universal suffrage, with a bad religion and a bad popular education, means perpetual wavering between anarchy and dictatorship, between the red and the black, between Danton and Loyola.

How many scapegoats will France sacrifice before it occurs to her to beat her own breast in penitence?

18th August 1873 (*Scheveningen*). — Yesterday, Sunday, the landscape was clear and distinct, the air bracing, the sea bright and gleaming, and of an ashy blue colour. There were beautiful effects of beach, sea, and distance; and dazzling tracks of gold upon the waves, after the sun had sunk below the bands of vapour drawn across the middle sky, and before it had disappeared in the mists of the sea horizon. The place was very full. All Scheveningen and the Hague, the village and the capital, had streamed out on to the terrace, amusing themselves at innumerable tables, and swamping the strangers and the bathers. The orchestra played some Wagner, some Auber, and some waltzes. What was all the world doing? Simply enjoying life.

A thousand thoughts wandered through my brain. I thought how much history it had taken to make what I saw possible; Judæa, Egypt, Greece, Germany, Gaul; all the centuries from Moses to Napoleon, and all the zones from Batavia to Guiana, had united in the formation of this gathering. The industry, the science, the art, the geography, the commerce, the religion of the whole human race, are repeated in every human combination; and what we see before our own eyes at any given moment is inexplicable without reference to all that has ever been. This interlacing of the ten thousand threads which Necessity weaves into the production of one single phenomenon is a stupefying thought. One feels oneself in the presence of Law itself — allowed a glimpse of the mysterious workshop of Nature. The ephemeral perceives the eternal.

What matters the brevity of the individual span, seeing that the generations, the centuries, and the worlds themselves are but occupied for ever with the ceaseless reproduction of the hymn of life, in all the hundred thousand modes and variations which make up the universal symphony? The motive is always the same; the monad has but one law: all truths are but the variation of one single truth. The universe represents the infinite wealth of the Spirit seeking in vain to exhaust all possibilities, and the goodness of the Creator, who would fain share with the created all that sleeps within the limbo of Omnipotence.

To contemplate and adore, to receive and give back, to have uttered one's note and moved one's grain of sand, is all which is expected from such insects as we are; it is enough to give motive and meaning to our fugitive apparition in existence. . . .

After the concert was over the paved esplanade behind the hotels and the two roads leading to the Hague were alive with people. One might have fancied oneself upon one of the great Parisian boulevards just when the theatres are emptying themselves — there were so many carriages, omnibuses, and cabs. Then, when the human tumult had disappeared, the peace of the starry heaven shone out resplendent, and the dreamy glimmer of the Milky Way was only answered by the distant murmur of the ocean.

Later. — What is it which has always come between real life and me? What glass screen has, as it were, interposed itself between me and the enjoyment, the possession, the contact of things, leaving me only the *rôle* of the looker-on?

False shame, no doubt. I have been ashamed to desire. Fatal result of timidity, aggravated by intellectual delusion! This renunciation beforehand of all natural ambitions, this systematic putting aside of all longings and all desires, has perhaps been false in idea; it has been too like a foolish, self-inflicted mutilation.

Fear, too, has had a large share in it —

'La peur de ce que j'aime est ma fatalité.'

I very soon discovered that it was simpler for me to give up a wish than to satisfy it. Not being able to obtain all that my nature longed for, I renounced the whole *en bloc*, without even taking the trouble to determine in detail what might have attracted me; for what was the good of stirring up trouble in oneself and evoking images of inaccessible treasure?

Thus I anticipated in spirit all possible disillusions, in the true stoical fashion. Only, with singular lack of logic, I have sometimes allowed regret to overtake me, and I have looked at conduct founded upon exceptional principles with the eyes of the ordinary man. I should have been ascetic to the end; contemplation ought to have been enough for me, especially now, when the hair begins to whiten. But, after all, I am a man, and not a theorem. A system cannot suffer, but I suffer. Logic makes only one demand — that of consequence; but life makes a thousand; the body wants health, the imagination cries out for beauty, and the heart for love; pride asks for consideration, the soul yearns for peace, the conscience for holiness; our whole being is athirst for happiness and for perfection; and we, tottering, mutilated, and incomplete, cannot always feign philosophic insensibility; we stretch out our arms towards life, and we say to it under our breath, 'Why — why — hast thou deceived me?'

19th August 1873 (*Scheveningen*). — I have had a morning walk. It has been raining in the night. There are large clouds all round; the sea, veined with green and drab, has put on the serious air of labour. She is about her business, in no threatening but at the same time in no lingering mood. She is making her clouds, heaping up her sands, visiting her shores and bathing them with foam, gathering up her floods for the tide, carrying the ships to their destinations, and feeding the universal life. I found in a hidden nook a sheet of fine sand which the water had furrowed and folded like the pink palate of a kitten's mouth, or like a dappled sky. Everything repeats itself by analogy, and each little fraction of the earth reproduces in a smaller and individual form all the phenomena of the planet. — Farther on I came across a bank of crumbling shells, and it was borne in upon me that the sea-sand itself might well be only the detritus of the organic life of preceding eras, a vast monument or pyramid of immemorial age, built up by countless generations of molluscs who have laboured at the architecture of the shores like good workmen of God. If the dunes and the mountains are the dust of living creatures who have preceded us, how can we doubt but that our death will be as serviceable as our life, and that nothing which has been lent is lost? Mutual borrowing and temporary service seem to be the law of existence. Only, the strong prey upon and devour the weak, and the concrete inequality of lots within the abstract equality of destinies wounds and disquiets the sense of justice.

(*Same day.*) — A new spirit governs and inspires the generation which will succeed me. It is a singular sensation to feel the grass growing under one's feet, to see oneself intellectually uprooted. One must address one's contemporaries. Younger men will not listen to you. Thought, like love, will not tolerate a gray hair. Knowledge herself loves the young, as Fortune used to do in olden days. Contemporary civilisation does not know what to do with old age; in proportion as it deifies physical experiment, it despises moral experience. One sees therein the triumph of Darwinism; it is a state of war, and war must have young soldiers; it can only put up with age in its leaders when they have the strength and the mettle of veterans.

In point of fact, one must either be strong or disappear, either constantly rejuvenate oneself or perish. It is as though the humanity of our day had, like the migratory birds, an immense voyage to make across space; she can no longer support the weak or help on the laggards. The great assault upon the Future makes her hard and pitiless to all who fall by the way. Her motto is, 'The devil take the hindmost.'

The worship of strength has never lacked altars, but it looks as though the more we talk of justice and humanity, the more that other god sees his kingdom widen.

20th August 1873 (*Scheveningen*). — I have now watched the sea which beats upon this shore under many different aspects. On the whole, I should class it with the Baltic. As far as colour, effect, and landscape go, it is widely different from the Breton or Basque ocean, and, above all, from the Mediterranean. It never attains to the blue-green of the Atlantic, nor the indigo of the Ionian Sea. Its scale of colour runs from flint to emerald, and when it turns to blue, the blue is a turquoise shade splashed with gray. The sea here is not amusing itself; it has a busy and serious air, like an Englishman or a Dutchman.

Neither polyps nor jelly-fish, neither seaweed nor crabs, enliven the sands at low water; the sea life is poor and meagre. What is wonderful is the struggle of man against a miserly and formidable power. Nature has done little for him, but she allows herself to be managed. Stepmother though she be, she is accommodating, subject to the occasional destruction of a hundred thousand lives in a single inundation.

The air inside the dune is altogether different from that outside it. The air of the sea is life-giving, bracing, oxydised; the air inland is soft, relaxing, and warm. In the same way there are two Hollands in every Dutchman: there is the man of the *polder*, heavy, pale, phlegmatic, slow, patient himself, and trying to the patience of others, — and there is the man of the *dune*, of the harbour, the shore, the sea, who is tenacious, seasoned, persevering, sunburnt, daring. Where the two agree is in calculating prudence, and in methodical persistency of effort.

22d August 1873 (*Scheveningen*). — The weather is rainy, the whole atmosphere gray; it is a time favourable to thought and meditation. I have a liking for such days as these; they revive one's converse with oneself and make it possible to live the inner life: they are quiet and peaceful, like a song in a minor key. We are nothing but thought, but we feel our life to its very centre. Our very sensations turn to reverie. It is a strange state of mind; it is like those silences in worship which are not the empty moments of devotion, but the full moments, and which are so because at such times the soul, instead of being polarised, dispersed, localised, in a single impression or thought, feels her own totality and is conscious of herself. She tastes her own substance. She is no longer played upon, coloured, set in motion, affected, from without; she is in equilibrium and at rest. Openness and self-surrender become possible to her; she contemplates and she adores. She sees the changeless and the eternal enwrapping all the phenomena of time. She is in the religious state, in harmony with the general order, or at least in intellectual harmony. For *holiness*, indeed, more is wanted — a harmony of will, a perfect self-devotion, death to self and absolute submission.

Psychological peace — that harmony which is perfect but virtual — is but the zero, the potentiality of all numbers; it is not that moral peace which is victorious over all ills, which is real, positive, tried by experience, and able to face whatever fresh storms may assail it.

The peace of fact is not the peace of principle. There are indeed two happinesses, that of nature and that of conquest, — two equilibria, that of Greece and that of Nazareth, — two kingdoms, that of the natural man and that of the regenerate man.

Later (Scheveningen). — Why do doctors so often make mistakes? Because they are not sufficiently individual in their diagnoses or their treatment. They class a sick man under some given department of their nosology, whereas every invalid is really a special case, a unique example. How is it possible that so coarse a method of sifting should produce judicious therapeutics? Every illness is a factor simple or complex, which is multiplied by a second factor, invariably complex, — the individual, that is to say, who is suffering from it, so that the result is a special problem, demanding a special solution, the more so the greater the remoteness of the patient from childhood or from country life.

The principal grievance which I have against the doctors is that they neglect the real problem, which is to seize the unity of the individual who claims their care. Their methods of investigation are far too elementary; a doctor who does not read you to the bottom is ignorant of essentials. To me the ideal doctor would be a man endowed with profound knowledge of life and of the soul, intuitively divining any suffering or disorder of whatever kind, and restoring peace by his mere presence. Such a doctor is possible, but the greater number of them lack the higher and inner life, they know nothing of the transcendent laboratories of nature; they seem to me superficial, profane, strangers to divine things, destitute of intuition and sympathy. The model doctor should be at once a genius, a saint, a man of God.

11*th September* 1873 (*Amsterdam*). — The doctor has just gone. He says I have fever about me, and does not think that I can start for another three days without imprudence. I dare not write to my Genevese friends and tell them that I am coming back from the sea in a radically worse state of strength and throat than when I went there, and that I have only wasted my time, my trouble, my money, and my hopes. . . .

This contradictory double fact — on the one side an eager hopefulness springing up afresh after all disappointments, and on the other an experience almost invariably unfavourable — can be explained like all illusions by the whim of nature, which either wills us to be deceived or wills us to act as if we were so.

Scepticism is the wiser course, but in delivering us from error it tends to paralyse life. Maturity of mind consists in taking part in the prescribed game as seriously as though one believed in it. Good-humoured compliance, tempered by a smile, is, on the whole, the best line to take; one lends oneself to an optical illusion, and the voluntary concession has an air of liberty. Once imprisoned in existence, we must submit to its laws with a good grace; to rebel against it only ends in impotent rage, when once we have denied ourselves the solution of suicide.

Humility and submission, or the religious point of view; clear-eyed indulgence with a touch of irony, or the point of view of worldly wisdom, — these two attitudes are possible. The second is sufficient for the minor ills of life, the other is perhaps necessary in the greater ones. The pessimism of Schopenhauer supposes at least health and intellect as means of enduring the rest of life. But optimism either of the stoical or the Christian sort is needed to make it possible for us to bear the worst sufferings of flesh, heart, and soul. If we are to escape the grip of despair, we must believe either that the whole of things at least is good, or that grief is a fatherly grace, a purifying trial.

There can be no doubt that the idea of a happy immortality, serving as a harbour of refuge from the tempests of this mortal existence, and rewarding the fidelity, the patience, the submission, and the courage of the travellers on life's sea — there can be no doubt that this idea, the strength of so many generations, and the faith of the Church, carries with it inexpressible consolation to those who are wearied, burdened, and tormented by pain and suffering. To feel oneself individually cared for and protected by God gives a special dignity and beauty to life. Monotheism lightens the struggle for existence. But does the study of nature allow of the maintenance of those local revelations which are called Mosaism, Christianity, Islamism? These religions, founded upon an infantine cosmogony, and upon a chimerical history of humanity, can they bear confronting with modern astronomy and geology? The present mode of escape, which consists in trying to satisfy the claims of both science and faith, — of the science which contradicts all the ancient beliefs, and the faith which, in the case of things that are beyond nature and incapable of verification, affirms them on her own responsibility only, — this mode of escape cannot last for ever. Every fresh cosmical conception demands a religion which corresponds to it. Our age of transition stands bewildered between the two incompatible methods, the scientific method and the religious method, and between the two certitudes, which contradict each other.

Surely the reconciliation of the two must be sought for in the moral law, which is also a fact, and every step of which requires for its explanation another cosmos than the cosmos of necessity. Who knows if necessity is not a particular case of liberty, and its condition? Who knows if nature is not a laboratory for the fabrication of thinking beings who are ultimately to become free creatures? Biology protests, and indeed the supposed existence of souls, independently of time, space, and matter, is a fiction of faith, less logical than the Platonic dogma. But the question remains open. We may eliminate the idea of purpose from nature, yet, as the guiding conception of the highest being of our planet, it is a fact, and a fact which postulates a meaning in the history of the universe.

My thought is straying in vague paths: why? — because I have no creed. All my studies end in notes of interrogation, and that I may not draw premature or arbitrary conclusions I draw none.

Later on. — My creed has melted away, but I believe in good, in the moral order, and in salvation; religion for me is to live and die in God, in complete abandonment to the holy will which is at the root of nature and destiny. I believe even in the Gospel, the Good News — that is to say, in the reconciliation of the sinner with God, by faith in the love of a pardoning Father.

4th October 1873 (*Geneva*). — I have been dreaming a long while in the moonlight, which floods my room with a radiance, full of vague mystery. The state of mind induced in us by this fantastic light is itself so dim and ghost-like that analysis loses its way in it, and arrives at nothing articulate. It is something indefinite and intangible, like the noise of waves which is made up of a thousand fused and mingled sounds. It is the reverberation of all the unsatisfied desires of the soul, of all the stifled sorrows of the heart, mingling in a vague sonorous whole, and dying away in cloudy murmurs. All those imperceptible regrets, which never individually reach the consciousness, accumulate at last into a definite result; they become the voice of a feeling of emptiness and aspiration; their tone is melancholy itself. In youth the tone of these Æolian vibrations of the heart is all hope — a proof that these thousands of indistinguishable accents make up indeed the fundamental note of our being, and reveal the tone of our whole situation. Tell me what you feel in your solitary room when the full moon is shining in upon you and your lamp is dying out, and I will tell you how old you are, and I shall know if you are happy.

. . . .

The best path through life is the high road, which initiates us at the right moment into all experience. Exceptional itineraries are suspicious, and matter for anxiety. What is normal is at once most convenient, most honest, and most wholesome. Cross roads may tempt us for one reason or another, but it is very seldom that we do not come to regret having taken them.

. . . . . .

Each man begins the world afresh, and not one fault of the first man has been avoided by his remotest descendant. The collective experience of the race accumulates, but individual experience dies with the individual, and the result is that institutions become wiser and knowledge as such increases; but the young man, although more cultivated, is just as presumptuous, and not less fallible to-day than he ever was. So that absolutely there is progress, and relatively there is none. Circumstances improve, but merit remains the same. The whole is better, perhaps, but man is not positively better — he is only different. His defects and his virtues change their form, but the total balance does not show him to be the richer. A thousand things advance, nine hundred and ninety-eight fall back: this is progress. There is nothing in it to be proud of, but something, after all, to console one.

4th February 1874. — I am still reading the *Origines du Christianisme* by Ernest Havet.[14] I like the book and I dislike it. I like it for its independence and courage; I dislike it for the insufficiency of its fundamental ideas, and the imperfection of its categories.

The author, for instance, has no clear idea of religion; and his philosophy of history is superficial. He is a Jacobin. 'The Republic and Free Thought' — he cannot get beyond that. This curt and narrow school of opinion is the refuge of men of independent mind, who have been scandalised by the colossal fraud of ultramontanism; but it leads rather to cursing history than to understanding it. It is the criticism of the eighteenth century, of which the general result is purely negative. But Voltairianism is only the half of the philosophic mind. Hegel frees thought in a very different way.

Havet, too, makes another mistake. He regards Christianity as synonymous with Roman Catholicism and with the Church. I know very well that the Roman Church does the same, and that with her the assimilation is a matter of sound tactics; but scientifically it is inexact. We ought not even to identify Christianity with the Gospel, nor the Gospel with religion in general. It is the business of critical precision to clear away these perpetual confusions in which Christian practice and Christian preaching abound. To disentangle ideas, to distinguish and limit them, to fit them into their true place and order, is the first duty of science whenever it lays hands upon such chaotic and complex things as manners, idioms, or beliefs. Entanglement is the condition of life; order and clearness are the signs of serious and successful thought.

Formerly it was the ideas of nature which were a tissue of errors and incoherent fancies; now it is the turn of moral and psychological ideas. The best issue from the present Babel would be the formation or the sketching out of a truly scientific science of man.

16th February 1874. — The multitude, who already possess force, and even, according to the Republican view, right, have always been persuaded by the Cleons of the day that enlightenment, wisdom, thought, and reason, are also theirs. The game of these conjurors and quacks of universal suffrage has always been to flatter the crowd in order to make an instrument of it. They pretend to adore the puppet of which they pull the threads.

The theory of radicalism is a piece of juggling, for it supposes premisses of which it knows the falsity: it manufactures the oracle whose revelations it pretends to adore; it proclaims that the multitude creates a brain for itself, while all the time it is the clever man who is the brain of the multitude, and suggests to it what it is supposed to invent. To reign by flattery has been the common practice of the courtiers of all despotisms, the favourites of all tyrants; it is an old and trite method, but none the less odious for that.

The honest politician should worship nothing but reason and justice, and it is his business to preach them to the masses, who represent, on an average, the age of childhood and not that of maturity. We corrupt childhood if we tell it that it cannot be mistaken, and that it knows more than its elders. We corrupt the masses when we tell them that they are wise and far-seeing and possess the gift of infallibility.

It is one of Montesquieu's subtle remarks, that the more wise men you heap together the less wisdom you will obtain. Radicalism pretends that the greater number of illiterate, passionate, thoughtless — above all, young people, you heap together, the greater will be the enlightenment resulting. The second thesis is no doubt the repartee to the first, but the joke is a bad one. All that can be got from a crowd is instinct or passion; the instinct may be good, but the passion may be bad, and neither is the instinct capable of producing a clear idea, nor the passion of leading to a just resolution.

A crowd is a material force, and the support of numbers gives a proposition the force of law; but that wise and ripened temper of mind which takes everything into account, and therefore tends to truth, is never engendered by the impetuosity of the masses. The masses are the material of democracy, but its form — that is to say, the laws which express the general reason, justice, and utility — can only be rightly shaped by wisdom, which is by no means a universal property. The fundamental error of the radical theory is to confound the right to do good with good itself, and universal suffrage with universal wisdom. It rests upon a legal fiction, which assumes a real equality of enlightenment and merit among those whom it declares electors. It is quite possible, however, that these electors may not desire the public good, and that even if they do, they may be deceived as to the manner of realising it. Universal suffrage is not a dogma — it is an instrument; and according to the population in whose hands it is placed, the instrument is serviceable or deadly to the proprietor.

27th February 1874. — Among the peoples, in whom the social gifts are strongest, the individual fears ridicule above all things, and ridicule is the certain result of originality. No one, therefore, wishes to make a party of his own; every one wishes to be on the side of all the world. 'All the world' is the greatest of powers; it is sovereign, and calls itself *we*. *We* dress, *we* dine, *we* walk, *we* go out, *we* come in, like this, and not like that. This *we* is always right, whatever it does. The subjects of *We* are more prostrate than the slaves of the East before the Padishah. The good pleasure of the sovereign decides every appeal; his caprice is law. What *we* does or says is called custom, what it thinks is called opinion, what it believes to be beautiful or good is called fashion. Among such nations as these *we* is the brain, the conscience, the reason, the taste, and the judgment of all. The individual finds everything decided for him without his troubling about it. He is dispensed from the task of finding out anything whatever. Provided that he imitates, copies, and repeats the models furnished by *we*, he has nothing more to fear. He knows all that he need know, and has entered into salvation.

29th April 1874.— Strange reminiscence! At the end of the terrace of La Treille, on the eastern side, as I looked down the slope, it seemed to me that I saw once more in imagination a little path which existed there when I was a child, and ran through the bushy underwood, which was thicker then than it is now. It is at least forty years since this impression disappeared from my mind. The revival of an image so dead and so forgotten set me thinking. Consciousness seems to be like a book, in which the leaves turned by life successively cover and hide each other in spite of their semi-transparency; but although the book may be open at the page of the present, the wind, for a few seconds, may blow back the first pages into view.

And at death will these leaves cease to hide each other, and shall we see all our past at once? Is death the passage from the successive to the simultaneous — that is to say, from time to eternity? Shall we then understand, in its unity, the poem or mysterious episode of our existence, which till then we have spelled out phrase by phrase? And is this the secret of that glory which so often enwraps the brow and countenance of those who are newly dead? If so, death would be like the arrival of a traveller at the top of a great mountain, whence he sees spread out before him the whole configuration of the country, of which till then he had had but passing glimpses. To be able to overlook one's own history, to divine its meaning in the general concert and in the divine plan, would be the beginning of eternal felicity. Till then we had sacrificed ourselves to the universal order, but then we should understand and appreciate the beauty of that order. We had toiled and laboured under the conductor of the orchestra; and we should find ourselves become surprised and delighted hearers. We had seen nothing but our own little path in the mist; and suddenly a marvellous panorama and boundless distances would open before our dazzled eyes. Why not?

31st May 1874. — I have been reading the philosophical poems of Madame Ackermann. She has rendered in fine verse that sense of desolation which has been so often stirred in me by the philosophy of Schopenhauer, of Hartmann, Comte, and Darwin. What tragic force and power! What thought and passion! She has courage for everything, and attacks the most tremendous subjects.

Science is implacable; will it suppress all religions? All those which start from a false conception of nature, certainly. But if the scientific conception of nature proves incapable of bringing harmony and peace to man, what will happen? Despair is not a durable situation. We shall have to build a moral city without God, without an immortality of the soul, without hope. Buddhism and Stoicism present themselves as possible alternatives.

But even if we suppose that there is no finality in the cosmos, it is certain that man has ends at which he aims, and if so the notion of end or purpose is a real phenomenon, although a limited one. Physical science may very well be limited by moral science, and *vice versa*. But if these two conceptions of the world are in opposition, which must give way?

I still incline to believe that nature is the virtuality of mind, — that the soul is the fruit of life, and liberty the flower of necessity, — that all is bound together, and that nothing can be done without. Our modern philosophy has returned to the point of view of the Ionians, the φυσικοί, or naturalist thinkers. But it will have to pass once more through Plato and through Aristotle, through the philosophy of 'goodness' and 'purpose,' through the science of mind.

3d July 1874. — Rebellion against common sense is a piece of childishness of which I am quite capable. But it does not last long. — I am soon brought back to the advantages and obligations of my situation; I return to a calmer self-consciousness. It is disagreeable to me, no doubt, to realise all that is hopelessly lost to me, all that is now and will be for ever denied to me; but I reckon up my privileges as well as my losses, — I lay stress on what I have, and not only on what I want. And so I escape from that terrible dilemma of 'all or nothing,' which for me always ends in the adoption of the second alternative. It seems to me at such times that a man may without shame content himself with being *some* thing and *some* one —

'Ni si haut, ni si bas . . .'

These brusque lapses into the formless, indeterminate state, are the price of my critical faculty. All my former habits become suddenly fluid; it seems to me that I am beginning life over again, and that all my acquired capital has disappeared at a stroke. I am for ever new-born; I am a mind which has never taken to itself a body, a country, an avocation, a sex, a species. Am I even quite sure of being a man, a European, an inhabitant of this earth? It seems to me so easy to be something else, that to be what I am appears to me a mere piece of arbitrary choice. I cannot possibly take an accidental structure of which the value is purely relative, seriously. When once a man has touched the absolute, all that might be other than what it is seems to him indifferent. All these ants pursuing their private ends excite his mirth. He looks down from the moon upon his hovel; he beholds the earth from the heights of the sun; he considers his life from the point of view of the Hindoo pondering the days of Brahma; he sees the finite from the distance of the infinite, and thenceforward the insignificance of all those things which men hold to be important makes effort ridiculous, passion burlesque, and prejudice absurd.

7th August 1874 (*Clarens*). — A day perfectly beautiful, luminous, limpid, brilliant.

I passed the morning in the churchyard; the 'Oasis' was delightful. Innumerable sensations, sweet and serious, peaceful and solemn, passed over me. . . . Around me Russians, English, Swedes, Germans, were sleeping their last sleep under the shadow of the Cubly. The landscape was one vast splendour; the woods were deep and mysterious, the roses full blown; all round me were butterflies — a noise of wings — the murmur of birds. I caught glimpses through the trees of distant mists, of soaring mountains, of the tender blue of the lake. . . . A little conjunction of things struck me. Two ladies were tending and watering a grave; two nurses were suckling their children. This double protest against death had something touching and poetical in it. 'Sleep, you who are dead; we, the living, are thinking of you, or at least carrying on the pilgrimage of the race!' — such seemed to me the words in my ear. It was clear to me that the Oasis of Clarens is the spot in which I should like to rest. Here I am surrounded with memories; here death is like a sleep — a sleep instinct with hope.

. . . .

Hope is not forbidden us, but peace and submission are the essentials.

1st September 1874 (*Clarens*). — On waking it seemed to me that I was staring into the future with wide startled eyes. Is it indeed to *me* that these things apply? Incessant and growing humiliation, my slavery becoming heavier, my circle of action steadily narrower! . . . What is hateful in my situation is that deliverance can never be hoped for, and that one misery will succeed another in such a way as to leave me no breathing space, not even in the future, not even in hope. All possibilities are closed to me, one by one. It is difficult for the natural man to escape from a dumb rage against inevitable agony.

Noon. — An indifferent nature ? A Satanic principle of things ? A good and just God ? Three points of view. The second is improbable and horrible. The first appeals to our stoicism. My organic combination has never been anything but mediocre; it has lasted as long as it could. Every man has his turn, and all must submit. To die quickly is a privilege; I shall die by inches. Well, submit. Rebellion would be useless and senseless. After all, I belong to the better-endowed half of human-kind, and my lot is superior to the average.

But the third point of view alone can give joy. Only is it tenable ? *Is* there a particular Providence directing all the circumstances of our life, and therefore imposing all our trials upon us for educational ends ? Is this heroic faith compatible with our actual knowledge of the laws of nature ? Scarcely. But what this faith makes objective we may hold as subjective truth. The moral being may moralise his sufferings by using natural facts for his own inner education. What he cannot change he calls the will of God, and to will what God wills brings him peace.

To nature both our continued existence and our morality are equally indifferent. But God, on the other hand, if God is, desires our sanctification; and if suffering purifies us, then we may console ourselves for suffering. This is what makes the great advantage of the Christian faith; it is the triumph over pain, the victory over death. There is but one thing necessary — death unto sin, the immolation of our selfish will, the filial sacrifice of our desires. Evil consists in living for *self* — that is to say, for one's own vanity, pride, sensuality, or even health. Righteousness consists in willingly accepting one's lot, in submitting to and espousing the destiny assigned us, in willing what God commands, in renouncing what He forbids us, in consenting to what He takes from us or refuses us.

In my own particular case, what has been taken from me is health — that is to say, the surest basis of all independence; but friendship and material comfort are still left to me; I am neither called upon to bear the slavery of poverty nor the hell of absolute isolation.

Health cut off, means marriage, travel,

study, and work forbidden or endangered. It means life reduced in attractiveness and utility by five-sixths.

Thy will be done!

14th September 1874 (*Charnex*). — A long walk and conversation with ——. We followed a high mountain path. Seated on the turf, and talking with open heart, our eyes wandered over the blue immensity below us, and the smiling outlines of the shore. All was friendly, azure-tinted, caressing, to the sight. The soul I was reading was profound and pure. Such an experience is like a flight into Paradise. — A few light clouds climbed the broad spaces of the sky, steamers made long tracks upon the water at our feet, white sails were dotted over the vast distance of the lake, and sea-gulls like gigantic butterflies quivered above its rippling surface.

21st September 1874 (*Charnex*). — A wonderful day! Never has the lake been bluer, or the landscape softer. It was enchanting. — But tragedy is hidden under the eclogue; the serpent crawls under the flowers. All the future is dark. The phantoms which for three or four weeks I have been able to keep at bay, wait for me behind the door, as the Eumenides waited for Orestes. Hemmed in on all sides!

> 'On ne croit plus à son étoile,
> On sent que derrière la toile
> Sont le deuil, les maux et la mort.'

For a fortnight I have been happy, and now this happiness is going.

There are no more birds, but a few white or blue butterflies are still left. Flowers are becoming rare — a few daisies in the fields, some blue or yellow chicories and colchicums, some wild geraniums growing among fragments of old walls, and the brown berries of the privet — this is all we were able to find. In the fields they are digging potatoes, beating down the nuts, and beginning the apple harvest. The leaves are thinning and changing colour; I watch them turning red on the pear-trees, gray on the plums, yellow on the walnut-trees, and tinging the thickly-strewn turf with shades of reddish-brown. We are nearing the end of the fine weather; the colouring is the colouring of late autumn; there is no need now to keep out of the sun. Everything is soberer, more measured, more fugitive, less emphatic. Energy is gone, youth is past, prodigality at an end, the summer over. The year is on the wane and tends towards winter; it is once more in harmony with my own age and position, and next Sunday it will keep my birthday. All these different consonances form a melancholy harmony.

. . . . . .

The distinguishing mark of religion is not so much liberty as obedience, and its value is measured by the sacrifices which it can extract from the individual.

. . . . . .

A young girl's love is a kind of piety. We must approach it with adoration if we are not to profane it, and with poetry if we are to understand it. If there is anything in the world which gives us a sweet, ineffable impression of the ideal, it is this trembling modest love. To deceive it would be a crime. Merely to watch its unfolding life is bliss to the beholder; he sees in it the birth of a divine marvel. When the garland of youth fades on our brow, let us try at least to have the virtues of maturity; may we grow better, gentler, graver, like the fruit of the vine, while its leaf withers and falls.

. . . .

To know how to grow old is the masterwork of wisdom, and one of the most difficult chapters in the great art of living.

. . . .

He who asks of life nothing but the improvement of his own nature, and a continuous moral progress towards inward contentment and religious submission, is less liable than any one else to miss and waste life.

2d January 1875 (*Hyères*). — In spite of my sleeping-draught I have had a bad night. Once it seemed as if I must choke, for I could breathe neither way.

Could I be more fragile, more sensitive, more vulnerable! People talk to me as if there were still a career before me, while all the time I know that the ground is slipping from under me, and that the defence of my health is already a hopeless task. At bottom, I am only living on out of complaisance and without a shadow of self-delusion. I know that not one of my desires will be realised, and for a long time I have had no desires at all. I simply accept what comes to me as though it were a bird perching on my window. I smile at it, but I know very well that my visitor has wings and will not stay long. The resignation which comes from despair has a kind of melancholy sweetness. It looks at life as a man sees it from his death-bed, and judges it without bitterness and without vain regrets.

I no longer hope to get well, or to be useful, or to be happy. I hope that those who have loved me will love me to the end; I should wish to have done them some good, and to leave them a tender memory of myself. I wish to die without rebellion and without weakness; that is about all. Is this relic of hope and of desire still too much? Let all be as God will. I resign myself into His hands.

22d January 1875 (*Hyères*).—The French mind, according to Gioberti, apprehends only the outward form of truth, and exaggerates it by isolating it, so that it acts as a solvent upon the realities with which it works. It takes the shadow for the substance, the word for the thing, appearance for reality, and abstract formula for truth. It lives in a world of intellectual *assignats*. If you talk to a Frenchman of art, of language, of religion, of the state, of duty, of the family, you feel in his way of speaking that his thought remains outside the subject, that he never penetrates into its substance, its inmost core. He is not striving to understand it in its essence, but only to say something plausible about it. On his lips the noblest words become thin and empty; for example, — mind, idea, religion. The French mind is superficial and yet not comprehensive; it has an extraordinarily fine edge, and yet no penetrating power. Its desire is to enjoy its own resources by the help of things, but it has none of the respect, the disinterestedness, the patience, and the self-forgetfulness, which are indispensable if we wish to see things as they are. Far from being the philosophic mind, it is a mere counterfeit of it, for it does not enable a man to solve any problem whatever, and remains incapable of understanding all that is living, complex, and concrete. Abstraction is its original sin, presumption its incurable defect, and plausibility its fatal limit.

The French language has no power of expressing truths of birth and germination; it paints effects, results, the *caput mortuum*, but not the cause, the motive power, the native force, the development of any phenomenon whatever. It is analytic and descriptive, but it explains nothing, for it avoids all beginnings and processes of formation. With it crystallisation is not the mysterious act itself by which a substance passes from the fluid state to the solid state. It is the product of that act.

The thirst for truth is not a French passion. In everything appearance is preferred to reality, the outside to the inside, the fashion to the material, that which shines to that which profits, opinion to conscience. That is to say, the Frenchman's centre of gravity is always outside him, — he is always thinking of others, playing to the gallery. To him individuals are so many zeros; the unit which turns them into a number must be added from outside; it may be royalty, the writer of the day, the favourite newspaper, or any other temporary master of fashion. — All this is probably the result of an exaggerated sociability, which weakens the soul's forces of resistance, destroys its capacity for investigation and personal conviction, and kills in it the worship of the ideal.

27th January 1875 (*Hyères*). — The whole atmosphere has a luminous serenity, a limpid clearness. The islands are like swans swimming in a golden stream. Peace, splendour, boundless space! . . . And I meanwhile look quietly on while the soft hours glide away. I long to catch the wild bird, happiness, and tame it. Above all, I long to share it with others. These delicious mornings impress me indescribably. They intoxicate me, they carry me away. I feel beguiled out of myself, dissolved in sunbeams, breezes, perfumes, and sudden impulses of joy. And yet all the time I pine for I know not what intangible Eden.

Lamartine in the *Préludes* has admirably described this oppressive effect of happiness on fragile human nature. I suspect that the reason for it is that the finite creature feels itself invaded by the infinite, and the invasion produces dizziness, a kind of vertigo, a longing to fling oneself into the great gulf of being. To feel life too intensely is to yearn for death; and for man, to die means to become like unto the gods — to be initiated into the great mystery. Pathetic and beautiful illusion.

Ten o'clock in the evening. — From one end to the other the day has been perfect, and my walk this afternoon to Beau Vallon was one long delight. It was like an expedition into Arcadia. Here was a wild and woodland corner, which would have made a fit setting for a dance of nymphs, and there an ilex overshadowing a rock, which reminded me of an ode of Horace or a drawing of Tibur. I felt a kind of certainty that the landscape had much that was Greek in it. And what made the sense of resemblance the more striking was the sea, which one feels to be always near, though one may not see it, and which any turn of the valley may bring into view. We found out a little tower with an overgrown garden, of which the owner might have been taken for a husbandman of the Odyssey. He could scarcely speak any French, but was not without a certain grave dignity. I translated to him the inscription on his sun-dial, '*Hora est benefaciendi*,' which is beautiful, and pleased him greatly. It would be an inspiring place to write a novel in. Only I do not know whether the little den would have a decent room, and one would certainly have to live upon eggs, milk, and figs, like Philemon.

15*th February* 1875 (*Hyères*). — I have just been reading the two last *Discours* at the French Academy, lingering over every word and weighing every idea. This kind of writing is a sort of intellectual dainty, for it is the art 'of expressing truth with all the courtesy and finesse possible;' the art of appearing perfectly at ease without the smallest loss of manners; of being gracefully sincere, and of making criticism itself a pleasure to the person criticised. — Legacy as it is from the monarchical tradition, this particular kind of eloquence is the distinguishing mark of those men of the world who are also men of breeding, and those men of letters who are also gentlemen. Democracy could never have invented it, and in this delicate *genre* of literature France may give points to all rival peoples, for it is the fruit of that refined and yet vigorous social sense which produced by court and drawing-room life, by literature and good company, by means of a mutual education continued for centuries. This complicated product is as original in its way as Athenian eloquence, but it is less healthy and less durable. If ever France becomes Americanised this *genre* at least will perish, without hope of revival.

16*th April* 1875 (*Hyères*). — I have already gone through the various emotions of leave-taking. I have been wandering slowly through the streets and up the castle hill, gathering a harvest of images and recollections. Already I am full of regret that I have not made a better study of the country, in which I have now spent four months and more. It is like what happens when a friend dies; we accuse ourselves of having loved him too little, or loved him ill; or it is like our own death, when we look back upon life and feel that it has been misspent.

16th August 1875. — Life is but a daily oscillation between revolt and submission, between the instinct of the *ego*, which is to expand, to take delight in its own tranquil sense of inviolability, if not to triumph in its own sovereignty, and the instinct of the soul, which is to obey the universal order, to accept the will of God.

The cold renunciation of disillusioned reason brings no real peace. Peace is only to be found in reconciliation with destiny, when destiny seems, in the religious sense of the word, *good;* that is to say, when man feels himself directly in the presence of God. Then, and then only, does the will acquiesce. Nay more, it only completely acquiesces when it adores. The soul only submits to the hardness of fate by virtue of its discovery of a sublime compensation — the lovingkindness of the Almighty. That is to say, it cannot resign itself to lack or famine, it shrinks from the void around it, and the happiness either of hope or faith is essential to it. It may very well vary its object, but some object it must have. It may renounce its former idols, but it will demand another cult. The soul hungers and thirsts after happiness, and it is in vain that everything deserts it, — it will never submit to its abandonment.

28th August 1875 *(Geneva).* — A word used by Sainte-Beuve *à propos* of Benjamin Constant has struck me: it is the word *consideration*. To possess or not to possess *consideration* was to Madame de Staël a matter of supreme importance, — the loss of it an irreparable evil, the acquirement of it a pressing necessity. What, then, is this good thing? The esteem of the public. And how is it gained? By honourable character and life, combined with a certain aggregate of services rendered and of successes obtained. It is not exactly a good conscience, but it is something like it, for it is the witness from without, if not the witness from within. *Consideration* is not reputation, still less celebrity, fame, or glory; it has nothing to do with *savoir faire*, and is not always the attendant of talent or genius. It is the reward given to constancy in duty, to probity of conduct. It is the homage rendered to a life held to be irreproachable. It is a little more than esteem, and a little less than admiration. To enjoy public consideration is at once a happiness and a power. The loss of it is a misfortune and a source of daily suffering. — Here am I, at the age of fifty-three, without ever having given this idea the smallest place in my life. It is curious, but the desire for consideration has been to me so little of a motive that I have not even been conscious of such an idea at all. The fact shows, I suppose, that for me the audience, the gallery, the public, has never had more than a negative importance. I have neither asked nor expected anything from it, not even justice; and to be a dependant upon it, to solicit its suffrages and its good graces, has always seemed to me an act of homage and flunkeyism against which my pride has instinctively rebelled. I have never even tried to gain the goodwill of a *coterie* or a newspaper, nor so much as the vote of an elector. And yet it would have been a joy to me to be smiled upon, loved, encouraged, welcomed, and to obtain what I was so ready to give, kindness and goodwill. But to hunt down consideration and reputation, — to force the esteem of others, — seemed to me an effort unworthy of myself, almost a degradation. I have never even thought of it.

Perhaps I have lost consideration by my indifference to it. Probably I have disappointed public expectation by thus allowing an over-sensitive and irritable consciousness to lead me into isolation and retreat. I know that the world, which is only eager to silence you when you do speak, is angry with your silence as soon as its own action has killed in you the wish to speak. No doubt, to be silent with a perfectly clear conscience a man must not hold a public office. I now indeed say to myself that a professor is morally bound to justify his position by publication; that students, authorities, and public are placed thereby in a healthier relation towards him; that it is necessary for his good repute in the world, and for the proper maintenance of his position. But this point of view has not been a familiar one to me. I have endeavoured to give conscientious lectures, and I have discharged all the subsidiary duties of my post to the best of my ability; but I have never been able to bend myself to a struggle with hostile opinion, for all the while my heart has been full of sadness and disappointment, and I have known and felt that I have been systematically and deliberately isolated. Premature despair and the deepest discouragement have been my constant portion. Incapable of taking any interest in my talents for my own sake, I let everything slip as soon as the hope of being loved for them and by them had forsaken me. A hermit against my will, I have not even found peace in solitude, because my inmost conscience has not been any better satisfied than my heart.

Does not all this make up a melancholy lot, a barren failure of a life? What use have I made of my gifts, of my special circumstances, of my half-century of existence? What have I paid back to my country? Are all the documents I have produced, taken together, my correspondence, these thousands of journal pages, my lectures, my articles, my poems, my notes of different kinds, anything better than withered leaves? To whom and to what have I been useful? Will my name survive me a single day, and will it ever mean anything to anybody? — A life of no account! A great many comings and goings, a great many scrawls, — for nothing. When all is added up, — nothing! And worst of all, it has not been a life used up in the service of some adored object, or sacrificed to any future hope. Its sufferings will have been vain, its renunciations useless, its sacrifices gratuitous, its dreariness without reward. . . . No, I am wrong; it will have had its secret treasure, its sweetness, its reward. It will have inspired a few affections of great price; it will have given joy to a few souls; its hidden existence will have had some value. Besides, if in itself it has been nothing, it has understood much. If it has not been in harmony with the great order, still it has loved it. If it has missed happiness and duty, it has at least felt its own nothingness, and implored its pardon.

Later on. — There is a great affinity in me with the Hindoo genius — that mind, vast, imaginative, loving, dreamy, and speculative, but destitute of ambition, personality, and will. Pantheistic disinterestedness, the effacement of the self in the great whole, womanish gentleness, a horror of slaughter, antipathy to action, — these are all present in my nature, in the nature at least which has been developed by years and circumstances. Still the West has also had its part in me. — What I have found difficult is to keep up a prejudice in favour of any form, nationality, or individuality whatever. Hence my indifference to my own person, my own usefulness, interest, or opinions of the moment. What does it all matter? *Omnis determinatio est negatio.* Grief localises us, love particularises us, but thought delivers us from personality. . . . To be a man is a poor thing, to be a man is well; to be *the* man — man in essence and in principle — that alone is to be desired.

Yes, but in these Brahmanic aspirations what becomes of the subordination of the individual to duty? Pleasure may lie in ceasing to be individual, but duty lies in performing the microscopic task allotted to us. The problem set before us is to bring our daily task into the temple of contemplation and ply it there, to act as in the presence of God, to interfuse one's little part with religion. So only can we inform the detail of life, all that is passing, temporary, and insignificant, with beauty and nobility. So may we dignify and consecrate the meanest of occupations. So may we feel that we are paying our tribute to the universal work and the eternal will. So are we reconciled with life and delivered from the fear of death. So are we in order and at peace.

1st September 1875. — I have been working for some hours at my article on Mme. de Staël, but with what labour, what painful effort! When I write for publication every word is misery, and my pen stumbles at every line, so anxious am I to find the ideally best expression, and so great is the number of possibilities which open before me at every step.

Composition demands a concentration, decision, and pliancy which I no longer possess. I cannot fuse together materials and ideas. If we are to give anything a form, we must, so to speak, be the tyrants of it.[16] We must treat our subject brutally, and not be always trembling lest we are doing it a wrong. We must be able to transmute and absorb it into our own substance. This sort of confident effrontery is beyond me: my whole nature tends to that impersonality which respects and subordinates itself to the object; it is love of truth which holds me back from concluding and deciding. — And then I am always retracing my steps: instead of going forwards I work in a circle: I am afraid of having forgotten a point, of having exaggerated an expression, of having used a word out of place, while all the time I ought to have been thinking of essentials and aiming at breadth of treatment. I do not know how to sacrifice anything, how to give up anything whatever. Hurtful timidity, unprofitable conscientiousness, fatal slavery to detail!

In reality I have never given much thought to the art of writing, to the best way of making an article, an essay, a book, nor have I ever methodically undergone the writer's apprenticeship; it would have been useful to me, and I was always ashamed of what was useful. I have felt, as it were, a scruple against trying to surprise the secret of the masters of literature, against picking *chef-d'œuvres* to pieces. When I think that I have always postponed the serious study of the art of writing, from a sort of awe of it, and a secret love of its beauty, I am furious with my own stupidity, and with my own respect. Practice and routine would have given me that ease, lightness, and assurance, without which the natural gift and impulse dies away. But on the contrary, I have developed two opposed habits of mind, the habit of scientific analysis which exhausts the material offered to it, and the habit of immediate notation of passing impressions. The art of composition lies between the two; you want for it both the living unity of the thing, and the sustained operation of thought.

25th October 1875. — I have been listening to M. Taine's first lecture (on the *Ancien Régime*) delivered in the University hall. It was an extremely substantial piece of work — clear, instructive, compact, and full of matter. As a writer he shows great skill in the French method of simplifying his subject by massing it in large striking divisions; his great defect is a constant straining after points; his principal merit is the sense he has of historical reality, his desire to see things as they are. For the rest, he has extreme openness of mind, freedom of thought, and precision of language. — The hall was crowded.

26th October 1875. — All origins are secret; the principle of every individual or collective life is a mystery — that is to say, something irrational, inexplicable, not to be defined. We may even go farther and say, — Every individuality is an insoluble enigma, and no beginning explains it. In fact, all that has *become* may be explained retrospectively, but the beginning of anything whatever did not *become*. It represents always the '*fiat lux*,' the initial miracle, the act of creation; for it is the consequence of nothing else, it simply appears among anterior things which make a *milieu*, an occasion, a surrounding for it, but which are witnesses of its appearance without understanding whence it comes.

Perhaps also there are no true individuals, and, if so, no beginning but one only, the primordial impulse, the first movement. All men on this hypothesis would be but *man* in two sexes; man again might be reduced to the animal, the animal to the plant, and the only individuality left would be a living nature, reduced to a living matter, to the hylozoism of Thales. However, even upon this hypothesis, if there were but one absolute beginning, relative beginnings would still remain to us as multiple symbols of the absolute. Every life, called individual for convenience' sake and by analogy, would represent in miniature the history of the world, and would be to the eye of the philosopher a microscopic compendium of it.

. . . . . .

The history of the formation of ideas is what frees the mind.

. . . . . .

A philosophic truth does not become popular until some eloquent soul has humanised it or some gifted personality has translated and embodied it. Pure truth cannot be assimilated by the crowd; it must be communicated by contagion.

30th January 1876. — After dinner I went two steps off, to Marc Monnier's, to hear the *Luthier de Crémone*, a one-act comedy in verse, read by the author, François Coppée.

It was a feast of fine sensations, of literary dainties. For the little piece is a pearl. It is steeped in poetry, and every line is a fresh pleasure to one's taste.

This young *maestro* is like the violin he writes about, vibrating and passionate; he has, besides delicacy, point, grace, all that a writer wants to make what is simple, naïve, heartfelt, and out of the beaten track, acceptable to a cultivated society.

How to return to nature through art: there is the problem of all highly composite literatures like our own. Rousseau himself attacked letters with all the resources of the art of writing, and boasted the delights of savage life with a skill and adroitness developed only by the most advanced civilisation. And it is indeed this marriage of contraries which charms us; this spiced gentleness, this learned innocence, this calculated simplicity, this yes and no, this foolish wisdom. It is the supreme irony of such combinations which tickles the taste of advanced and artificial epochs, epochs when men ask for two sensations at once, like the contrary meanings fused by the smile of La Gioconda. And our satisfaction too in work of this kind is best expressed by that ambiguous curve of the lip which says:—I feel your charm, but I am not your dupe; I see the illusion both from within and from without; I yield to you, but I understand you; I am complaisant, but I am proud; I am open to sensations, yet not the slave of any; you have talent, I have subtlety of perception; we are quits, and we understand each other.

1st February 1876. — This evening we talked of the infinitely great and the infinitely small. The great things of the universe are for —— so much easier to understand than the small, because all greatness is a multiple of herself, whereas she is incapable of analysing what requires a different sort of measurement.

It is possible for the thinking being to place himself in all points of view, and to teach his soul to live under the most different modes of being. But it must be confessed that very few profit by the possibility. Men are in general imprisoned, held in a vice by their circumstances almost as the animals are, but they have very little suspicion of it because they have so little faculty of self-judgment. It is only the critic and the philosopher who can penetrate into all states of being, and realise their life from within.

When the imagination shrinks in fear from the phantoms which it creates, it may be excused because it is imagination. But when the intellect allows itself to be tyrannised over or terrified by the categories to which itself gives birth, it is in the wrong, for it is not allowed to intellect, — the critical power of man, — to be the dupe of anything.

Now, in the superstition of size the mind is merely the dupe of itself, for it creates the notion of space. The created is not more than the creator, the son not more than the father. The point of view wants rectifying. The mind has to free itself from space, which gives it a false notion of itself, but it can only attain this freedom by reversing things and by learning to see space in the mind instead of the mind in space. How can it do this? Simply by reducing space to its virtuality. Space is dispersion; mind is concentration.

And that is why God is present everywhere, without taking up a thousand millions of cube leagues, nor a hundred times more nor a hundred times less.

In the state of thought the universe occupies but a single point; but in the state of dispersion and analysis this thought requires the heaven of heavens for its expansion.

In the same way, time and number are contained in the mind. Man, as mind, is not their inferior, but their superior.

It is true that before he can reach this state of freedom his own body must appear to him at will either speck or world — that is to say, he must be independent of it. So long as the self still feels itself spatial, dispersed, corporeal, it is but a soul, it is not a mind; it is conscious of itself only as the animal is, the impressionable, affectionate, active and restless animal.

The mind being the subject of phenomena cannot be itself phenomenal; the mirror of an image, if it was an image, could not be a mirror. There can be no echo without a noise. Consciousness means some one who experiences something. And all the some-things together cannot take the place of the some one. The phenomenon exists only for a point which is not itself, and for which it is an object. The perceptible supposes the perceiver.

15th May 1876.—This morning I corrected the proofs of the *Etrangères*.* Here at least is one thing off my hands. The piece of prose theorising which ends the volume pleased and satisfied me a good deal more than my new metres. The book, as a whole, may be regarded as an attempt to solve the problem of French verse-translation considered as a special art. It is science applied to poetry. It ought not, I

* *Les Etrangères: Poésies traduites de diverses littératures*, par H. F. Amiel, 1876.

think, to do any discredit to a philosopher, for, after all, it is nothing but applied psychology.

Do I feel any relief, any joy, pride, hope? Hardly. It seems to me that I feel nothing at all, or at least my feeling is so vague and doubtful that I cannot analyse it. On the whole, I am rather tempted to say to myself, how much labour for how small a result, — *Much ado about nothing!* And yet the work in itself is good, is successful. But what does verse-translation matter? Already my interest in it is fading; my mind and my energies clamour for something else.

What will Edmond Scherer say to the volume?

. . . .

To the inmost self of me this literary attempt is quite indifferent, — a Lilliputian affair. In comparing my work with other work of the same kind, I find a sort of relative satisfaction; but I see the intrinsic futility of it, and the insignificance of its success or failure. I do not believe in the public; I do not believe in my own work; I have no ambition, properly speaking, and I blow soap-bubbles for want of something to do.

'Car le néant peut seul bien cacher l'infini.'

Self-satire, disillusion, absence of prejudice, may be freedom, but they are not strength.

12th July 1876. — Trouble on trouble. My cough has been worse than ever. I cannot see that the fine weather or the holidays have made any change for the better in my state of health. On the contrary, the process of demolition seems more rapid. It is a painful experience, this premature decay! . . . '*Après tant de malheurs, que vous reste-t-il? Moi.*' This '*moi*' is the central consciousness, the trunk of all the branches which have been cut away, that which bears every successive mutilation. Soon I shall have nothing else left than bare intellect. Death reduces us to the mathematical 'point'; the destruction which precedes it forces us back, as it were, by a series of ever-narrowing concentric circles to this last inaccessible refuge. Already I have a foretaste of that zero in which all forms and all modes are extinguished. I see how we return into the night, and inversely I understand how we issue from it. Life is but a meteor, of which the whole brief course is before me. Birth, life, death assume a fresh meaning to us at each phase of our existence. To see oneself as a firework in the darkness — to become a witness of one's own fugitive phenomenon — this is practical psychology. I prefer indeed the spectacle of the world, which is a vaster and more splendid firework; but when illness narrows my horizon and makes me dwell perforce upon my own miseries, these miseries are still capable of supplying food for my psychological curiosity. What interests me in myself, in spite of my repulsions, is that I find in my own case a genuine example of human nature, and therefore a specimen of general value. The sample enables me to understand a multitude of similar situations, and numbers of my fellow-men.

To enter consciously into all possible modes of being would be sufficient occupation for hundreds of centuries — at least for our finite intelligences, which are conditioned by time. The progressive happiness of the process, indeed, may be easily poisoned and embittered by the ambition which asks for everything at once, and clamours to reach the absolute at a bound. But it may be answered that aspirations are necessarily prophetic, for they could only have come into being under the action of the same cause which will enable them to reach their goal. The soul can only imagine the absolute because the absolute exists; our consciousness of a possible perfection is the guarantee that perfection will be realised.

Thought itself is eternal. It is the consciousness of thought which is gradually achieved through the long succession of ages, races, and humanities. Such is the doctrine of Hegel. The history of the mind is, according to him, one of approximation to the absolute, and the absolute differs at the two ends of the story. It *was* at the beginning: it *knows itself* at the end. Or rather it advances in the possession of itself with the gradual unfolding of creation. Such also was the conception of Aristotle.

If the history of the mind and of consciousness is the very marrow and essence of being, then to be driven back on psychology, even personal psychology, is to be still occupied with the main question of things, to keep to the subject, to feel oneself in the centre of the universal drama. There is comfort in the idea. Everything else may be taken away from us, but if thought remains we are still connected by a magic thread with the axis of the world. But we may lose thought and speech. Then nothing remains but simple feeling, the sense of the presence of God and of death in God, — the last relic of the human privilege, which is to participate in the whole, to commune with the absolute.

'Ta vie est un éclair qui meurt dans son nuage,
Mais l'éclair t'a sauvé s'il t'a fait voir le ciel.'

26th July 1876. — A private journal is a friend to idleness. It frees us from the necessity of looking all round a subject, it puts up with every kind of repetition, it accompanies all the caprices and meanderings of the inner life, and proposes to itself no definite end. This journal of mine represents the material of a good many volumes: what prodigious waste of time, of thought, of strength! It will be useful to nobody, and even for myself, — it has rather helped me to shirk life than to practise it. A journal takes the place of a confidant, that is, of friend or wife; it becomes a substitute for production, a substitute for country and public. It is a grief-cheating device, a mode of escape and withdrawal; but, factotum as it is, though it takes the place of everything, properly speaking it represents nothing at all. . . .

What is it which makes the history of a soul? It is the stratification of its different stages of progress, the story of its acquisitions and of the general course of its destiny. Before my history can teach anybody anything, or even interest myself, it must be disentangled from its materials, distilled and simplified. These thousands of pages are but the pile of leaves and bark from which the essence has still to be extracted. A whole forest of cinchonas are worth but one cask of quinine. A whole Smyrna rose-garden goes to produce one phial of perfume.

This mass of written talk, the work of twenty-nine years, may in the end be worth nothing at all; for each is only interested in his own romance, his own individual life. Even I perhaps shall never have time to read them over myself. So — so what? I shall have lived my life, and life consists in repeating the human type, and the burden of the human song, as myriads of my kindred have done, are doing, and will do, century after century. To rise to consciousness of this burden and this type is something, and we can scarcely achieve anything further. The realisation of the type is more complete, and the burden a more joyous one, if circumstances are kind and propitious, but whether the puppets have done this or that—

'Trois p'tits tours et puis s'en vont!'

everything falls into the same gulf at last, and comes to very much the same thing.

To rebel against fate — to try to escape the inevitable issue — is almost puerile. When the duration of a centenarian and that of an insect are quantities sensibly equivalent, — and geology and astronomy enable us to regard such durations from this point of view, — what is the meaning of all our tiny efforts and cries, the value of our anger, our ambition, our hope? For the dream of a dream it is absurd to raise these make-believe tempests. The forty millions of infusoria which make up a cube-inch of chalk — do they matter much to us? and do the forty millions of men who make up France matter any more to an inhabitant of the moon or Jupiter?

To be a conscious monad — a nothing which knows itself to be the microscopic phantom of the universe: this is all we can ever attain to.

12*th September* 1876. — What is your own

particular absurdity? Why, simply that you exhaust yourself in trying to understand wisdom without practising it, that you are always making preparations for nothing, that you live without living. Contemplation which has not the courage to be purely contemplative, renunciation which does not renounce completely, chronic contradiction — there is your case. Inconsistent scepticism, irresolution, not convinced but incorrigible, weakness which will not accept itself and cannot transform itself into strength — there is your misery. The comic side of it lies in capacity to direct others becoming incapacity to direct oneself, in the dream of the infinitely great stopped short by the infinitely little, in what seems to be the utter uselessness of talent. To arrive at immobility by excess of motion, at zero from abundance of numbers, is a strange farce, a sad comedy; the poorest gossip can laugh at its absurdity.

19*th September* 1876. — My reading to-day has been Doudan's *Lettres et Mélanges*.[17] A fascinating book! Wit, grace, subtlety, imagination, thought, — these letters possess them all. How much I regret that I never knew the man himself. He was a

Frenchman of the best type, *un délicat né sublime*, to quote Sainte-Beuve's expression. Fastidiousness of temper, and a too keen love of perfection, led him to withhold his talent from the public, but while still living, and within his own circle, he was the recognised equal of the best. He scarcely lacked anything except that fraction of ambition, of brutality and material force which are necessary to success in this world; but he was appreciated by the best society of Paris, and he cared for nothing else. He reminds me of Joubert.

20th September. — To be witty is to satisfy another's wits by the bestowal on him of two pleasures, that of understanding one thing and that of guessing another, and so achieving a double stroke.

Thus Doudan scarcely ever speaks out his thought directly; he disguises and suggests it by imagery, allusion, hyperbole; he overlays it with light irony and feigned anger, with gentle mischief and assumed humility. The more the thing to be guessed differs from the thing said, the more pleasant surprise there is for the interlocutor or the correspondent concerned. These charming and delicate ways of expression allow a man to teach what he will without pedantry, and to venture what he will without offence. There is something Attic and aërial in them; they mingle grave and gay, fiction and truth, with a light grace of touch such as neither La Fontaine nor Alcibiades would have been ashamed of. Socratic *badinage* like this presupposes a free and equal mind, victorious over physical ill and inward discontents. Such delicate playfulness is the exclusive heritage of those rare natures in whom subtlety is the disguise of superiority, and taste its revelation. What balance of faculties and cultivation it requires! What personal distinction it shows! Perhaps only a valetudinarian would have been capable of this *morbidezza* of touch, this marriage of virile thought and feminine caprice. If there is excess anywhere, it lies perhaps in a certain effeminacy of sentiment. Doudan can put up with nothing but what is perfect — nothing but what is absolutely harmonious; all that is rough, harsh, powerful, brutal, and unexpected, throws him into convulsions. Audacity — boldness of all kinds — repels him. This Athenian of the Roman time is a true disciple of Epicurus in all matters of sight, hearing, and intelligence — a crumpled rose-leaf disturbs him.

'Une ombre, un souffle, un rien, tout lui donnait la fièvre.'

What all this softness wants is strength, creative and muscular force. His range is not as wide as I thought it at first. The classical world and the Renaissance — that is to say, the horizon of La Fontaine — is his horizon. He is out of his element in the German or Slav literatures. He knows nothing of Asia. Humanity for him is not much larger than France, and he has never made a bible of Nature. In music and painting he is more or less exclusive. In philosophy he stops at Kant. To sum up: he is a man of exquisite and ingenious taste, but he is not a first-rate critic, still less a poet, philosopher, or artist. He was an admirable talker, a delightful letter-writer, who might have become an author had he chosen to concentrate himself. I must wait for the second volume in order to review and correct this preliminary impression.

Mid-day. — I have now gone once more through the whole volume, lingering over the Attic charm of it, and meditating on the originality and distinction of the man's organisation. Doudan was a keen penetrating psychologist, a diviner of aptitudes, a trainer of minds, a man of infinite taste and talent, capable of every *nuance* and of every delicacy; but his defect was a want of persevering energy of thought, a lack of patience in execution. Timidity, unworldliness, indolence, indifference, confined him to the *rôle* of the literary counsellor and made him judge of the field in which he ought rather to have fought. But do I mean to blame him? — no indeed! In the first place, it would be to fire on my allies; in the second, very likely he chose the better part.

Was it not Goethe who remarked that in the neighbourhood of all famous men we find men who never achieve fame, and yet were esteemed by those who did, as their equals or superiors? Descartes, I think, said the same thing. Fame will not run after the men who are afraid of her. She makes mock of those trembling and respectful lovers who deserve but cannot force her favours. The public is won by the bold, imperious talents — by the enterprising and the skilful. It does not believe in modesty, which it regards as a device of impotence. The golden book contains but a section of the true geniuses; it names those only who have taken glory by storm.

15th November 1876. — I have been reading *L'Avenir Religieux des Peuples Civilisés*, by Emile de Laveleye. The theory of this writer is that the Gospel, in its pure form, is capable of providing the religion of the future, and that the abolition of all religious principle, which is what the socialism of the present moment demands, is as much to be feared as Catholic superstition. The Protestant method, according to him, is the means of transition whereby sacerdotal Christianity passes into the pure religion of the Gospel. Laveleye does not think that civilisation can last without the belief in God and in another life. Perhaps he forgets that Japan and China prove the contrary. But it is enough to determine him against Atheism if it can be shown that a general Atheism would bring about a lowering of the moral average. After all, however, this is nothing but a religion of utilitarianism. A belief is not true because it is useful. And it is truth alone — scientific, established, proved, and rational truth — which is capable of satisfying nowadays the awakened minds of all classes. We may still say perhaps, 'faith governs the world,' — but the faith of the present is no longer in revelation or in the priest — it is in reason and in science. Is there a science of goodness and happiness? — that is the question. Do justice and goodness depend upon any particular religion? How are men to be made free, honest, just, and good? — there is the point.

On my way through the book I perceived many new applications of my law of irony. Every epoch has two contradictory aspirations which are logically antagonistic and practically associated. Thus the philosophic materialism of the last century was the champion of liberty. And at the present moment we find Darwinians in love with equality, while Darwinism itself is based on the right of the stronger. Absurdity is interwoven with life: real beings are animated contradictions, absurdities brought into action. Harmony with self would mean peace, repose, and perhaps immobility. By far the greater number of human beings can only conceive action, or practise it, under the form of war — a war of competition at home, a bloody war of nations abroad, and finally war with self. So that life is a perpetual combat; it wills that which it wills not, and wills not that it wills. Hence what I call the law of irony — that is to say, the refutation of the self by itself, the concrete realisation of the absurd,

Is such a result inevitable? I think not. Struggle is the caricature of harmony, and harmony, which is the association of contraries, is also a principle of movement. War is a brutal and fierce means of pacification; it means the suppression of resistance by the destruction or enslavement of the conquered. Mutual respect would be a better way out of difficulties. Conflict is the result of the selfishness which will acknowledge no other limit than that of external force. The laws of animality govern almost the whole of history. The history of man is essentially zoological; it becomes human late in the day, and then only in the beautiful souls, the souls alive to justice, goodness, enthusiasm, and devotion. The angel shows itself rarely and with difficulty through the highly-organised brute. The divine aureole plays only with a dim and fugitive light around the brows of the world's governing race.

The Christian nations offer many illustrations of the law of irony. They profess the citizenship of heaven, the exclusive worship of eternal good; and never has the hungry pursuit of perishable joys, the love of this world, or the thirst for conquest, been stronger or more active than among these nations. Their official motto is exactly the reverse of their real aspiration. Under a false flag they play the smuggler with a droll ease of conscience. Is the fraud a conscious one? No — it is but an application of the law of irony. The deception is so common a one that the delinquent becomes unconscious of it. Every nation gives itself the lie in the course of its daily life, and not one feels the ridicule of its position. A man must be a Japanese to perceive the burlesque contradictions of the Christian civilisation. He must be a native of the moon to understand the stupidity of man and his state of constant delusion. The philosopher himself falls under the law of irony, for after having mentally stripped himself of all prejudice — having, that is to say, wholly laid aside his own personality, he finds himself slipping back perforce into the rags he had taken off, obliged to eat and drink, to be hungry, cold, thirsty, and to behave like all other mortals, after having for a moment behaved like no other. This is the point where the comic poets are lying in wait for him; the animal needs revenge themselves for his flight into the Empyrean, and mock him by their cry: — *Thou art dust, thou art nothing, thou art man!*

26th November 1876. — I have just finished a novel of Cherbuliez, *Le fiancé de Mademoiselle de St. Maur.* It is a jewelled mosaic of precious stones, sparkling with a thousand lights. But the heart gets little from it. The Mephistophelian type of novel leaves one sad. This subtle, refined world is strangely near to corruption; these artificial women have an air of the Lower Empire. There is not a character who is not witty, and neither is there one who has not bartered conscience for cleverness. The elegance of the whole is but a mask of immorality. These stories of feeling in which there is no feeling make a strange and painful impression upon me.

4th December 1876. — I have been thinking a great deal of Victor Cherbuliez. Perhaps his novels make up the most disputable part of his work, — they are so much wanting in simplicity, feeling, reality. And yet what knowledge, style, wit, and subtlety — how much thought everywhere, and what mastery of language! He astonishes one; I cannot but admire him.

Cherbuliez's mind is of immense range, clear-sighted, keen, full of resource; he is an Alexandrian exquisite, substituting for the feeling which makes men earnest the irony which leaves them free. Pascal would say of him — 'He has never risen from the order of thought to the order of charity.' But we must not be ungrateful. A Lucian is not worth an Augustine, but still he is Lucian. Those who enfranchise the mind render service to man as well as those who persuade the heart. After the leaders come the liberators, and the negative and critical minds have their place and function beside the men of affirmation, the convinced and inspired souls. The positive element in Victor Cherbuliez's work is beauty, not goodness, not moral or religious life. Æsthetically he is serious; what he respects is style. And therefore he has found his vocation; for he is first and foremost a writer — a consummate, exquisite, and model writer. He does not win our love, but he claims our homage.

. . . .

In every union there is a mystery — a certain invisible bond which must not be disturbed. This vital bond in the filial relation is respect; in friendship, esteem; in marriage, confidence; in the collective life, patriotism; in the religious life, faith. Such points are best left untouched by speech, for to touch them is almost to profane them.

. . . .

Men of genius supply the substance of history, while the mass of men are but the critical filter, the limiting, slackening, passive force needed for the modification of the ideas supplied by genius. Stupidity is dynamically the necessary balance of intellect. To make an atmosphere which human life can breathe, oxygen must be combined with a great deal — with three-fourths — of azote. And so, to make history, there must be a great deal of resistance to conquer and of weight to drag.

5th January 1877. — This morning I am altogether miserable, half stifled by bronchitis — walking a difficulty — the brain weak — this last the worst misery of all, for thought is my only weapon against my other ills. Rapid deterioration of all the bodily powers, a dull continuous waste of vital organs, brain-decay; — this is the trial laid upon me, a trial that no one suspects! Men pity you for growing old outwardly; but what does that matter? — nothing, so long as the faculties are intact. This boon of mental soundness to the last has been granted to so many students that I hoped for it a little. Alas, must I sacrifice that too? Sacrifice is almost easy when we believe it laid upon us, asked of us, rather, by a fatherly God and a watchful Providence; but I know nothing of this religious joy. The mutilation of the self which is going on in me lowers and lessens me without doing good to anybody. Supposing I became blind, who would be the gainer? Only one motive remains to me, — that of manly resignation to the inevitable, — the wish to set an example to others, — the Stoic view of morals pure and simple.

This moral education of the individual soul, — is it then wasted? When our planet has accomplished the cycle of its destinies, of what use will it have been to any one or anything in the universe? Well, it will have sounded its note in the symphony of creation. And for us, individual atoms, seeing monads, we appropriate a momentary consciousness of the whole and the unchangeable, and then we disappear. Is not this enough? No, it is not enough, for if there is not progress, increase, profit, there is nothing but a mere chemical play and balance of combinations. Brahma, after having created, draws his creation back into the gulf. If we are a laboratory of the universal mind, may that mind at least profit and grow by us! If we realise the supreme will, may God have the joy of it! If the trustful humility of the soul rejoices Him more than the greatness of intellect, let us enter into His plan, His intention. This, in theological language, is to live to the glory of God. Religion consists in the filial acceptation of the Divine Will whatever it be, provided we see it distinctly. Well, can we doubt that decay, sickness, death, are in the programme of our existence? Is not destiny the inevitable? And is not destiny the anonymous title of Him or of That which the religions call God? To descend without murmuring the stream of destiny, to pass without revolt through loss after loss, and diminution after diminution, with no other limit than zero before us,— this is what is demanded of us. Involution is as natural as evolution. We sink gradually back into the darkness, just as we issued gradually from it. The play of faculties and organs, the grandiose apparatus of life, is put back bit by bit into the box. We begin by instinct; at the end comes a clearness of vision which we must learn to bear with and to employ without murmuring upon our own failure and decay. A musical theme once exhausted, finds its due refuge and repose in silence.

6th February 1877. — I spent the evening with the ——, and we talked of the anarchy of ideas, of the general want of culture, of what it is which keeps the world going, and of the assured march of science in the midst of universal passion and superstition.

What is rarest in the world is fair-mindedness, method, the critical view, the sense of proportion, the capacity for distinguishing. The common state of human thought is one of confusion, incoherence, and presumption, and the common state of human hearts is a state of passion, in which equity, impartiality, and openness to impressions are unattainable. Men's wills are always in advance of their intelligence, their desires ahead of their will, and accident the source of their desires; so that they express merely fortuitous opinions which are not worth the trouble of taking seriously, and which have no other account to give of themselves than this childish one: I am, because I am. The art of finding truth is very little practised; it scarcely exists, because there is no personal humility, nor even any love of truth among us. We are covetous enough of such knowledge as may furnish weapons to our hand or tongue, as may serve our vanity or gratify our craving for power; but self-knowledge, the criticism of our own appetites and prejudices, is unwelcome and disagreeable to us.

Man is a wilful and covetous animal, who makes use of his intellect to satisfy his inclinations, but who cares nothing for truth, who rebels against personal discipline, who hates disinterested thought and the idea of self-education. Wisdom offends him, because it rouses in him disturbance and confusion, and because he will not see himself as he is.

The great majority of men are but tangled skeins, imperfect key-boards, so many specimens of restless or stagnant chaos, — and what makes their situation almost hopeless is the fact that they take pleasure in it. There is no curing a sick man who believes himself in health.

5th April 1877. — I have been thinking over the pleasant evening of yesterday, an experience in which the sweets of friendship, the charm of mutual understanding, æsthetic pleasure, and a general sense of comfort, were happily combined and intermingled. There was not a crease in the rose-leaf. Why? Because 'all that is pure, all that is honest, all that is excellent, all that is lovely and of good report,' was there gathered together. 'The incorruptibility of a gentle and quiet spirit,' innocent mirth, faithfulness to duty, fine taste and sympathetic imagination, form an attractive and wholesome *milieu* in which the soul may rest.

The party — which celebrated the last day of vacation — gave much pleasure, and not to me only. Is not making others happy the best happiness? To illuminate for an instant the depths of a deep soul, to cheer those who bear by sympathy the burdens of so many sorrow-laden hearts and suffering lives, is to me a blessing and a precious privilege. There is a sort of religious joy in helping to renew the strength and courage of noble minds. We are surprised to find ourselves the possessors of a power of which we are not worthy, and we long to exercise it purely and seriously.

I feel most strongly that man, in all that he does or can do which is beautiful, great, or good, is but the organ and the vehicle of something or some one higher than himself. This feeling is religion. The religious man takes part with a tremor of sacred joy in these phenomena of which he is the intermediary but not the source, of which he is the scene, but not the author, or rather, the poet. He lends them voice, hand, will, and help, but he is respectfully careful to efface himself, that he may alter as little as possible the higher work of the Genius who is making a momentary use of him. A pure emotion deprives him of personality and annihilates the self in him. Self must perforce disappear when it is the Holy Spirit who speaks, when it is God who acts. This is the mood in which the prophet hears the call, the young mother feels the movement of the child within, the preacher watches the tears of his audience. So long as we are conscious of self we are limited, selfish, held in bondage; when we are in harmony with the universal order, when we vibrate in unison with God, self disappears. Thus, in a perfectly harmonious choir, the individual cannot hear himself unless he makes a false note. The religious state is one of deep enthusiasm, of moved contemplation, of tranquil ecstasy.

But how rare a state it is for us poor creatures harassed by duty, by necessity, by the wicked world, by sin, by illness! It is the state which produces inward happiness; but alas! the foundation of existence, the common texture of our days, is made up of action, effort, struggle, and therefore dissonance. Perpetual conflict, interrupted by short and threatened truces, — there is a true picture of our human condition.

Let us hail, then, as an echo from heaven, as the foretaste of a more blessed economy, these brief moments of perfect harmony, these halts between two storms. Peace is not in itself a dream, but we know it only as the result of a momentary equilibrium, — an accident. 'Happy are the peacemakers, for they shall be called the children of God.'

26th April 1877. — I have been turning over again the *Paris* of Victor Hugo (1867). For ten years event after event has given the lie to the prophet, but the confidence of the prophet in his own imaginings is not therefore a whit diminished. Humility and common sense are only fit for Lilliputians. Victor Hugo superbly ignores everything that he has not foreseen. He does not see that pride is a limitation of the mind, and that a pride without limitations is a littleness of soul. If he could but learn to compare himself with other men, and France with other nations, he would see things more truly, and would not fall into these mad exaggerations, these extravagant judgments. But proportion and fairness will never be among the strings at his command. He is vowed to the Titanic; his gold is always mixed with lead, his insight with childishness, his reason with madness. He cannot be simple; the only light he has to give blinds you like that of a fire. He astonishes a reader and provokes him, he moves him and annoys him. There is always some falsity of note in him, which accounts for the *malaise* he so constantly excites in me. The great poet in him cannot shake of the charlatan. A few shafts of Voltairean irony would have shrivelled the inflation of his genius and made it stronger by making it saner. It is a public misfortune that the most powerful poet of a nation should not have better understood his *rôle*, and that, unlike those Hebrew prophets who scourged because they loved, he should devote himself proudly and systematically to the flattery of his countrymen. France is the world; Paris is France; Hugo is Paris; peoples, bow down!

2d May 1877. — Which nation is best worth belonging to? There is not one in which the good is not counterbalanced by evil. Each is a caricature of man, a proof that no one among them deserves to crush the others, and that all have something to learn from all. I am alternately struck with the qualities and with the defects of each, which is perhaps lucky for a critic. I am conscious of no preference for the defects of north or south, of west or east; and I should find a difficulty in stating my own predilections. Indeed I myself am wholly indifferent in the matter, for to me the question is not one of liking or of blaming, but of understanding. My point of view is philosophical — that is to say, impartial and impersonal. The only type which pleases me is perfection — *man*, in short, the ideal man. As for the national man, I bear with and study him, but I have no admiration for him. I can only admire the fine specimens of the race, the great men, the geniuses, the lofty characters and noble souls, and specimens of these are to be found in all the ethnographical divisions. The 'country of my choice' (to quote Madame de Staël) is with the chosen souls. I feel no greater inclination towards the French, the Germans, the Swiss, the English, the Poles, the Italians, than towards the Brazilians or the Chinese. The illusions of patriotism, of Chauvinist, family, or professional feeling, do not exist for me. My tendency, on the contrary, is to feel with increased force the lacunæ, deformities, and imperfections of the group to which I belong. My inclination is to see things as they are, abstracting my own individuality, and suppressing all personal will and desire ; so that I feel antipathy, not towards this or that, but towards error, prejudice, stupidity, exclusiveness, exaggeration. I love only justice and fairness. Anger and annoyance are with me merely superficial; the fundamental tendency is towards impartiality and detachment. Inward liberty and aspiration towards the true — these are what I care for and take pleasure in.

4th June 1877. — I have just heard the *Romeo and Juliet* of Hector Berlioz. The work is entitled — 'Dramatic symphony for orchestra, with choruses.' The execution was extremely good. The work is interesting, careful, curious, and suggestive, but it leaves one cold. — When I come to reason out my impression I explain it in this way. To subordinate man to things — to annex the human voice, as a mere supplement, to the orchestra — is false in idea. To make simple narrative out of dramatic material, is a derogation, a piece of levity. A Romeo and Juliet in which there is no Romeo and no Juliet is an absurdity. To substitute the inferior, the obscure, the vague, for the higher and the clear, is a challenge to common sense. It is a violation of that natural hierarchy of things which is never violated with impunity. The musician has put together a series of symphonic pictures, without any inner connection, a string of riddles, to which a prose text alone supplies meaning and unity. The only intelligible voice which is allowed to appear in the work is that of Friar Laurence: his sermon could not be expressed in chords, and is therefore plainly sung. But the moral of a play is not the play, and the play itself has been elbowed out by recitative.

The musician of the present day, not being able to give us what is beautiful, torments himself to give us what is new. False originality, false grandeur, false genius! This laboured art is wholly antipathetic to me. Science simulating genius is but a form of quackery.

Berlioz as a critic is cleverness itself; as a musician he is learned, inventive, and ingenious, but he is trying to achieve the greater when he cannot compass the lesser. Thirty years ago, at Berlin, the same impression was left upon me by his *Infancy of Christ*, which I heard him conduct himself. His art seems to me neither fruitful nor wholesome; there is no true and solid beauty in it.

I ought to say, however, that the audience, which was a fairly full one, seemed very well satisfied.

17th July 1877. — Yesterday I went through my La Fontaine, and noticed the omissions in him. He has neither butterfly nor rose. He utilises neither the crane, nor the quail, nor the dromedary, nor the lizard. There is not a single echo of chivalry in him. For him, the history of France dates from Louis XIV. His geography only ranges, in reality, over a few square miles, and touches neither the Rhine nor the Loire, neither the mountains nor the sea. He never invents his subjects, but indolently takes them ready-made from elsewhere. But with all this what an adorable writer, what a painter, what an observer, what a humorist, what a story-teller! I am never tired of reading him, though I know half his fables by heart. In the matter of vocabulary, turns, tones, phrases, idioms, his style is perhaps the richest of the great period, for it combines, in the most skilful way, archaism and classic finish, the Gallic and the French elements. Variety, satire, *finesse*, feeling, movement, terseness, suavity, grace, gaiety, at times even nobleness, gravity, grandeur, — everything, — is to be found in him. And then the happiness of the epithets, the piquancy of the sayings, the felicity of his rapid sketches and unforeseen audacities, and the unforgettable sharpness of phrase! His defects are eclipsed by his immense variety of different aptitudes.

One has only to compare his 'Woodcutter and Death' with that of Boileau in order to estimate the enormous difference between the artist and the critic who found fault with his work. La Fontaine gives you a picture of the poor peasant under the monarchy; Boileau shows you nothing but a man perspiring under a heavy load. The first is a historical witness, the second a mere academic rhymer. From La Fontaine it is possible to reconstruct the whole society of his epoch, and the old Champenois with his beasts remains the only Homer France has ever possessed. He has as many portraits of men and women as La Bruyère, and Molière is not more humorous.

His weak side is his epicureanism, with its tinge of grossness. This, no doubt, was what made Lamartine dislike him. The religious note is absent from his lyre; there is nothing in him which shows any contact with Christianity, any knowledge of the sublimer tragedies of the soul. Kind nature is his goddess, Horace his prophet, and Montaigne his gospel. In other words, his horizon is that of the Renaissance. This pagan island in the full Catholic stream is very curious; the paganism of it is so perfectly sincere and naïve. But indeed, Rabelais, Molière, Saint Evremond, are much more pagan than Voltaire. It is as though, for the genuine Frenchman, Christianity was a mere pose or costume — something which has nothing to do with the heart, with the real man, or his deeper nature. This division of things is common in Italy too. It is the natural effect of political religions: the priest becomes separated from the layman, the believer from the man, worship from sincerity.

18th July 1877. — I have just come across a character in a novel with a passion for synonyms, and I said to myself: Take care — that is your weakness too. In your search for close and delicate expression, you run through the whole gamut of synonyms, and your pen works too often in series of three. Beware! Avoid mannerisms and tricks; they are signs of weakness. Subject and occasion only must govern the use of words. Procedure by single epithet gives strength; the doubling of a word gives clearness, because it supplies the two extremities of the series; the trebling of it gives completeness by suggesting at once the beginning, middle, and end of the idea; while a quadruple phrase may enrich by force of enumeration.

Indecision being my principal defect, I am fond of a plurality of phrases which are but so many successive approximations and corrections. I am especially fond of them in this journal, where I write as it comes.

In serious composition *two* is, on the whole, my category. But it would be well to practise oneself in the use of the single word — of the shaft delivered promptly and once for all. I should have indeed to cure myself of hesitation first. I see too many ways of saying things; a more decided mind hits on the right way at once. Singleness of phrase implies courage, self-confidence, clear-sightedness. To attain it there must be no doubting, and I am always doubting. And yet —

> 'Quiconque est loup agisse en loup;
> C'est le plus certain de beaucoup.'

I wonder whether I should gain anything by the attempt to assume a character which is not mine. My wavering manner, born of doubt and scruple, has at least the advantage of rendering all the different shades of my thought, and of being sincere. If it were to become terse, affirmative, resolute, would it not be a mere imitation?

A private journal, which is but a vehicle for meditation and reverie, beats about the bush as it pleases without being bound to make for any definite end. Conversation with self is a gradual process of thought-clearing. Hence all these synonyms, these waverings, these repetitions and returns upon oneself. Affirmation may be brief; inquiry takes time; and the line which thought follows is necessarily an irregular one.

I am conscious indeed that at bottom there is but one right expression;[18] but in order to find it I wish to make my choice among all that are like it; and my mind instinctively goes through a series of verbal modulations in search of that shade which may most accurately render the idea. Or sometimes it is the idea itself which has to be turned over and over, that I may know it and apprehend it better. I think, pen in hand; it is like the disentanglement, the winding-off of a skein. Evidently the corresponding form of style cannot have the qualities which belong to thought which is already sure of itself, and only seeks to communicate itself to others. The function of the private journal is one of observation, experiment, analysis, contemplation; that of the essay or article is to provoke reflection; that of the book is to demonstrate.

21st July 1877. — A superb night, — a starry sky, — Jupiter and Phœbe holding converse before my windows. Grandiose effects of light and shade over the courtyard. A sonata rose from the black gulf of shadow like a repentant prayer wafted from purgatory. The picturesque was lost in poetry, and admiration in feeling.

30th July 1877.— . . . makes a very true remark about Renan, *à propos* of the volume of *Les Évangiles*. He brings out the contradiction between the literary taste of the artist, which is delicate, individual, and true, and the opinions of the critic, which are borrowed, old-fashioned, and wavering. — This hesitancy of choice between the beautiful and the true, between poetry and prose, between art and learning, is, in fact, characteristic. Renan has a keen love for science, but he has a still keener love for good writing, and, if necessary, he will sacrifice the exact phrase to the beautiful phrase. Science is his material rather than his object; his object is style. A fine passage is ten times more precious in his eyes than the discovery of a fact or the rectification of a date. And on this point I am very much with him, for a beautiful piece of writing is beautiful by virtue of a kind of truth which is truer than any mere record of authentic facts. Rousseau also thought the same. A chronicler may be able to correct Tacitus, but Tacitus survives all the chroniclers. I know well that the æsthetic temptation is the French temptation; I have often bewailed it, and yet, if I desired anything, it would be to be a writer, a great writer. To leave a monument behind, *aere perennius*, an imperishable work which might stir the thoughts, the feelings, the dreams of men, generation after generation, — this is the only glory which I could wish for, if I were not weaned even from this wish also. A book would be my ambition, if ambition were not vanity and vanity of vanities.

11*th August* 1877. — The growing triumph of Darwinism — that is to say of materialism, or of force — threatens the conception of justice. But justice will have its turn. The higher human law cannot be the offspring of animality. Justice is the right to the maximum of individual independence compatible with the same liberty for others; — in other words, it is respect for man, for the immature, the small, the feeble; it is the guarantee of those human collectivities, associations, states, nationalities — those voluntary or involuntary unions — the object of which is to increase the sum of happiness, and to satisfy the aspiration of the individual. That some should make use of others for their own purposes is an injury to justice. The right of the stronger is not a right, but a simple fact, which obtains only so long as there is neither protest nor resistance. It is like cold, darkness, weight, which tyrannise over man until he has invented artificial warmth, artificial light, and machinery. Human industry is throughout an emancipation from brute nature, and the advances made by justice are in the same way a series of rebuffs inflicted upon the tyranny of the stronger. As the medical art consists in the conquest of disease, so goodness consists in the conquest of the blind ferocities and untamed appetites of the human animal. I see the same law throughout: — increasing emancipation of the individual, a continuous ascent of being towards life, happiness, justice, and wisdom. Greed and gluttony are the starting-point, intelligence and generosity the goal.

21st August 1877 (*Baths of Ems*). — In the *salon* there has been a performance in chorus of 'Lorelei' and other popular airs. What in our country is only done for worship is done also in Germany for poetry and music. Voices blend together; art shares the privilege of religion. It is a trait which is neither French nor English, nor, I think, Italian. The spirit of artistic devotion, of impersonal combination, of common, harmonious, disinterested action, is specially German; it makes a welcome balance to certain clumsy and prosaic elements in the race.

Later. — Perhaps the craving for independence of thought — the tendency to go back to first principles — is really proper to the Germanic mind only. The Slavs and the Latins are governed rather by the collective wisdom of the community, by tradition, usage, prejudice, fashion; or, if they break through these, they are like slaves in revolt, without any real living apprehension of the law inherent in things, — the true law, which is neither written, nor arbitrary, nor imposed. The German wishes to get at Nature; the Frenchman, the Spaniard, the Russian, stop at conventions. The root of the problem is in the question of the relations between God and the world. Immanence or transcendence, — that, step by step, decides the meaning of everything else. If the mind is radically external to things, it is not called upon to conform to them. If the mind is destitute of native truth, it must get its truth from outside, by revelations. And so you get thought despising Nature, and in bondage to the Church — so you have the Latin world!

6th November 1877 (*Geneva*). — We talk of love many years before we know anything about it, and we think we know it because we talk of it, or because we repeat what other people say of it, or what books tell us about it. So that there are ignorances of different degrees, and degrees of knowledge which are quite deceptive. One of the worst plagues of society is this thoughtless inexhaustible verbosity, this careless use of words, this pretence of knowing a thing because we talk about it, — these counterfeits of belief, thought, love, or earnestness, which all the while are mere babble. The worst of it is, that as self-love is behind the babble, these ignorances of society are in general ferociously affirmative; chatter mistakes itself for opinion, prejudice poses as principle. Parrots behave as though they were thinking beings; imitations give themselves out as originals;

and politeness demands the acceptance of the convention. It is very wearisome.

Language is the vehicle of this confusion, the instrument of this unconscious fraud, and all evils of the kind are enormously increased by universal education, by the periodical press, and by all the other processes of vulgarisation in use at the present time. Every one deals in paper money; few have ever handled gold. We live on symbols, and even on the symbols of symbols; we have never grasped or verified things for ourselves; we judge everything, and we know nothing.

How seldom we meet with originality, individuality, sincerity, nowadays! — with men who are worth the trouble of listening to! The true self in the majority is lost in the borrowed self. How few are anything else than a bundle of inclinations — anything more than animals — whose language and whose gait alone recall to us the highest rank in nature!

The immense majority of our species are candidates for humanity, and nothing more. Virtually we are men; we might be, we ought to be, men; but practically we do not succeed in realising the type of our race. Semblances and counterfeits of men fill up the habitable earth, people the islands and the continents, the country and the town. If we wish to respect men we must forget what they are, and think of the ideal which they carry hidden within them, of the just man and the noble, the man of intelligence and goodness, inspiration and creative force, who is loyal and true, faithful and trustworthy, of the higher man, in short, and that divine thing we call a soul. The only men who deserve the name are the heroes, the geniuses, the saints, the harmonious, puissant, and perfect samples of the race.

Very few individuals deserve to be listened to, but all deserve that our curiosity with regard to them should be a pitiful curiosity — that the insight we bring to bear on them should be charged with humility. Are we not all shipwrecked, diseased, condemned to death? Let each work out his own salvation, and blame no one but himself; so the lot of all will be bettered. Whatever impatience we may feel towards our neighbour, and whatever indignation our race may rouse in us, we are chained one to another, and, companions in labour and misfortune, have everything to lose by mutual recrimination and reproach. Let us be silent as to each other's weakness, helpful, tolerant, nay, tender towards each other! Or, if we cannot feel tenderness, may we at least feel pity! May we put away from us the satire which scourges and the anger which brands: the oil and wine of the good Samaritan are of more avail. We may make the ideal a reason for contempt; but it is more beautiful to make it a reason for tenderness.

9th December 1877. — The modern haunters of Parnassus [19] carve urns of agate and of onyx, but inside the urns what is there? — ashes. Their work lacks feeling, seriousness, sincerity, and pathos — in a word, soul and moral life. I cannot bring myself to sympathise with such a way of understanding poetry. The talent shown is astonishing, but stuff and matter are wanting. It is an effort of the imagination to stand alone — a substitute for everything else. We find metaphors, rhymes, music, colour, but not man, not humanity. Poetry of this factitious kind may beguile one at twenty, but what can one make of it at fifty? It reminds me of Pergamos, of Alexandria, of all the epochs of decadence when beauty of form hid poverty of thought and exhaustion of feeling. I strongly share the repugnance which this poetical school arouses in simple people. It is as though it only cared to please the world-worn, the over-subtle, the corrupted, while it ignores all normal healthy life, virtuous habits, pure affections, steady labour, honesty, and duty. It is an affectation, and because it is an affectation the school is struck with sterility. The reader desires in the poet something better than a juggler in rhyme, or a conjuror in verse; he looks to find in him a painter of life, a being who thinks, loves, and has a conscience, who feels passion and repentance.

. . . .

Composition is a process of combination, in which thought puts together complementary truths, and talent fuses into harmony the most contrary qualities of style. So that there is no composition without effort, without pain even, as in all bringing forth. The reward is the giving birth to something living — something, that is to say, which, by a kind of magic, makes a living unity out of such opposed attributes as orderliness and spontaneity, thought and imagination, solidity and charm.

The true critic strives for a clear vision of things as they are — for justice and fairness; his effort is to get free from himself, so that he may in no way disfigure that which he wishes to understand or reproduce. His superiority to the common herd lies in this effort, even when its success is only partial. He distrusts his own senses, he sifts his own impressions, by returning upon them from different sides and at different times, by comparing, moderating, shading, distinguishing, and so endeavouring to approach more and more nearly to the formula which represents the maximum of truth.

* * * * * * *

Is it not the sad natures who are most tolerant of gaiety? They know that gaiety means impulse and vigour, that generally speaking it is disguised kindliness, and that if it were a mere affair of temperament and mood, still it is a blessing.

* * * * * *

The art which is grand and yet simple is that which presupposes the greatest elevation both in artist and in public.

* * * * * *

How much folly is compatible with ultimate wisdom and prudence? It is difficult to say. The cleverest folk are those who discover soonest how to utilise their neighbour's experience, and so get rid in good time of their natural presumption.

. . . .

We must try to grasp the spirit of things, to see correctly, to speak to the point, to give practicable advice, to act on the spot, to arrive at the proper moment, to stop in time. Tact, measure, occasion — all these deserve our cultivation and respect.

. . . .

22d April 1878.—Letter from my cousin Julia. These kind old relations find it very difficult to understand a man's life, especially a student's life. The hermits of reverie are scared by the busy world, and feel themselves out of place in action. But after all, we do not change at seventy, and a good, pious old lady, half-blind and living in a village, can no longer extend her point of view, nor form any idea of existences which have no relation with her own.

What is the link by which these souls, shut in and encompassed as they are by the details of daily life, lay hold on the ideal? The link of religious aspiration. Faith is the plank which saves them. They know the meaning of the higher life; their soul is athirst for Heaven. Their opinions are defective, but their moral experience is great; their intellect is full of darkness, but their soul is full of light. We scarcely know how to talk to them about the things of earth, but they are ripe and mature in the things of the heart. If they cannot understand us, it is for us to make advances to them, to speak their language, to enter into their range of ideas, their modes of feeling. We must approach them on their noble side, and, that we may show them the more respect, induce them to open to us the casket of their most treasured thoughts. There is always some grain of gold at the bottom of every honourable old age. Let it be our business to give it an opportunity of showing itself to affectionate eyes.

10*th May* 1878. — I have just come back from a solitary walk. I heard nightingales, saw white lilac and orchard trees in bloom. My heart is full of impressions showered upon it by the chaffinches, the golden orioles, the grasshoppers, the hawthorns, and the primroses. A dull, gray, fleecy sky brooded with a certain melancholy over the nuptial splendours of vegetation. Many painful memories stirred afresh in me; at Pré l'Evèque, at Jargonnant, at Villereuse, a score of phantoms — phantoms of youth — rose with sad eyes to greet me. The walls had changed, and roads which were once shady and dreamy I found now waste and treeless. But at the first trills of the nightingale a flood of tender feeling filled my heart. I felt myself soothed, grateful, melted; a mood of serenity and contemplation took possession of me. A certain little path, a very kingdom of green, with fountain, thickets, gentle ups and downs, and an abundance of singing-birds, delighted me, and did me inexpressible good. Its peaceful remoteness brought back the bloom of feeling. I had need of it.

19th May 1878. — Criticism is above all a gift, an intuition, a matter of tact and *flair;* it cannot be taught or demonstrated, — it is an art. Critical genius means an aptitude for discerning truth under appearances or in disguises which conceal it; for discovering it in spite of the errors of testimony, the frauds of tradition, the dust of time, the loss or alteration of texts. It is the sagacity of the hunter whom nothing deceives for long, and whom no ruse can throw off the trail. It is the talent of the

Juge d'Instruction, who knows how to interrogate circumstances, and to extract an unknown secret from a thousand falsehoods. The true critic can understand everything, but he will be the dupe of nothing, and to no convention will he sacrifice his duty, which is to find out and proclaim truth. Competent learning, general cultivation, absolute probity, accuracy of general view, human sympathy and technical capacity, — how many things are necessary to the critic, without reckoning grace, delicacy, *savoir vivre*, and the gift of happy phrase-making!

26th July 1878. — Every morning I wake up with the same sense of vain struggle against a mountain tide which is about to overwhelm me. I shall die by suffocation, and the suffocation has begun; the progress it has already made stimulates it to go on.

How can one make any plans when every day brings with it some fresh misery? I cannot even decide on a line of action in a situation so full of confusion and uncertainty, in which I look forward to the worst, while yet all is doubtful. Have I still a few years before me or only a few months? Will death be slow or will it come upon me as a sudden catastrophe? How am I to bear the days as they come? how am I to fill them? How am I to die with calmness and dignity? I know not. Everything I do for the first time I do badly; but here everything is new; there can be no help from experience; the end must be a chance! How mortifying for one who has set so great a price upon independence — to depend upon a thousand unforeseen contingencies! He knows not how he will act or what he will become; he would fain speak of these things with a friend of good sense and good counsel — but who? He dares not alarm the affections which are most his own, and he is almost sure that any others would try to distract his attention, and would refuse to see the position as it is.

And while I wait (wait for what? — health? — certainty?) the weeks flow by like water, and strength wastes away like a smoking candle. . . .

Is one free to let oneself drift into death without resistance? Is self-preservation a duty? Do we owe it to those who love us to prolong this desperate struggle to its utmost limit? I think so, but it is one fetter the more. For we must then feign a hope which we do not feel, and hide the absolute discouragement of which the heart is really full. Well, why not? Those who succumb are bound in generosity not to cool the ardour of those who are still battling, still enjoying.

Two parallel roads lead to the same result; meditation paralyses me, physiology condemns me. My soul is dying, my body is dying. In every direction the end is closing upon me. My own melancholy anticipates and endorses the medical judgment which says, 'Your journey is done.' The two verdicts point to the same result — that I have no longer a future. And yet there is a side of me which says, 'Absurd!' which is incredulous, and inclined to regard it all as a bad dream. In vain the reason asserts it; the mind's inward assent is still refused. Another contradiction!

I have not the strength to hope, and I have not the strength to submit. I believe no longer, and I believe still. I feel that I am dying, and yet I cannot realise that I am dying. Is it madness already? No, it is human nature taken in the act; it is life itself which is a contradiction, for life means an incessant death and a daily resurrection; it affirms and it denies, it destroys and reconstructs, it gathers and scatters, it humbles and exalts at the same time. To live is to die partially — to feel oneself in the heart of a whirlwind of opposing forces — to be an enigma.

If the invisible type moulded by these two contradictory currents — if this form which presides over all my changes of being — has itself general and original value, what does it matter whether it carries on the game a few months or years longer, or not? It has done what it had to do, it has represented a certain unique combination, one particular expression of the race. These types are shadows — *manes*. Century after century employs itself in fashioning them. Glory — fame — is the proof that one type has seemed to the other types newer, rarer, and more beautiful than the rest. The common types are souls too, only they have no interest except for the Creator, and for a small number of individuals.

To feel one's own fragility is well, but to be indifferent to it is better. To take the measure of one's own misery is profitable, but to understand its *raison d'être* is still more profitable. To mourn for oneself is a last sign of vanity; we ought only to regret that which has real value, and to regret oneself, is to furnish involuntary evidence that one had attached importance to oneself. At the same time it is a proof of ignorance of our true worth and function. It is not necessary to live, but it is necessary to preserve one's type unharmed, to remain faithful to one's idea, to protect one's monad against alteration and degradation.

7th November 1878. — To-day we have been talking of realism in painting, and, in connection with it, of that poetical and artistic illusion which does not aim at being confounded with reality itself. Realism wishes to entrap sensation; the object of true art is only to charm the imagination, not to deceive the eye. When we see a good portrait we say, 'It is alive!' — in other words, our imagination lends it life. On the other hand, a wax figure produces a sort of terror in us; its frozen lifelikeness makes a deathlike impression on us, and we say, 'It is a ghost!' In the one case we see what is lacking, and demand it; in the other we see what is given us, and we give on our side. Art, then, addresses itself to the imagination; everything that appeals to sensation only is below art, almost outside art. A work of art ought to set the poetical faculty in us to work, it ought to stir us to imagine, to complete our perception of a thing. And we can only do this when the artist leads the way Mere copyist's painting, realistic reproduction, pure imitation, leave us cold because their author is a machine, a mirror, an iodised plate, and not a soul.

Art lives by appearances, but these appearances are spiritual visions, fixed dreams. Poetry represents to us nature become consubstantial with the soul, because in it nature is only a reminiscence touched with emotion, an image vibrating with our own life, a form without weight, — in short, a mode of the soul. The poetry which is most real and objective is the expression of a soul which throws itself into things, and forgets itself in their presence more readily than others; but still, it is the expression of a soul, and hence what we call style. Style may be only collective, hieratic, national, so long as the artist is still the interpreter of the community; it tends to become personal in proportion as society makes room for individuality and favours its expansion.

. . . . . .

There is a way of killing truth by truths. Under the pretence that we want to study it more in detail we pulverise the statue — it is an absurdity of which our pedantry is constantly guilty. Those who can only see the fragments of a thing are to me *esprits faux*, just as much as those who disfigure the fragments. The good critic ought to be master of the three capacities, the three modes of seeing men and things — he should be able simultaneously to see them as they are, as they might be, and as they ought to be.

. . . . . .

Modern culture is a delicate electuary made up of varied savours and subtle colours, which can be more easily felt than measured or defined. Its very superiority consists in the complexity, the association of contraries, the skilful combination it implies. The man of to-day, fashioned by the historical and geographical influences of twenty countries and of thirty centuries, trained and modified by all the sciences and all the arts, the supple recipient of all literatures, is an entirely new product. He finds affinities, relationships, analogies everywhere, but at the same time he condenses and sums up what is elsewhere scattered. He is like the smile of La Gioconda, which seems to reveal a soul to the spectator only to leave him the more certainly under a final impression of mystery, so many different things are expressed in it at once.

* * * * *

To understand things we must have been once in them and then have come out of them; so that first there must be captivity and then deliverance, illusion followed by disillusion, enthusiasm by disappointment. He who is still under the spell, and he who has never felt the spell, are equally incompetent. We only know well what we have first believed, then judged. To understand we must be free, yet not have been always free. The same truth holds, whether it is a question of love, of art, of religion, or of patriotism. Sympathy is a first condition of criticism; reason and justice presuppose, at their origin, emotion.

* * * * *

What is an intelligent man? A man who enters with ease and completeness into the spirit of things and the intention of persons, and who arrives at an end by the shortest route. Lucidity and suppleness of thought, critical delicacy and inventive resource, these are his attributes.

. . . .

Analysis kills spontaneity. The grain once ground into flour springs and germinates no more.

. . . .

3d January 1879. — Letter from ——. This kind friend of mine has no pity. . . . I have been trying to quiet his over-delicate susceptibilities. . . . It is difficult to write perfectly easy letters when one finds them studied with a magnifying glass, and treated like monumental inscriptions, in which each character has been deliberately engraved with a view to an eternity of life. Such disproportion between the word and its commentary, between the playfulness of the writer and the analytical temper of the reader, is not favourable to ease of style. One dares not be one's natural self with these serious folk who attach importance to everything; it is difficult to write openheartedly if one must weigh every phrase and every word.

Esprit means taking things in the sense which they are meant to have, entering into the tone of other people, being able to place oneself on the required level; *esprit* is that just and accurate sense which divines, appreciates, and weighs quickly, lightly, and well. The mind must have its play, the Muse is winged — the Greeks knew it, and Socrates.

13th January 1879. — It is impossible for me to remember what letters I wrote yesterday. A single night digs a gulf between the self of yesterday and the self of to-day. My life is without unity of action, because my actions themselves are escaping from the control of memory. My mental power, occupied in gaining possession of itself under the form of consciousness, seems to be letting go its hold on all that generally peoples the understanding, as the glacier throws off the stones and fragments fallen into its crevasses, that it may remain pure crystal. The philosophic mind is loth to overweight itself with too many material facts or trivial memories. Thought clings only to thought, — that is to say, to itself, to the psychological process. The mind's only ambition is for an enriched experience. It finds its pleasure in studying the play of its own faculties, and the study passes easily into an aptitude and habit. Reflection becomes nothing more than an apparatus for the registration of the impressions, emotions, and ideas which pass across the mind. The whole moulting process is carried on so energetically that the mind is not only unclothed, but stripped of itself, and, so to speak, *de-substantiated*. The wheel turns so quickly that it melts around the mathematical axis, which alone remains cold because it is impalpable, and has no thickness. — All this is natural enough, but very dangerous.

So long as one is numbered among the living, — so long, that is to say, as one is still plunged in the world of men, a sharer of their interests, conflicts, vanities, passions, and duties, one is bound to deny oneself this subtle state of consciousness; one must consent to be a separate individual, having one's special name, position, age, and sphere of activity. In spite of all the temptations of impersonality, one must resume the position of a being imprisoned within certain limits of time and space, an individual with special surroundings, friends, enemies, profession, country, bound to house and feed himself, to make up his accounts and look after his affairs; in short, one must behave like all the world. There are days when all these details seem to me a dream, — when I wonder at the desk under my hand, at my body itself, —

when I ask myself if there is a street before my house, and if all this geographical and topographical phantasmagoria is indeed real. Time and space become then mere specks; I become a sharer in a purely spiritual existence; I see myself *sub specie æternitatis.*

Is not mind simply that which enables us to merge finite reality in the infinite possibility around it? Or, to put it differently, is not mind the universal virtuality, the universe latent? If so, its zero would be the germ of the infinite, which is expressed mathematically by the double zero (00).

Deduction: — that the mind may experience the infinite in itself; that in the human individual there arises sometimes the divine spark which reveals to him the existence of the original, fundamental, principal Being, within which all is contained like a series within its generating formula. The universe is but a radiation of mind; and the radiations of the Divine mind are for us more than appearances; they have a reality parallel to our own. The radiations of our mind are imperfect reflections from the great show of fireworks set in motion by Brahma, and great art is great only because of its conformities with the Divine order — with that which is.

Ideal conceptions are the mind's anticipation of such an order. The mind is capable of them because it is mind, and, as such, perceives the Eternal. The real, on the contrary, is fragmentary and passing. Law alone is eternal. The ideal is then the imperishable hope of something better, the mind's involuntary protest against the present, the leaven of the future working in it. It is the supernatural in us, or rather the super-animal, and the ground of human progress. He who has no ideal contents himself with what is; he has no quarrel with facts, which for him are identical with the just, the good, and the beautiful.

But why is the Divine radiation imperfect? Because it is still going on. Our planet, for example, is in the midcourse of its experience. Its flora and fauna are still changing. The evolution of humanity is nearer its origin than its close. The complete spiritualisation of the animal element in nature seems to be singularly difficult, and it is the task of our species. Its performance is hindered by error, evil, selfishness, and death, without counting telluric catastrophes. The edifice of a common happiness, a common science of morality and justice, is sketched, but only sketched. A thousand retarding and perturbing causes hinder this giant's task, in which nations, races, and continents take part. At the present moment humanity is not yet constituted as a physical unity, and its general education is not yet begun. All our attempts at order as yet have been local crystallisations. Now, indeed, the different possibilities are beginning to combine (union of posts and telegraphs, universal exhibitions, voyages round the globes, international congresses, etc.). Science and common interest are binding together the great fractions of humanity, which religion and language have kept apart. A year in which there has been talk of a network of African railways, running from the coast to the centre and bringing the Atlantic, the Mediterranean, and the Indian Ocean into communication with each other — such a year is enough to mark a new epoch. The fantastic has become the conceivable, the possible tends to become the real; the earth becomes the garden of man. Man's chief problem is how to make the cohabitation of the individuals of his species possible; how, that is to say, to secure for each successive epoch the law, the order, the equilibrium which befits it. Division of labour allows him to explore in every direction at once; industry, science, art, law, education, morals, religion, politics, and economical relations, — all are in process of birth.

Thus everything may be brought back to zero by the mind, but it is a fruitful zero — a zero which contains the universe and, in particular, humanity. The mind has no more difficulty in tracking the real within the innumerable than in apprehending infinite possibility. 00 may issue from 0, or may return to it.

19th January 1879. — Charity — goodness — places a voluntary curb on acuteness of perception; it screens and softens the rays of a too vivid insight; it refuses to see too clearly the ugliness and misery of the great intellectual hospital around it. True goodness is loth to recognise any privilege in itself; it prefers to be humble and charitable; it tries not to see what stares it in the face, — that is to say, the imperfections, infirmities, and errors of humankind; its pity puts on airs of approval and encouragement.

It triumphs over its own repulsions that it may help and raise.

It has often been remarked that Vinet praised weak things. If so, it was not from any failure in his own critical sense; it was from charity. 'Quench not the smoking flax,' — to which I add, 'Never give unnecessary pain.' The cricket is not the nightingale; why tell him so? Throw yourself into the mind of the cricket — the process is newer and more ingenious; and it is what charity commands.

Intellect is aristocratic, charity is democratic. In a democracy the general equality of pretensions, combined with the inequality of merits, creates considerable practical difficulty; some get out of it by making their prudence a muzzle on their frankness; others, by using kindness as a corrective of perspicacity. On the whole, kindness is safer than reserve; it inflicts no wound, and kills nothing.

Charity is generous; it runs a risk willingly, and in spite of a hundred successive experiences, it thinks no evil at the hundred-and-first. We cannot be at the same time kind and wary, nor can we serve two masters, — love and selfishness. We must be knowingly rash, that we may not be like the clever ones of the world, who never forget their own interests. We must be able to submit to being deceived; it is the sacrifice which interest and self-love owe to conscience. The claims of the soul must be satisfied first if we are to be the children of God.

Was it not Bossuet who said, 'It is only the great souls who know all the grandeur there is in charity'?

21st January 1879. — At first religion holds the place of science and philosophy; afterwards she has to learn to confine herself to her own domain — which is in the inmost depths of conscience, in the secret recesses of the soul, where life communes with the Divine will and the universal order. Piety is the daily renewing of the ideal, the steadying of our inner being, agitated, troubled, and embittered by the common accidents of existence. Prayer is the spiritual balm, the precious cordial which restores to us peace and courage. It reminds us of pardon and of duty. It says to us, 'Thou art loved — love; thou hast received — give; thou must die — labour while thou canst; overcome anger by kindness; overcome evil with good. What does the blindness of opinion matter, or misunderstanding, or ingratitude? Thou art neither bound to follow the common example nor to succeed. *Fais ce que dois, advienne que pourra.* Thou hast a witness in thy conscience; and thy conscience is God speaking to thee!'

3d March 1879. — The sensible politician is governed by considerations of social utility, the public good, the greatest attainable good; the political windbag starts from the idea of the rights of the individual, — abstract rights, of which the extent is affirmed, not demonstrated, for the political right of the individual is precisely what is in question. The revolutionary school always forgets that right apart from duty is a compass with one leg. The notion of right inflates the individual, fills him with thoughts of self and of what others owe him, while it ignores the other side of the question, and extinguishes his capacity for devoting himself to a common cause. The State becomes a shop with self-interest for a principle, — or rather an arena, in which every combatant fights for his own hand only. In either case self is the motive power.

Church and State ought to provide two opposite careers for the individual; in the State he should be called on to give proof of merit — that is to say, he should earn his rights by services rendered; in the Church his task should be to do good while suppressing his own merits, by a voluntary act of humility.

Extreme individualism dissipates the moral substance of the individual. It leads him to subordinate everything to himself, and to think the world, society, the State, made for him. I am chilled by its lack of gratitude, of the spirit of deference, of the instinct of solidarity. It is an ideal without beauty and without grandeur.

But, as a consolation, the modern zeal for equality makes a counterpoise for Darwinism, just as one wolf holds another wolf in check. Neither, indeed, acknowledges the claim of duty. The fanatic for equality affirms his right not to be eaten by his neighbour; the Darwinian states the fact that the big devour the little, and adds — so much the better. Neither the one nor the other has a word to say of love, of eternity, of kindness, of piety, of voluntary submission, of self-surrender.

All forces and all principles are brought

into action at once in this world. The result is, on the whole, good. But the struggle itself is hateful because it dislocates truth and shows us nothing but error pitted against error, party against party; that is to say, mere halves and fragments of being—monsters against monsters. A nature in love with beauty cannot reconcile itself to the sight; it longs for harmony, for something else than perpetual dissonance. The common condition of human society must indeed be accepted; tumult, hatred, fraud, crime, the ferocity of self-interest, the tenacity of prejudice, are perennial; but the philosopher sighs over it; his heart is not in it; his ambition is to see human history from a height; his ear is set to catch the music of the eternal spheres.

15th March 1879.—I have been turning over *Les histoires de mon Parrain* by Stahl, and a few chapters of *Nos Fils et nos Filles* by Legouvé. These writers press wit, grace, gaiety, and charm into the service of goodness; their desire is to show that virtue is not so dull nor common sense so tiresome as people believe. They are persuasive moralists, captivating story-

tellers; they rouse the appetite for good.
This pretty manner of theirs, however, has
its dangers. A moral wrapped up in sugar
goes down certainly, but it may be feared
that it only goes down because of its sugar.
The Sybarites of to-day will tolerate a sermon which is delicate enough to flatter
their literary sensuality; but it is their
taste which is charmed, not their conscience which is awakened: their principle
of conduct escapes untouched.

Amusement, instruction, morals, are distinct *genres*. They may no doubt be mingled and combined, but if we wish to obtain
direct and simple effects, we shall do best
to keep them apart. The well-disposed
child, besides, does not like mixtures which
have something of artifice and deception in
them. Duty claims obedience; study requires application; for amusement, nothing
is wanted but good temper. To convert
obedience and application into means of
amusement is to weaken the will and the
intelligence. These efforts to make virtue
the fashion are praiseworthy enough, but
if they do honour to the writers, on the
other hand they prove the moral anæmia
of society. When the digestion is unspoilt,
so much persuading is not necessary to
give it a taste for bread.

what suffering is, and yearn for happiness. All know what sin is, and feel the need of pardon.

Christianity reduced to its original simplicity is the reconciliation of the sinner with God, by means of the certainty that God loves in spite of everything, and that He chastises because He loves. Christianity furnished a new motive and a new strength for the achievement of moral perfection. It made holiness attractive by giving to it the air of filial gratitude.

28th June 1879. — Last lecture of the term and of the academic year. I finished the exposition of modern philosophy, and wound up my course with the precision I wished. The circle has returned upon itself. In order to do this I have divided my hour into minutes, calculated my material, and counted every stitch and point. This, however, is but a very small part of the professorial science. It is a more difficult matter to divide one's whole material into a given number of lectures, to determine the right proportions of the different parts, and the normal speed of delivery to be attained. The ordinary lecturer may achieve a series of complete *séances*, — the unity being the *séance*. But a scientific course ought to aim at something more — at a general unity of subject and of exposition.

Has this concise, substantial, closely-reasoned kind of work been useful to my class? I cannot tell. Have my students liked me this year? I am not sure, but I hope so. It seems to me they have. Only, if I have pleased them, it cannot have been in any case more than a *succès d'estime;* I have never aimed at any oratorical success. My only object is to light up for them a complicated and difficult subject. I respect myself too much, and I respect my class too much, to attempt rhetoric. My *rôle* is to help them to understand. Scientific lecturing ought to be, above all things, clear, instructive, well put together, and convincing. A lecturer has nothing to do with paying court to the scholars, or with showing off the master; his business is one of serious study and impersonal exposition. To yield anything on this point would seem to me a piece of mean utilitarianism. I hate everything that savours of cajoling and coaxing. All such ways are mere attempts to throw dust in men's eyes, mere forms of coquetry and stratagem. A pro-

The only positive good is order, the return therefore to order and to a state of equilibrium. Thought without action is an evil, and so is action without thought. The ideal is a poison unless it be fused with the real, and the real becomes corrupt without the perfume of the ideal. Nothing is good singly without its complement and its contrary. Self-examination is dangerous if it encroaches upon self-devotion; reverie is hurtful when it stupefies the will; gentleness is an evil when it lessens strength; contemplation is fatal when it destroys character. 'Too much' and 'too little' sin equally against wisdom. Excess is one evil, apathy another. Duty may be defined as energy tempered by moderation; happiness, as inclination calmed and tempered by self-control.

Just as life is only lent us for a few years, but is not inherent in us, so the good which is in us is not our own. It is not difficult to think of oneself in this detached spirit. It only needs a little self-knowledge, a little intuitive perception of the ideal, a little religion. There is even much sweetness in this conception that we are nothing of ourselves, and that yet it is granted to us to summon each other to life, joy, poetry and holiness.

Another application of the law of irony: Zeno, a fatalist by theory, makes his disciples heroes: Epicurus, the upholder of liberty, makes his disciples languid and effeminate. The ideal pursued is the decisive point; the Stoical ideal is duty, whereas the Epicureans make an ideal out of an interest. Two tendencies, two systems of morals, two worlds. In the same way the Jansenists, and before them the great reformers, are for predestination, the Jesuits for free-will, — and yet the first founded liberty, the second slavery of conscience. What matters then is not the theoretical principle; it is the secret tendency, the aspiration, the aim, which is the essential thing.

. . . .

At every epoch there lies, beyond the domain of what man knows, the domain of the unknown, in which faith has its dwelling. Faith has no proofs, but only itself, to offer. It is born spontaneously in certain commanding souls; it spreads its empire among the rest by imitation and contagion. A great faith is but a great hope which becomes certitude as we move farther and farther from the founder of it; time and distance strengthen it, until at last the passion for knowledge seizes upon it, questions, and examines it. Then all which had once made its strength becomes its weakness; the impossibility of verification, exaltation of feeling, distance.

. . . . . .

At what age is our view clearest, our eye truest? Surely in old age, before the infirmities come which weaken or embitter. The ancients were right. The old man who is at once sympathetic and disinterested, necessarily develops the spirit of contemplation, and it is given to the spirit of contemplation to see things most truly, because it alone perceives them in their relative and proportional value.

2d January 1880. — A sense of rest, of deep quiet even. Silence within and without. A quietly-burning fire. A sense of comfort. The portrait of my mother seems to smile upon me. I am not dazed or stupid, but only happy in this peaceful morning. Whatever may be the charm of emotion, I do not know whether it equals the sweetness of those hours of silent meditation, in which we have a glimpse and foretaste of the contemplative joys of Paradise. Desire and fear, sadness and care, are done away. Existence is reduced to the simplest form, the most ethereal mode of being, that is, to pure self-consciousness. It is a state of harmony, without tension and without disturbance, the dominical state of the soul, perhaps the state which awaits it beyond the grave. It is happiness as the Orientals understand it, the happiness of the anchorite, who neither struggles nor wishes any more, but simply adores and enjoys. It is difficult to find words in which to express this moral situation, for our languages can only render the particular and localised vibrations of life; they are incapable of expressing this motionless concentration, this divine quietude, this state of the resting ocean, which reflects the sky, and is master of its own profundities. Things are then re-absorbed into their principles; memories are swallowed up in memory; the soul is only soul, and is no longer conscious of itself in its individuality and separateness. It is something which feels the universal life, a sensible atom of the Divine, of God. It no longer appropriates anything to itself, it is conscious of no void. Only the Yoghis and Soufis perhaps have known in its profundity this humble and yet voluptuous state, which combines the joys of being and of non-being, which is neither reflection nor will, which is above both the moral existence and the intellectual existence, which is the return to unity, to the pleroma, the vision of Plotinus and of Proclus, — Nirvana in its most attractive form.

It is clear that the western nations in general, and especially the Americans, know very little of this state of feeling. For them life is devouring and incessant activity. They are eager for gold, for power, for dominion; their aim is to crush men and to enslave nature. They show an obstinate interest in means, and have not a thought for the end. They confound being with individual being, and the expansion of the self with happiness, — that is to say, they do not live by the soul; they ignore the unchangeable and the eternal; they live at the periphery of their being, because they are unable to penetrate to its axis. They are excited, ardent, positive, because they are superficial. Why so much effort, noise, struggle, and greed? — it is all a mere stunning and deafening of the self. When death comes they recognise that it is so, — why not then admit it sooner? Activity is only beautiful when it is holy — that is to say, when it is spent in the service of that which passeth not away.

6th February 1880. — A feeling article by Edmond Schérer on the death of Bersot, the director of the 'École Normale,' a philosopher who bore like a stoic a terrible disease, and who laboured to the last without a complaint. . . . I have just read the four orations delivered over his grave. They have brought the tears to my eyes. In the last days of this brave man everything was manly, noble, moral, and spiritual. Each of the speakers paid homage to the character, the devotion, the constancy, and the intellectual elevation of the dead. 'Let us learn from him how to live and how to die.' The whole funeral ceremony had an antique dignity.

7th February 1880. — Hoar-frost and fog, but the general aspect is bright and fairy-like, and has nothing in common with the gloom in Paris and London, of which the newspapers tell us.

This silvery landscape has a dreamy grace,

a fanciful charm, which is unknown both to the countries of the sun and to those of coal-smoke. The trees seem to belong to another creation, in which white has taken the place of green. As one gazes at these alleys, these clumps, these groves and arcades, these lace-like garlands and festoons, one feels no wish for anything else; their beauty is original and self-sufficing, all the more because the ground powdered with snow, the sky dimmed with mist, and the smooth soft distances, combine to form, a general scale of colour, and a harmonious whole, which charms the eye. No harshness anywhere — all is velvet. My enchantment beguiled me out both before and after dinner. The impression is that of a *fête*, and the subdued tints are, or seem to be, a mere coquetry of winter which has set itself to paint something without sunshine, and yet to charm the spectator.

9th February 1880. — Life rushes on — so much the worse for the weak and the stragglers. As soon as a man's tendo Achillis gives way he finds himself trampled under foot by the young, the eager, the voracious. '*Vae victis, vae debilibus!*' yells the crowd, which in its turn is storming the goods of this world. Every man is always in some other man's way, since, however small he may make himself, he still occupies *some* space, and however little he may envy or possess, he is still sure to be envied and his goods coveted by some one else. Mean world! — peopled by a mean race! To console ourselves we must think of the exceptions — of the noble and generous souls. There are such. What do the rest matter! — The traveller crossing the desert feels himself surrounded by creatures thirsting for his blood; by day vultures fly about his head; by night scorpions creep into his tent, jackals prowl around his camp-fire, mosquitoes prick and torture him with their greedy sting; everywhere menace, enmity, ferocity. But far beyond the horizon, and the barren sands peopled by these hostile hordes, the wayfarer pictures to himself a few loved faces and kind looks, a few true hearts which follow him in their dreams — and smiles. — When all is said, indeed, we defend ourselves a greater or lesser number of years, but we are always conquered and devoured in the end; there is no escaping the grave and its worm. Destruction is our destiny, and oblivion our portion. . . .

How near is the great gulf! My skiff is thin as a nutshell, or even more fragile still. Let the leak but widen a little and all is over for the navigator. A mere nothing separates me from idiocy, from madness, from death. The slightest breach is enough to endanger all this frail, ingenious edifice, which calls itself my being and my life.

Not even the dragonfly symbol is enough to express its frailty; the soap-bubble is the best poetical translation of all this illusory magnificence, this fugitive apparition of the tiny self, which is we, and we it.

. . . A miserable night enough. Awakened three or four times by my bronchitis. Sadness — restlessness. One of these winter nights, possibly, suffocation will come. I realise that it would be well to keep myself ready, to put everything in order. . . . To begin with, let me wipe out all personal grievances and bitternesses; forgive all, judge no one; in enmity and illwill, see only misunderstanding. 'As much as lieth in you, be at peace with all men.' On the bed of death the soul should have no eyes but for eternal things. All the littlenesses of life disappear. The fight is over. There should be nothing left now but remembrance of past blessings, — adoration of the ways of God. Our natural instinct leads us back to Christian humility and pity. 'Father, forgive us our trespasses, as we forgive them who trespass against us.'

Prepare thyself as though the coming Easter were thy last, for thy days henceforward shall be few and evil.

11*th February* 1880. — Victor de Laprade[20] has elevation, grandeur, nobility, and harmony. What is it, then, that he lacks? Ease, and perhaps humour. Hence the monotonous solemnity, the excess of emphasis, the over-intensity, the inspired air, the statue-like gait, which annoy one in him. He is a muse which never lays aside the cothurnus, and a royalty which never puts off its crown, even to sleep. The total absence in him of playfulness, simplicity, familiarity, is a great defect. De Laprade is to the ancients as the French tragedy is to that of Euripides, or as the wig of Louis XIV. to the locks of Apollo. His majestic airs are wearisome and factitious. If there is not exactly affectation in them, there is at least a kind of theatrical and sacerdotal posing, a sort of professional attitudinising. Truth is not as fine as this, but it is more living, more pathetic, more varied. Marble images are cold. Was it not Musset who said, 'If De Laprade is a poet, then I am not one'?

27th February 1880.—I have finished translating twelve or fourteen little poems by Petöfi. They have a strange kind of savour. There is something of the Steppe, of the East, of Mazeppa, of madness, in these songs, which seem to go to the beat of a riding-whip. What force and passion, what savage brilliancy, what wild and grandiose images, there are in them! One feels that the Magyar is a kind of Centaur, and that he is only Christian and European by accident. The Hun in him tends towards the Arab.

20th March 1880.—I have been reading *La Bannière Bleue*—a history of the world at the time of Genghis Khan, under the form of memoirs. It is a Turk, Ouïgour, who tells the story. He shows us civilisation from the wrong side, or the other side, and the Asiatic nomads appear as the scavengers of its corruptions.

Genghis proclaimed himself the scourge of God, and he did in fact realise the vastest empire known to history, stretching from the Blue Sea to the Baltic, and from the vast plains of Siberia to the banks of the sacred Ganges. The most solid empires of the ancient world were overthrown by the tramp of his horsemen and the shafts of his archers. From the tumult into which he threw the western continent there issued certain vast results: the fall of the Byzantine Empire, involving the Renaissance, the voyages of discovery in Asia, undertaken from both sides of the globe — that is to say, Gama and Columbus; the formation of the Turkish Empire; and the preparation of the Russian Empire. This tremendous hurricane, starting from the high Asiatic tablelands, felled the decaying oaks and worm-eaten buildings of the whole ancient world. The descent of the yellow, flat-nosed Mongols upon Europe is a historical cyclone which devastated and purified our thirteenth century, and broke, at the two ends of the known world, through two great Chinese walls — that which protected the ancient empire of the

Centre, and that which made a barrier of ignorance and superstition round the little world of Christendom. Attila, Genghis, Tamerlane, ought to range in the memory of men with Cæsar, Charlemagne, and Napoleon. They roused whole peoples into action, and stirred the depths of human life, they powerfully affected ethnography, they let loose rivers of blood, and renewed the face of things. The Quakers will not see that there is a law of tempests in history as in Nature. The revilers of war are like the revilers of thunder, storms, and volcanoes; they know not what they do. Civilisation tends to corrupt men, as large towns tend to vitiate the air.

'Nos patimur longæ pacis mala.'

Catastrophes bring about a violent restoration of equilibrium; they put the world brutally to rights. Evil chastises itself, and the tendency to ruin in human things supplies the place of the regulator who has not yet been discovered. No civilisation can bear more than a certain proportion of abuses, injustice, corruption, shame, and crime. When this proportion has been reached, the boiler bursts, the palace falls, the scaffolding breaks down; institutions, cities, states, empires, sink into ruin. The evil contained in an organism is a virus which preys upon it, and if it is not eliminated ends by destroying it. And as nothing is perfect, nothing can escape death.

19th May 1880. — *Inadaptablility*, due either to mysticism or stiffness, delicacy or disdain, is the misfortune or at all events the characteristic of my life. I have not been able to fit myself to anything, to content myself with anything. I have never had the quantum of illusion necessary for risking the irreparable. I have made use of the ideal itself to keep me from any kind of bondage. It was thus with marriage: only perfection would have satisfied me; and, on the other hand, I was not worthy of perfection. . . . So that, finding no satisfaction in things, I tried to extirpate desire, by which things enslave us. Independence has been my refuge; detachment my stronghold. I have lived the impersonal life, — in the world, yet not in it, thinking much, desiring nothing. It is a state of mind which corresponds with what in women is called a broken heart; and it is in fact like it, since the characteristic common to both is despair. When one knows that one will never possess what one could have loved, and that one can be content with nothing less, one has, so to speak, left the world, one has cut the golden hair, parted with all that makes human life — that is to say, illusion — the incessant effort towards an apparently attainable end.

31*st May* 1880. — Let us not be over-ingenious. There is no help to be got out of subtleties. Besides, one must live. It is best and simplest not to quarrel with any illusion, and to accept the inevitable good-temperedly. Plunged as we are in human existence, we must take it as it comes, not too bitterly, nor too tragically, without horror and without sarcasm, without misplaced petulance or a too exacting expectation; cheerfulness, serenity, and patience, these are best, — let us aim at these. Our business is to treat life as the grandfather treats his granddaughter, or the grandmother her grandson; to enter into the pretences of childhood and the fictions of youth, even when we ourselves have long passed beyond them. It is probable that God Himself looks kindly upon the illusions of the human race, so long as they are innocent. There is nothing evil but sin — that is, egotism and revolt. And as for error, man changes his errors frequently, but error of some sort is always with him. Travel as one may, one is always somewhere, and one's mind rests on some point of truth, as one's feet rest upon some point of the globe.

Society alone represents a more or less complete unity. The individual must content himself with being a stone in the building, a wheel in the immense machine, a word in the poem. He is a part of the family, of the State, of humanity, of all the special fragments formed by human interests, beliefs, aspirations, and labours. The loftiest souls are those who are conscious of the universal symphony, and who give their full and willing collaboration to this vast and complicated concert which we call civilisation.

In principle the mind is capable of suppressing all the limits which it discovers in itself, limits of language, nationality, religion, race, or epoch. But it must be admitted that the more the mind spiritualises and generalises itself, the less hold it has on other minds, which no longer understand it or know what to do with it. Influence belongs to men of action, and for purposes of action nothing is more useful than narrowness of thought combined with energy of will.

The forms of dreamland are gigantic, those of action are small and dwarfed. To the minds imprisoned in things, belong success, fame, profit; a great deal no doubt; but they know nothing of the pleasures of liberty or the joy of penetrating the infinite. However, I do not mean to put one class before another; for every man is happy according to his nature. History is made by combatants and specialists; only it is perhaps not a bad thing that in the midst of the devouring activities of the western world, there should be a few *Brahmanising* souls.

... This soliloquy means — what? That reverie turns upon itself as dreams do; that impressions added together do not always produce a fair judgment; that a private journal is like a good king, and permits repetitions, outpourings, complaint. ... These unseen effusions are the conversation of thought with itself, the arpeggios, involuntary but not unconscious, of that Æolian harp we bear within us. Its vibrations compose no piece, exhaust no theme, achieve no melody, carry out no programme, but they express the innermost life of man.

1st June 1880.— Stendhal's *La Chartreuse de Parme.* A remarkable book. It is even typical, the first of a class. Stendhal opens the series of naturalist novels, which suppress the intervention of the moral sense, and scoff at the claim of free-will. Individuals are irresponsible ; they are governed by their passions, and the play of human passions is the observer's joy, the artist's material. Stendhal is a novelist after Taine's heart, a faithful painter who is neither touched nor angry, and whom everything amuses — the knave and the adventuress as well as honest men and women, but who has neither faith, nor preference, nor ideal. In him literature is subordinated to natural history, to science. It no longer forms part of the *humanities*, it no longer gives man the honour of a separate rank. It classes him with the ant, the beaver, and the monkey. And this moral indifference to morality leads direct to immorality.

The vice of the whole school is cynicism, contempt for man, whom they degrade to the level of the brute ; it is the worship of strength, disregard of the soul, a want of generosity, of reverence, of nobility, which shows itself in spite of all protestations to the contrary; in a word, it is *inhumanity*. No man can be a naturalist with impunity: he will be coarse even with the most refined culture. A free mind is a great thing no doubt, but loftiness of heart, belief in goodness, capacity for enthusiasm and devotion, the thirst after perfection and holiness, are greater things still.

7th June 1880. — I am reading Madame Necker de Saussure [21] again. *L'Éducation progressive* is an admirable book. What moderation and fairness of view, what reasonableness and dignity of manner! Everything in it is of high quality, — observation, thought, and style. The reconciliation of science with the ideal, of philosophy with religion, of psychology with morals, which the book attempts, is sound and beneficent. It is a fine book — a classic — and Geneva may be proud of a piece of work which shows such high cultivation and so much solid wisdom. Here we have the true Genevese literature, the central tradition of the country.

Later. — I have finished the third volume

of Madame Necker. The elevation and delicacy, the sense and seriousness, the beauty and perfection of the whole, are astonishing. A few harshnesses or inaccuracies of language do not matter. I feel for the author a respect mingled with emotion. How rare it is to find a book in which everything is sincere and everything is true!

26th June 1880. — Democracy exists; it is mere loss of time to dwell upon its absurdities and defects. Every *régime* has its weaknesses, and this *régime* is a lesser evil than others. On things its effect is unfavourable, but on the other hand men profit by it, for it develops the individual by obliging every one to take interest in a multitude of questions. It makes bad work, but it produces citizens. This is its excuse, and a more than tolerable one; in the eyes of the philanthropist, indeed, it is a serious title to respect, for, after all, social institutions are made for man, and not *vice versâ*.

27th June 1880. — I paid a visit to my friends ——, and we resumed the conversation of yesterday. We talked of the ills which threaten democracy and which are derived from the legal fiction at the root of it. Surely the remedy consists in insisting everywhere upon the truth which democracy systematically forgets, and which is its proper makeweight, — on the inequalities of talent, of virtue, and merit, and on the respect due to age, to capacity, to services rendered. Juvenile arrogance and jealous ingratitude must be resisted all the more strenuously because social forms are in their favour; and when the institutions of a country lay stress only on the rights of the individual, it is the business of the citizen to lay all the more stress on duty. There must be a constant effort to correct the prevailing tendency of things. All this, it is true, is nothing but palliative, but in human society one cannot hope for more.

Later. — Alfred de Vigny is a sympathetic writer, with a meditative turn of thought, a strong and supple talent. He possesses elevation, independence, seriousness, originality, boldness and grace; he has something of everything. He paints, describes, and judges well; he thinks, and has the courage of his opinions. His defect lies in an excess of self-respect, in a British pride and reserve which give him a horror of familiarity and a terror of letting himself go. This tendency has naturally injured his popularity as a writer with a public whom he holds at arm's length as one might a troublesome crowd. The French race has never cared much about the inviolability of personal conscience; it does not like stoics shut up in their own dignity as in a tower, and recognising no master but God, duty or faith. Such strictness annoys and irritates it; it is merely piqued and made impatient by anything solemn. It repudiated Protestantism for this very reason, and in all crises it has crushed those who have not yielded to the passionate current of opinion.

1st July 1880 (*Three o'clock*).—The temperature is oppressive; I ought to be looking over my notes, and thinking of tomorrow's examinations. Inward distaste — emptiness — discontent. Is it trouble of conscience, or sorrow of heart? or the soul preying upon itself? or merely a sense of strength decaying and time running to waste? Is sadness — or regret — or fear — at the root of it? I do not know; but this dull sense of misery has danger in it; it leads to rash efforts and mad decisions. Oh for escape from self, for something to stifle the importunate voice of want and yearning! Discontent is the father of temptation. How can we gorge the invisible serpent hidden at the bottom of our well, — gorge it so that it may sleep?

At the heart of all this rage and vain rebellion there lies — what? Aspiration, yearning! We are athirst for the infinite — for love — for I know not what. It is the instinct of happiness, which, like some wild animal, is restless for its prey. It is God calling — God avenging Himself.

4th July 1880 (*Sunday, half-past eight in the morning*). — The sun has come out after heavy rain. May one take it as an omen on this solemn day? The great voice of *Clémence* has just been sounding in our ears. The bell's deep vibrations went to my heart. For a quarter of an hour the pathetic appeal went on — 'Geneva, Geneva, remember! I am called *Clémence* — I am the voice of Church and of Country. People of Geneva, serve God and be at peace together.' *

---

* A law to bring about separation between Church and State, adopted by the Great Council, was on this day submitted to the vote of the Genevese people. It was rejected by a large majority (9306 against 4044). — [S.]

Seven o'clock in the evening. — *Clémence* has been ringing again, during the last half-hour of the *scrutin*. Now that she has stopped, the silence has a terrible seriousness, like that which weighs upon a crowd when it is waiting for the return of the judge and the delivery of the death sentence. The fate of the Genevese church and country is now in the voting box.

Eleven o'clock in the evening. — Victory along the whole line. The Ayes have carried little more than two-sevenths of the vote. At my friend ——'s house I found them all full of excitement, gratitude, and joy.

5th July 1880. — There are some words which have still a magical virtue with the mass of the people: those of State, Republic, Country, Nation, Flag, and even, I think, Church. Our sceptical and mocking culture knows nothing of the emotion, the exaltation, the delirium, which these words awaken in simple people. The *blasés* of the world have no idea how the popular mind vibrates to these appeals, by which they themselves are untouched. It is their punishment; it is also their infirmity.

Their temper is satirical and separatist; they live in isolation and sterility.

I feel again what I felt at the time of the Rousseau centenary; my feeling and imagination are chilled and repelled by those Pharisaical people who think themselves too good to associate with the crowd.

At the same time, I suffer from an inward contradiction, from a twofold, instinctive repugnance — an æsthetic repugnance towards vulgarity of every kind, a moral repugnance towards barrenness and coldness of heart.

So that personally I am only attracted by the individuals of cultivation and eminence, while on the other hand nothing is sweeter to me than to feel myself vibrating in sympathy with the national spirit, with the feeling of the masses. I only care for the two extremes, and it is this which separates me from each of them.

Our everyday life, split up as it is into clashing parties and opposed opinions, and harassed by perpetual disorder and discussion, is painful and almost hateful to me. A thousand things irritate and provoke me. But perhaps it would be the same elsewhere. Very likely it is the inevitable way of the world which displeases me — the sight of what succeeds, of what men approve or blame, of what they excuse or accuse. I need to admire, to feel myself in sympathy and in harmony with my neighbour, with the march of things, and the tendencies of those around me, and almost always I have had to give up the hope of it. I take refuge in retreat, to avoid discord. But solitude is only a *pis-aller*.

6th July 1880. — Magnificent weather. The college prize-day.* Towards evening I went with our three ladies to the plain of Plainpalais. There was an immense crowd, and I was struck with the bright look of the faces. The festival wound up with the traditional fireworks, under a calm and starry sky. Here we have the Republic indeed, I thought as I came in. For a whole week this people has been out-of-doors, camping, like the Athenians on the Agora. Since Wednesday lectures and public meetings have followed one another without intermission; at home there are pamphlets and the newspapers to be read; while speech-making goes on at the clubs. On Sunday, *plebiscite;* Monday, public pro-

* The prize-giving at the College of Geneva is made the occasion of a national festival.

cession, service at St. Pierre, speeches on the Molard, festival for the adults. Tuesday, the college fête-day. Wednesday, the fête-day of the primary schools.

Geneva is a cauldron always at boiling-point, a furnace of which the fires are never extinguished. Vulcan had more than one forge, and Geneva is certainly one of those world-anvils on which the greatest number of projects have been hammered out. When one thinks that the martyrs of all causes have been at work here, the mystery is explained a little; but the truest explanation is that Geneva, — republican, protestant, democratic, learned, and enterprising Geneva — has for centuries depended on herself alone for the solution of her own difficulties. Since the Reformation she has been always on the alert, marching with a lantern in her left hand and a sword in her right. It pleases me to see that she has not yet become a mere copy of anything, and that she is still capable of deciding for herself. Those who say to her, 'Do as they do at New York, at Paris, at Rome, at Berlin,' are still in the minority. The *doctrinaires* who would split her up and destroy her unity waste their breath upon her. She divines the snare laid for her and turns away. I like this proof of vitality. Only that which is original has a sufficient reason for existence. A country in which the word of command comes from elsewhere is nothing more than a province. This is what our Jacobins and our Ultramontanes never will recognise. Neither of them understand the meaning of self-government, and neither of them have any idea of the dignity of a historical state and an independent people.

Our small nationalities are ruined by the hollow cosmopolitan formulæ which have an equally disastrous effect upon art and letters. The modern *isms* are so many acids which dissolve everything living and concrete. No one achieves a masterpiece, nor even a decent piece of work, by the help of realism, liberalism, or romanticism. Separatism has even less virtue than any of the other *isms*, for it is the abstraction of a negation, the shadow of a shadow. The various *isms* of the present are not fruitful principles: they are hardly even explanatory formulæ. They are rather names of disease, for they express some element in excess, some dangerous and abusive exaggeration. Examples: empiricism, idealism, radicalism. What is best among things and most perfect among beings slips through these categories. The man who is perfectly well is neither sanguineous — [to use the old medical term] — nor bilious nor nervous. A normal republic contains opposing parties and points of view, but it contains them, as it were, in a state of chemical combination. All the colours are contained in a ray of light, while red alone does not contain a sixth part of the perfect ray.

8th July 1880. — It is thirty years since I read Waagen's book on *Museums*, which my friend —— is now reading. It was in 1842 that I was wild for pictures; in 1845 that I was studying Krause's philosophy; in 1850 that I became professor of æsthetics. —— may be the same age as I am; it is none the less true that when a particular stage has become to me a matter of history, he is just arriving at it. This impression of distance and remoteness is a strange one. I begin to realise that my memory is a great catacomb, and that below my actual standing-ground there is layer after layer of historical ashes.

Is the life of mind something like that of great trees of immemorial growth? Is the living layer of consciousness superimposed upon hundreds of dead layers? *Dead?* No doubt this is too much to say, but still, when memory is slack the past becomes almost as though it had never been. To remember that we did know once is not a sign of possession but a sign of loss; it is like the number of an engraving which is no longer on its nail, the title of a volume no longer to be found on its shelf. My mind is the empty frame of a thousand vanished images. Sharpened by incessant training, it is all culture, but it has retained hardly anything in its meshes. It is without matter, and is only form. It no longer has knowledge; it has become method. It is etherealised, algebraicised. Life has treated it as death treats other minds; it has already prepared it for a further metamorphosis. Since the age of sixteen onwards I have been able to look at things with the eyes of a blind man recently operated upon —that is to say, I have been able to suppress in myself the results of the long education of sight, and to abolish distances; and now I find myself regarding existence as though from beyond the tomb, from another world; all is strange to me; I am, as it were, outside my own body and individuality; I am *depersonalised*, detached, cut adrift. — Is this madness? No. Madness means the impossibility of recovering one's normal balance after the mind has thus played truant among alien forms of being, and followed Dante to invisible worlds. Madness means incapacity for self-judgment and self-control. Whereas it seems to me that my mental transformations are but philosophical experiences. I am tied to none. I am but making psychological investigations. At the same time I do not hide from myself that such experiences weaken the hold of common sense, because they act as solvents of all personal interests and prejudices. I can only defend myself against them by returning to the common life of men, and by bracing and fortifying the will.

14th July 1880. — What is the book which, of all Genevese literature, I would soonest have written? Perhaps that of Madame Necker de Saussure, or Madame de Staël's *L'Allemagne*. To a Genevese, moral philosophy is still the most congenial and remunerative of studies. Intellectual seriousness is what suits us least ill. History, politics, economical science, education, practical philosophy — these are our subjects. We have everything to lose in the attempt to make ourselves mere Frenchified copies of the Parisians : by so doing we are merely carrying water to the Seine. Independent criticism is perhaps easier at Geneva than at Paris, and Geneva ought to remain faithful to her own special line, which, as compared with that of France, is one of greater freedom from the tyranny of taste and fashion on the one hand, and the tyranny of ruling opinion on the other — of Catholicism or Jacobinism. Geneva should be to *La Grande Nation* what Diogenes was to Alexander ; her *rôle* is to represent the independent thought and the free speech which is not dazzled by prestige, and does not blink the truth. It is true that the *rôle* is an ungrateful one, that it lends itself to sarcasm and misrepresentation — but what matter ?

28th July 1880. — This afternoon I have had a walk in the sunshine, and have just come back rejoicing in a renewed communion with nature. The waters of the Rhone and the Arve, the murmur of the river, the austerity of its banks, the brilliancy of the foliage, the play of the leaves, the splendour of the July sunlight, the rich fertility of the fields, the lucidity of the distant mountains, the whiteness of the glaciers under the azure serenity of the sky, the sparkle and foam of the mingling rivers, the leafy masses of the La Bâtie woods — all and everything delighted me. It seemed to me as though the years of strength had come back to me. I was overwhelmed with sensations. I was surprised and grateful. The universal life carried me on its breast; the summer's caress went to my heart. Once more my eyes beheld the vast horizons, the soaring peaks, the blue lakes, the winding valleys, and all the free outlets of old days. And yet there was no painful sense of longing. The scene left upon me an indefinable impression, which was neither hope, nor desire, nor regret, but rather a sense of emotion, of passionate impulse, mingled with admiration and anxiety. I am conscious at once of joy and of want; beyond what I possess I see the impossible and the unattainable; I gauge my own wealth and poverty: in a word, I am and I am not, — my inner state is one of contradiction, because it is one of transition. The ambiguity of it is characteristic of human nature, which is ambiguous, because it is flesh becoming spirit, space changing into thought, the Finite looking dimly out upon the Infinite, intelligence working its way through love and pain.

Man is the *sensorium commune* of nature, the point at which all values are interchanged. Mind is the plastic medium, the principle, and the result of all; at once material and laboratory, product and formula, sensation, expression, and law; that which is, that which does, that which knows. All is not mind, but mind is in all, and contains all. It is the consciousness of being — that is, Being raised to the second power. — If the universe subsists, it is because the Eternal mind loves to perceive its own content, in all its wealth and expansion — especially in its stages of preparation. Not that God is an egotist. He allows myriads upon myriads of suns to disport themselves in His shadow; He grants life and consciousness to innumerable multitudes of creatures who thus participate in being and in nature; and all these animated monads multiply, so to speak, His divinity.

4th August 1880. — I have read a few numbers of the *Feuille Centrale de Zofingen*.* It is one of those perpetual new beginnings of youth which thinks it is pro-

---

* The journal of a students' society, drawn from the different cantons of Switzerland, which meets every year in the little town of Zofingen.

ducing something fresh when it is only repeating the old.

Nature is governed by continuity — the continuity of repetition; it is like an oft-told tale, or the recurring burthen of a song. The rose-trees are never tired of rose-bearing, the birds of nest-building, young hearts of loving, or young voices of singing the thoughts and feelings which have served their predecessors a hundred thousand times before. Profound monotony in universal movement, — there is the simplest formula furnished by the spectacle of the world. All circles are alike, and every existence tends to trace its circle.

How, then, is *fastidium* to be avoided? By shutting our eyes to the general uniformity, by laying stress upon the small differences which exist, and then by learning to enjoy repetition. What to the intellect is old and worn-out is perennially young and fresh to the heart; curiosity is insatiable, but love is never tired. The natural preservative against satiety, too, is work. What we do may weary others, but the personal effort is at least useful to its author. Where every one works, the general life is sure to possess charm and savour, even though it repeat for ever the same song, the same aspirations, the same prejudices, and the same sighs. 'To every man his turn,' is the motto of mortal beings. If what they do is old, they themselves are new; when they imitate, they think they are inventing. They have received, and they transmit. *E sempre bene!*

24th August 1880. — As years go on I love the beautiful more than the sublime, the smooth more than the rough, the calm nobility of Plato more than the fierce holiness of the world's Jeremiahs. The vehement barbarian is to me the inferior of the mild and playful Socrates. My taste is for the well-balanced soul and the well-trained heart — for a liberty which is not harsh and insolent, like that of the newly enfranchised slave, but lovable. The temperament which charms me is that in which one virtue leads naturally to another. All exclusive and sharply-marked qualities are but so many signs of imperfection.

29th August 1880. — To-day I am conscious of improvement. I am taking advantage of it to go back to my neglected work and my interrupted habits; but in a week I have grown several months older,

— that is easy to see. The affection of those around me makes them pretend not to see it; but the looking-glass tells the truth. The fact does not take away from the pleasure of convalescence; but still one hears in it the shuttle of destiny, and death seems to be nearing rapidly, in spite of the halts and truces which are granted one. — The most beautiful existence, it seems to me, would be that of a river which should get through all its rapids and waterfalls not far from its rising, and should then in its widening course form a succession of rich valleys, and in each of them a lake equally but diversely beautiful, to end, after the plains of age were past, in the ocean where all that is weary and heavy-laden comes to seek for rest. How few there are of these full, fruitful, gentle lives! What is the use of wishing for or regretting them? It is wiser and harder to see in one's own lot the best one could have had, and to say to oneself that after all the cleverest tailor cannot make us a coat to fit us more closely than our skin.

'Le vrai nom du bonheur est le contentement.'

. . . The essential thing for every one is to accept his destiny. Fate has deceived you; you have sometimes grumbled at your lot; well, no more mutual reproaches; go to sleep in peace.

30th August 1880 (*Two o'clock*). — Rumblings of a grave and distant thunder. The sky is gray but rainless; the sharp little cries of the birds show agitation and fear; one might imagine it the prelude to a symphony or a catastrophe.

' Quel éclair te traverse, ô mon cœur soucieux ? '

Strange — all the business of the immediate neighbourhood is going on; there is even more movement than usual; and yet all these noises are, as it were, held suspended in the silence — in a soft, positive silence, which they cannot disguise — silence akin to that which, in every town, on one day of the week, replaces the vague murmur of the labouring hive. Such silence at such an hour is extraordinary. There is something expectant, contemplative, almost anxious in it. Are there days on which 'the little breath' of Job produces more effect than tempest? on which a dull rumbling on the distant horizon is enough to suspend the concert of voices, like the roaring of a desert lion at the fall of night?

9th September 1880. — It seems to me that with the decline of my active force I am becoming more purely spirit; everything is growing transparent to me. I see the types, the foundation of beings, the sense of things.

All personal events, all particular experiences, are to me texts for meditation, facts to be generalised into laws, realities to be reduced to ideas. Life is only a document to be interpreted, matter to be spiritualised. Such is the life of the thinker. Every day he strips himself more and more of personality. If he consents to act and to feel, it is that he may the better understand; if he wills, it is that he may know what will is. Although it is sweet to him to be loved, and he knows nothing else so sweet, yet there also he seems to himself to be the occasion of the phenomenon rather than its end. He contemplates the spectacle of love, and love for him remains a spectacle. He does not even believe his body his own; he feels the vital whirlwind passing through him, — lent to him, as it were, for a moment, in order that he may perceive the cosmic vibrations. He is a mere thinking subject; he retains only the form of things; he attributes to himself the material possession of nothing whatsoever; he asks nothing from life but wisdom. This temper of mind makes him incomprehensible to all that loves enjoyment, dominion, possession. He is fluid as a phantom that we see but cannot grasp; he resembles a man, as the *manes* of Achilles or the shade of Creusa resembled the living. Without having died, I am a ghost. Other men are dreams to me, and I am a dream to them.

Later. — Consciousness in me takes no account of the category of time, and therefore all those partitions which tend to make of life a palace with a thousand rooms, do not exist in my case; I am still in the primitive unicellular state. I possess myself only as Monad and as Ego, and I feel my faculties themselves reabsorbed into the substance which they have individualised. All the endowment of animality is, so to speak, repudiated; all the product of study and of cultivation is in the same way annulled; the whole crystallisation is redissolved into fluid; the whole rainbow is withdrawn within the dewdrop; consequences return to the principle, effects to the cause, the bird to the egg, the organism to its germ.

This psychological reinvolution is an anticipation of death; it represents the life beyond the grave, the return to Scheol, the soul fading into the world of ghosts, or descending into the region of *Die Mütter;* it implies the simplification of the individual who, allowing all the accidents of personality to evaporate, exists henceforward only in the indivisible state, the state of point, of potentiality, of pregnant nothingness. Is not this the true definition of mind? is not mind, dissociated from space and time, just this? Its development, past or future, is contained in it just as a curve is contained in its algebraical formula. This nothing is an all. This *punctum* without dimensions is a *punctum saliens.* What is the acorn but the oak which has lost its branches, its leaves, its trunk, and its roots — that is to say, all its apparatus, its forms, its particularities — but which is still present in concentration, in essence, in a force which contains the possibility of complete revival?

This impoverishment, then, is only superficially a loss, a reduction. To be reduced to those elements in one which are eternal, is indeed to die, but not to be annihilated: it is simply to become virtual again.

9th October 1880 (*Clarens*). — A walk. Deep feeling and admiration. Nature was so beautiful, so caressing, so poetical, so maternal. The sunlight, the leaves, the sky, the bells, all said to me, — ' Be of good strength and courage, poor bruised one. This is nature's kindly season; here is forgetfulness, calm, and rest. Faults and troubles, anxieties and regrets, cares and wrongs, are but one and the same burden. We make no distinctions; we comfort all sorrows, we bring peace, and with us is consolation. Salvation to the weary, salvation to the afflicted, salvation to the sick, to sinners, to all that suffer in heart, in conscience, and in body. We are the fountain of blessing; drink and live! God maketh His sun to rise upon the just and upon the unjust. There is nothing grudging in His munificence; He does not weigh His gifts like a money-changer, or number them like a cashier. Come, — there is enough for all!'

29th October 1880 (*Geneva*). — The ideal which a man professes may itself be only a matter of appearance — a device for misleading his neighbour, or deluding himself. The individual is always ready to claim for himself the merits of the badge under which he fights; whereas, generally speaking, it is the contrary which happens. The nobler the badge, the less estimable is the wearer of it. Such at least is the presumption. It is extremely dangerous to pride oneself on any moral or religious specialty whatever. Tell me what you pique yourself upon, and I will tell you what you are not.

But how are we to know what an individual is? First of all by his acts; but by something else too — something which is only perceived by intuition. Soul judges soul by elective affinity, reaching through and beyond both words and silence, looks and actions.

The criterion is subjective, I allow, and liable to error; but in the first place there is no safer one, and in the next, the accuracy of the judgment is in proportion to the moral culture of the judge. Courage is an authority on courage, goodness on goodness, nobleness on nobleness, loyalty on uprightness. We only truly know what we have, or what we have lost and regret, as, for example, childish innocence, virginal purity, or stainless honour. The truest and best judge, then, is Infinite Goodness, and next to it, the regenerated sinner or the saint, the man tried by experience or the sage. Naturally, the touchstone in us becomes finer and truer the better we are.

3d November 1880. — What impression has the story I have just read made upon me? A mixed one. The imagination gets no pleasure out of it, although the intellect is amused. Why? Because the author's mood is one of incessant irony and *persiflage*. The Voltairean tradition has been his guide — a great deal of wit and satire, very little feeling, no simplicity. It is a combination of qualities which serves eminently well for satire, for journalism, and for paper warfare of all kinds, but which is much less suitable to the novel or short story, for cleverness is not poetry, and the novel is still within the domain of poetry, although on the frontier. The vague discomfort aroused in one by these epigrammatic productions is due probably to a confusion of kinds. Ambiguity of style keeps one in a perpetual state of tension and self-defence; we ought not to be left in doubt whether the speaker is jesting or serious, mocking or tender. Moreover, banter is not humour, and never will be. I think, indeed, that the professional wit finds a difficulty in being genuinely comic, for want of depth and disinterested feeling. To laugh at things and people is not really a joy; it is at best but a cold pleasure. Buffoonery is wholesomer, because it is a little more kindly. The reason why continuous sarcasm repels us is that it lacks two things — humanity and seriousness. Sarcasm implies pride, since it means putting oneself above others, — and levity, because conscience is allowed no voice in controlling it. In short, we read satirical books, but we only love and cling to the books in which there is *heart*.

22d November 1880. — How is ill-nature to be met and overcome? First, by humility: when a man knows his own weaknesses, why should he be angry with others for pointing them out? No doubt it is not very amiable of them to do so, but still, truth is on their side. Secondly, by reflection: after all we are what we are, and if we have been thinking too much of ourselves, it is only an opinion to be modified; the incivility of our neighbour leaves us what we were before. Above all, by pardon: there is only one way of not hating those who do us wrong, and that is by doing them good; anger is best conquered by kindness. Such a victory over feeling may not indeed affect those who have wronged us, but it is a valuable piece of self-discipline. It is vulgar to be angry on one's own account; we ought only to be angry for great causes. Besides, the poisoned dart can only be extracted from the wound by the balm of a silent and thoughtful charity. Why do we let human malignity embitter us? why should ingratitude, jealousy — perfidy even — enrage us? There is no end to recriminations, complaints, or reprisals. The simplest plan is to blot everything out. Anger, rancour, bitterness, trouble the soul. Every man is a dispenser of justice; but there is one wrong that he is not bound to punish — that of which he himself is the victim. Such a wrong is to be healed, not avenged. Fire purifies all.

'Mon âme est comme un feu qui dévore et parfume
Ce qu'on jette pour le ternir.'

27th December 1880. — In an article I have just read, Biedermann reproaches Strauss with being too negative, and with having broken with Christianity. The object to be pursued, according to him, should be the freeing of religion from the mythological element, and the substitution of another point of view for the antiquated dualism of orthodoxy, — this other point of view to be the victory over the world, produced by the sense of divine sonship.

It is true that another question arises: has not a religion which has separated itself from special miracle, from local interventions of the supernatural, and from mystery, lost its savour and its efficacy? For the sake of satisfying a thinking and instructed public, is it wise to sacrifice the influence of religion over the multitude? Answer. A pious fiction is still a fiction. Truth has the highest claim. It is for the world to accommodate itself to truth, and not *vice versâ*. Copernicus upset the astronomy of the Middle Ages, — so much the worse for it! The Eternal Gospel revolutionises modern churches — what matter! When symbols become transparent, they have no further binding force. We see in them a poem, an allegory, a metaphor; but we believe in them no longer.

Yes, but still a certain esotericism is inevitable, since critical, scientific, and philosophical culture is only attainable by a minority. The new faith must have its symbols too. At present the effect it produces on pious souls is a more or less profane one; it has a disrespectful, incredulous, frivolous look, and it seems to free a man from traditional dogma at the cost of seriousness of conscience. How are sensitiveness of feeling, the sense of sin, the desire for pardon, the thirst for holiness, to be preserved among us, when the errors which have served them so long for support and food have been eliminated? Is not illusion indispensable? is it not the divine process of education?

Perhaps the best way is to draw a deep distinction between opinion and belief, and between belief and science. The mind which discerns these different degrees may allow itself imagination and faith, and still remain within the lines of progress.

28th December 1880. — There are two modes of classing the people we know: the first is utilitarian — it starts from ourselves, divides our friends from our enemies, and distinguishes those who are antipathetic to us, those who are indifferent, those who can serve or harm us; the second is disinterested — it classes men according to their intrinsic value, their own qualities and defects, apart from the feelings which they have for us, or we for them.

My tendency is to the second kind of classification. I appreciate men less by the special affection which they show to me than by their personal excellence, and I cannot confuse gratitude with esteem. It is a happy thing for us when the two feelings can be combined; and nothing is more painful than to owe gratitude where yet we can feel neither respect nor confidence.

I am not very willing to believe in the permanence of accidental states. The generosity of a miser, the good-nature of an egotist, the gentleness of a passionate temperament, the tenderness of a barren nature, the piety of a dull heart, the humility of an excitable self-love, interest me as phenomena — nay, even touch me if I am the object of them, but they inspire me with very little confidence. I foresee the end of them too clearly. Every exception tends to disappear and to return to the rule. All privilege is temporary, and besides, I am less flattered than anxious when I find myself the object of a privilege.

A man's primitive character may be covered over by alluvial deposits of culture and acquisition, — none the less is it sure to come to the surface when years have worn away all that is accessory and adventitious. I admit indeed the possibility of great moral crises which sometimes revolutionise the soul, but I dare not reckon on them. It is a possibility — not a probability. In choosing one's friends we must choose those whose qualities are inborn, and their virtues virtues of temperament. To lay the foundations of friendship on borrowed or added virtues is to build on an artificial soil; we run too many risks by it.

Exceptions are snares, and we ought above all to distrust them when they charm our vanity. To catch and fix a fickle heart is a task which tempts all women; and a man finds something intoxicating in the tears of tenderness and joy which he alone has had the power to draw from a proud woman. But attractions of this kind are deceptive. Affinity of nature founded on worship of the same ideal, and perfect in proportion to perfectness of soul, is the only affinity which is worth anything. True love is that which ennobles the personality, fortifies the heart, and sanctifies the existence. And the being we love must not be mysterious and sphinx-like, but clear and limpid as a diamond; so that admiration and attachment may grow with knowledge.

. . . . . .

Jealousy is a terrible thing. It resembles love, only it is precisely love's contrary. Instead of wishing for the welfare of the object loved, it desires the dependence of that object upon itself, and its own triumph. Love is the forgetfulness of self; jealousy is the most passionate form of egotism, the glorification of a despotic, exacting, and vain *ego*, which can neither forget nor subordinate itself. The contrast is perfect.

. . . .

Austerity in women is sometimes the accompaniment of a rare power of loving. And when it is so their attachment is strong as death; their fidelity as resisting as the diamond; they are hungry for devotion and athirst for sacrifice. Their love is a piety, their tenderness a religion, and they triple the energy of love by giving to it the sanctity of duty.

. . . .

To the spectator over fifty, the world certainly presents a good deal that is new, but a great deal more which is only the old furbished up — mere plagiarism and modification, rather than amelioration. Almost everything is a copy of a copy, a reflection of a reflection, and the perfect being is as rare now as he ever was. Let us not complain of it; it is the reason why the world lasts. Humanity improves but slowly; that is why history goes on.

Is not progress the goad of Siva? It excites the torch to burn itself away; it hastens the approach of death. Societies which change rapidly only reach their final catastrophe the sooner. Children who are too precocious never reach maturity. Progress should be the aroma of life, not its substance.

. . . .

Man is a passion which brings a will into play, which works an intelligence, — and thus the organs which seem to be in the service of intelligence, are in reality only the agents of passion. For all the commoner sorts of being, determinism is true: inward liberty exists only as an exception and as the result of self-conquest. And even he who has tasted liberty is only free intermittently and by moments. True liberty, then, is not a continuous state: it is not an indefeasible and invariable quality. We are free only so far as we are not dupes of ourselves, our pretexts, our instincts, our temperament. We are freed by energy and the critical spirit — that is to say, by detachment of soul, by self-government. So that we are enslaved, but susceptible of freedom; we are bound, but capable of shaking off our bonds. The soul is caged, but it has power to flutter within its cage.

. . . . .

Material results are but the tardy sign of invisible activities. The bullet has started long before the noise of the report has reached us. The decisive events of the world take place in the intellect.

. . . . .

Sorrow is the most tremendous of all realities in the sensible world, but the transfiguration of sorrow after the manner of Christ is a more beautiful solution of the problem than the extirpation of sorrow, after the method of Çakyamouni.

Life should be a giving birth to the soul, the development of a higher mode of reality. The animal must be humanised: flesh must be made spirit; physiological activity must be transmuted into intellect and conscience, into reason, justice, and generosity, as the torch is transmuted into life and warmth. The blind, greedy, selfish nature of man must put on beauty and nobleness. This heavenly alchemy is what justifies our presence on the earth: it is our mission and our glory.

* * * * * *

To renounce happiness and think only of duty, to put conscience in the place of feeling; — this voluntary martyrdom has its nobility. The natural man in us flinches, but the better self submits. To hope for justice in the world is a sign of sickly sensibility; we must be able to do without it. True manliness consists in such independence. Let the world think what it will of us, it is its own affair. If it will not give us the place which is lawfully ours until after our death, or perhaps not at all, it is but acting within its right. It is our business to behave as though our country were grateful, as though the world were equitable, as though opinion were clear-sighted, as though life were just, as though men were good.

* * * * * *

Death itself may become matter of consent, and therefore a moral act. The animal expires; man surrenders his soul to the author of the soul.

[With the year 1881, beginning with the month of January, we enter upon the last period of Amiel's illness. Although he continued to attend to his professorial duties, and never spoke of his forebodings, he felt himself mortally ill, as we shall see by the following extracts from the Journal. Amiel wrote up to the end, doing little else, however, towards the last than record the progress of his disease, and the proofs of interest and kindliness which he received. After weeks of suffering and pain a state of extreme weakness gradually gained upon him. His last lines are dated the 29th April; it was on the 11th of May that he succumbed, without a struggle, to the complicated disease from which he suffered. — S.]

5th January 1881. — I think I fear shame more than death. Tacitus said: *Omnia serviliter pro dominatione.* My tendency is just the contrary. Even when it is voluntary, dependence is a burden to me. I should blush to find myself determined by interest, submitting to constraint, or becoming the slave of any will whatever. To me vanity is slavery, self-love degrading, and utilitarianism meanness. I detest the ambition which makes you the liege man of something or some one — I desire to be simply my own master.

If I had health I should be the freest man I know. Although perhaps a little hardness of heart would be desirable to make me still more independent.

Let me exaggerate nothing. My liberty is only negative. Nobody has any hold over me, but many things have become impossible to me, and if I were so foolish as to wish for them, the limits of my liberty would soon become apparent. Therefore I take care not to wish for them, and not to let my thoughts dwell on them. I only desire what I am able for, and in this way I run my head against no wall, I cease even to be conscious of the boundaries which enclose me. I take care to wish for rather less than is in my power, that I may not even be reminded of the obstacles in my way. Renunciation is the safeguard of dignity. Let us strip ourselves, if we would not be stripped. He who has freely given up his life may look death in the face: what more can it take away from him? Do away with desire and practise charity — there you have the whole method of Buddha, the whole secret of the great Deliverance. . . .

It is snowing, and my chest is troublesome. So that I depend on Nature and on God. But I do not depend on human caprice; this is the point to be insisted on.

It is true that my chemist may make a blunder and poison me, my banker may reduce me to pauperism, just as an earthquake may destroy my house without hope of redress. Absolute independence, therefore, is a pure chimera. But I do possess relative independence — that of the stoic who withdraws into the fortress of his will, and shuts the gates behind him.

'Jurons, excepté Dieu, de n'avoir point de maître.

This oath of old Geneva remains my motto still.

10th January 1881. — To let oneself be troubled by the ill-will, the ingratitude, the indifference, of others, is a weakness to which I am very much inclined. It is painful to me to be misunderstood, ill judged. I am wanting in manly hardihood, and the heart in me is more vulnerable than it ought to be. It seems to me, however, that I have grown tougher in this respect than I used to be. The malignity of the world troubles me less than it did. Is it the result of philosophy, or an effect of age, or simply caused by the many proofs of respect and attachment that I have received?

These proofs were just what were wanting to inspire me with some self-respect. Otherwise I should have so easily believed in my own nullity and in the insignificance of all my efforts. Success is necessary for the timid, praise is a moral stimulus, and admiration a strengthening elixir. We think we know ourselves, but as long as we are ignorant of our comparative value, our place in the social assessment, we do not know ourselves well enough. If we are to act with effect, we must count for something with our fellow-men; we must feel ourselves possessed of some weight and credit with them, so that our effort may be rightly proportioned to the resistance which has to be overcome. As long as we despise opinion we are without a standard by which to measure ourselves; we do not know our relative power. I have despised opinion too much, while yet I have been too sensitive to injustice. These two faults have cost me dear. I longed for kindness, sympathy, and equity, but my pride forbade me to ask for them, or to employ any address or calculation to obtain them. . . . I do not think I have been wrong altogether, for all through I have been in harmony with my best self, but my want of adaptability has worn me out, to no purpose. Now, indeed, I am at peace within, but my career is over, my strength is running out, and my life is near its end.

'Il n'est plus temps pour rien excepté pour mourir.'

This is why I can look at it all historically.

23d January 1881. — A tolerable night, but this morning the cough has been frightful. — Beautiful weather, the windows ablaze with sunshine. With my feet on the fender I have just finished the newspaper.

At this moment I feel well, and it seems strange to me that my doom should be so near. Life has no sense of kinship with death. This is why, no doubt, a sort of mechanical instinctive hope is for ever springing up afresh in us, troubling our reason, and casting doubt on the verdict of science. All life is tenacious and persistent. It is like the parrot in the fable, who, at the very moment when its neck is being wrung, still repeats with its last breath —

'Cela, cela, ne sera rien.'

The intellect puts the matter at its worst, but the animal protests. It will not believe in the evil till it comes. Ought one to regret it? Probably not. It is Nature's will that life should defend itself against death; hope is only the love of life; it is an organic impulse which religion has taken under its protection. Who knows? God may save us, may work a miracle. Besides, are we ever sure that there is no remedy? Uncertainty is the refuge of hope. We reckon the doubtful among the chances in our favour. Mortal frailty clings to every support. How be angry with it for so doing? Even with all possible aids it hardly ever escapes desolation and distress. The supreme solution is, and always will be, to see in necessity the fatherly will of God, and so to submit ourselves and bear our cross bravely, as an offering to the Arbiter of human destiny. The soldier does not dispute the order given him: he obeys and dies without murmuring. If he waited to understand the use of his sacrifice, where would his submission be?

It occurred to me this morning how little we know of each other's physical troubles; even those nearest and dearest to us know nothing of our conversations with the King of Terrors. There are thoughts which brook no confidant; there are griefs which cannot be shared. Consideration for others even bids us conceal them. We dream alone, we suffer alone, we die alone, we inhabit the last resting-place alone. But there is nothing to prevent us from opening our solitude to God. And so what was an austere monologue becomes dialogue, reluctance becomes docility, renunciation passes into peace, and the sense of painful defeat is lost in the sense of recovered liberty.

' Vouloir ce que Dieu veut est la seule science
 Qui nous met en repos.'

None of us can escape the play of contrary impulse ; but as soon as the soul has once recognised the order of things, and submitted itself thereto, then all is well.

'Comme un sage mourant puissions nous dire
 en paix :
J'ai trop longtemps erré, cherché ; je me
 trompais :
 Tout est bien, mon Dieu m'enveloppe.'

28th January 1881.—A terrible night. For three or four hours I struggled against suffocation and looked death in the face. . . . It is clear that what awaits me is suffocation — asphyxia. I shall die by choking.

I should not have chosen such a death ;

but when there is no option, one must simply resign oneself, and at once. . . . Spinoza expired in the presence of the doctor whom he had sent for. I must familiarise myself with the idea of dying unexpectedly, some fine night, strangled by laryngitis. The last sigh of a patriarch surrounded by his kneeling family is more beautiful: my fate indeed lacks beauty, grandeur, poetry; but stoicism consists in renunciation. *Abstine et sustine.*

I must remember besides that I have faithful friends; it is better not to torment them. The last journey is only made more painful by scenes and lamentations: one word is worth all others — 'Thy will, not mine, be done!' Leibnitz was accompanied to the grave by his servant only. The loneliness of the deathbed and the tomb is not an evil. The great mystery cannot be shared. The dialogue between the soul and the King of Terrors needs no witnesses. It is the living who cling to the thought of last greetings. And, after all, no one knows exactly what is reserved for him. What will be will be. We have but to say, 'Amen.'

4th February 1881. — It is a strange sensation that of laying oneself down to rest with the thought that perhaps one will never see the morrow. Yesterday I felt it strongly, and yet here I am. Humility is made easy by the sense of excessive frailty, but it cuts away all ambition.

'Quittez le long espoir et les vastes pensées.'

A long piece of work seems absurd — one lives but from day to day.

When a man can no longer look forward in imagination to five years, a year, a month, of free activity, — when he is reduced to counting the hours, and to seeing in the coming night the threat of an unknown fate, — it is plain that he must give up art, science, and politics, and that he must be content to hold converse with himself, the one possibility which is his till the end. Inward soliloquy is the only resource of the condemned man whose execution is delayed. He withdraws upon the fastnesses of conscience. His spiritual force no longer radiates outwardly; it is consumed in self-study. Action is cut off — only contemplation remains. He still writes to those who have claims upon him, but he bids farewell to the public, and retreats into himself. Like the hare, he comes back to die in his form, and this form is his consciousness, his intellect, — the journal, too, which has been the companion of his inner life. As long as he can hold a pen, as long as he has a moment of solitude, this echo of himself still claims his meditation, still represents to him his converse with his God.

In all this, however, there is nothing akin to self-examination: it is not an act of contrition, or a cry for help. It is simply an Amen of submission — 'My child, give me thy heart!'

Renunciation and acquiescence are less difficult to me than to others, for I desire nothing. I could only wish not to suffer, but Jesus on Gethsemane allowed himself to make the same prayer; let us add to it the words that he did: 'Nevertheless, not my will, but thine, be done,' — and wait.

. . . For many years past the immanent God has been more real to me than the transcendent God, and the religion of Jacob has been more alien to me than that of Kant, or even Spinoza. The whole Semitic dramaturgy has come to seem to me a work of the imagination. The apostolic documents have changed in value and meaning to my eyes. Belief and truth have become distinct to me with a growing distinctness. Religious psychology has become a simple phenomenon, and has lost its fixed and absolute value. The apologetics of Pascal, of Leibnitz, of Secrétan, are to me no more convincing than those of the middle ages, for they presuppose what is really in question, — a revealed doctrine, a definite and unchangeable Christianity. It seems to me that what remains to me from all my studies is a new phenomenology of mind, an intuition of universal metamorphosis. All particular convictions, all definite principles, all clear-cut formulas and fixed ideas, are but prejudices, useful in practice, but still narrownesses of the mind. The absolute in detail is absurd and contradictory. All political, religious, æsthetic, or literary parties are protuberances, misgrowths of thought. Every special belief represents a stiffening and thickening of thought; a stiffening, however, which is necessary in its time and place. Our monad, in its thinking capacity, overleaps the boundaries of time and space and of its own historical surroundings; but in its individual capacity, and for purposes of action, it adapts itself to current illusions, and puts before itself a definite end. It is lawful to be *man*, but it is needful also to be *a* man, to be an individual. Our *rôle* is thus a double one. Only, the philosopher is specially authorised to develop the first *rôle*, which the vast majority of humankind neglects.

7th February 1881. — Beautiful sunshine to-day. But I have scarcely spring enough left in me to notice it. Admiration, joy, presuppose a little relief from pain. Whereas my neck is tired with the weight of my head, and my heart is wearied with the weight of life; — this is not the æsthetic state.

I have been thinking over different things which I might have written. But generally speaking we let what is most original and best in us be wasted. We reserve ourselves for a future which never comes. *Omnis moriar.*

14th February 1881. — Supposing that my weeks are numbered, what duties still remain to me to fulfil, that I may leave all in order? I must give every one his due; justice, prudence, kindness must be satisfied; the last memories must be sweet ones. Try to forget nothing useful, nor anybody who has a claim upon thee!

15th February 1881. — I have, very reluctantly, given up my lecture at the University, and sent for my doctor. On my chimney-piece are the flowers which —— has sent me. Letters from London, Paris, Lausanne, Neuchâtel. . . . They seem to me like wreaths thrown into a grave.

Mentally I say farewell to all the distant friends whom I shall never see again.

18th February 1881. — Misty weather. A fairly good night. Still, the emaciation goes on. That is to say, the vulture allows me some respite, but he still hovers over his prey. The possibility of resuming my official work seems like a dream to me.

Although just now the sense of ghostly remoteness from life which I so often have is absent, I feel myself a prisoner for good, a hopeless invalid. This vague intermediate state, which is neither death nor life, has its sweetness, because if it implies renunciation, still it allows of thought. It is a reverie without pain, peaceful and meditative. Surrounded with affection and with books, I float down the stream of time, as once I glided over the Dutch canals, smoothly and noiselessly. It is as though I were once more on board the

Treckschute. Scarcely can one hear even the soft ripple of the water furrowed by the barge, or the hoof of the towing horse trotting along the sandy path. A journey under these conditions has something fantastic in it. One is not sure whether one still exists, still belongs to earth. It is like the *manes*, the shadows, flitting through the twilight of the *inania regna*. Existence has become fluid. From the standpoint of complete personal renunciation I watch the passage of my impressions, my dreams, thoughts, and memories. . . . It is a mood of fixed contemplation akin to that which we attribute to the Seraphim. It takes no interest in the individual self, but only in the specimen monad, the sample of the general history of mind. Everything is in everything, and the consciousness examines what it has before it. Nothing is either great or small. The mind adopts all modes, and everything is acceptable to it. In this state its relations with the body, with the outer world, and with other individuals, fade out of sight. *Selbst-bewusstsein* becomes once more impersonal *Bewusstsein*, and before personality can be reacquired, pain, duty, and will must be brought into action.

Are these oscillations between the personal and the impersonal, between pantheism and theism, between Spinoza and Leibnitz, to be regretted? No, for it is the one state which makes us conscious of the other. And as man is capable of ranging the two domains, why should he mutilate himself?

22d February 1881. — The march of mind finds its typical expression in astronomy — no pause, but no hurry; orbits, cycles, energy, but at the same time harmony; movement and yet order; everything has its own weight and its relative weight, receives and gives forth light. Cannot this cosmic and divine energy become ours? Is the war of all against all, the preying of man upon man, a higher type of balanced action? I shrink from believing it. Some theorists imagine that the phase of selfish brutality is the last phase of all. They must be wrong. Justice will prevail, and justice is not selfishness. Independence of intellect, combined with goodness of heart, will be the agents of a result, which will be the compromise required.

1st March 1881. — I have just been glancing over the affairs of the world in the newspaper. What a Babel it is! But it is very pleasant to be able to make the tour of the planet and review the human race in an hour. It gives one a sense of ubiquity. A newspaper in the twentieth century will be composed of eight or ten daily bulletins — political, religious, scientific, literary, artistic, commercial, meteorological, military, economical, social, legal, and financial; and will be divided into two parts only — *Urbs* and *Orbis*. The need of totalising, of simplifying, will bring about the general use of such graphic methods as permit of series and comparisons. We shall end by feeling the pulse of the race and the globe as easily as that of a sick man, and we shall count the palpitations of the universal life, just as we shall hear the grass growing, or the sun-spots clashing, and catch the first stirrings of volcanic disturbances. Activity will become consciousness; the earth will see herself. Then will be the time for her to blush for her disorders, her hideousness, her misery, her crime — and to throw herself at last with energy and perseverance into the pursuit of justice. When humanity has cut its wisdom-teeth, then perhaps it will have the grace to reform itself, and the will to attempt a systematic reduction of the share of the evil in the world. The *Weltgeist* will pass from the state of instinct to the moral state. War, hatred, selfishness, fraud, the right of the stronger, will be held to be old-world barbarisms, mere diseases of growth. The pretences of modern civilisation will be replaced by real virtues. Men will be brothers, peoples will be friends, races will sympathise one with another, and mankind will draw from love a principle of emulation, of invention, and of zeal, as powerful as any furnished by the vulgar stimulant of interest. This millennium — will it ever be? It is at least an act of piety to believe in it.

14th March 1881. — I have finished Mérimée's letters to Panizzi. Mérimée died of the disease which torments me — '*Je tousse, et j'étouffe.*' Bronchitis and asthma, whence defective assimilation, and finally exhaustion. He, too, tried arsenic, wintering at Cannes, compressed air. All was useless. Suffocation and inanition carried off the author of *Colomba*. *Hic tua res agitur.* The gray, heavy sky is of the same colour as my thoughts. And yet the irrevocable has its own sweetness and serenity. The fluctuations of illusion, the uncertainties of desire, the leaps and bounds of hope, give place to tranquil resignation. One feels as though one were already beyond the grave. It is this very week, too, I remember, that my corner of ground in the Oasis is to be bought. Everything draws towards the end. *Festinat ad eventum.*

15th March 1881. — The *Journal* is full of details of the horrible affair at Petersburg. How clear it is that such catastrophes as this, in which the innocent suffer, are the product of a long accumulation of iniquities. Historical justice is, generally speaking, tardy — so tardy that it becomes unjust. The Providential theory is really based on human solidarity. Louis XVI. pays for Louis XV., — Alexander II. for Nicholas. We expiate the sins of our fathers, and our grandchildren will be punished for ours. A double injustice! cries the individual. And he is right if the individualist principle is true. But is it true? That is the point. It seems as though the individual part of each man's destiny were but one section of that destiny. Morally we are responsible for what we ourselves

have willed, but socially, our happiness
and unhappiness depend on causes outside
our will. Religion answers — 'Mystery,
obscurity, submission, faith. Do your
duty ; leave the rest to God !'

16th March 1881. — A wretched night.
A melancholy morning. . . . The two
stand-bys of the doctor, digitalis and bro-
mide, seem to have lost their power over
me. Wearily and painfully I watch the
tedious progress of my own decay. What
efforts to keep oneself from dying ! I am
worn out with the struggle.

Useless and incessant struggle is a humiliation to one's manhood. The lion finds
the gnat the most intolerable of his foes.
The natural man feels the same. But the
spiritual man must learn the lesson of gentleness and long-suffering. The inevitable
is the will of God. We might have preferred something else, but it is our business
to accept the lot assigned us. . . . One
thing only is necessary —

'Garde en mon cœur la foi dans ta volonté
  sainte,
Et de moi fais, ô Dieu, tout ce que tu vou-
  dras.'

Later. — One of my students has just brought me a sympathetic message from my class. My sister sends me a pot of azaleas, rich in flowers and buds; —— sends roses and violets: every one spoils me, which proves that I am ill.

19th March 1881. — Distaste — discouragement. My heart is growing cold. And yet what affectionate care, what tenderness, surrounds me! ... But without health, what can one do with all the rest? What is the good of it all to me? What was the good of Job's trials? They ripened his patience; they exercised his submission.

Come, let me forget myself, let me shake off this melancholy, this weariness. Let me think, not of all that is lost, but of all that I might still lose. I will reckon up my privileges; I will try to be worthy of my blessings.

21st March 1881. — This invalid life is too Epicurean. For five or six weeks now I have done nothing else but wait, nurse myself, and amuse myself, and how weary one gets of it! What I want is work. It is work which gives flavour to life. Mere existence without object and without effort is a poor thing. Idleness leads to languor, and languor to disgust. Besides, here is the spring again, the season of vague desires, of dull discomforts, of dim aspirations, of sighs without a cause. We dream wide-awake. We search darkly for we know not what; invoking the while something which has no name, unless it be happiness or death.

28th March 1881. — I cannot work; I find it difficult to exist. One may be glad to let one's friends spoil one for a few months; it is an experience which is good for us all; but afterwards? How much better to make room for the living, the active, the productive.

'Tircis, voici le temps de prendre sa retraite.'

Is it that I care so much to go on living? I think not. It is health that I long for — freedom from suffering. And this desire being vain, I can find no savour in anything else. — Satiety. Lassitude. Renunciation. Abdication. 'In your patience possess ye your souls.'

10th April 1881 (*Sunday*). — Visit to ——. She read over to me letters of 1844 to 1845

— letters of mine. So much promise to end in so meagre a result! What creatures we are! I shall end like the Rhine, lost among the sands, and the hour is close by when my thread of water will have disappeared.

Afterwards I had a little walk in the sunset. There was an effect of scattered rays and stormy clouds; a green haze envelops all the trees —

> 'Et tout renaît, et déjà l'aubépine
> A vu l'abeille accourir à ses fleurs,'

— but to me it all seems strange already.

Later. — What dupes we are of our own desires! ... Destiny has two ways of crushing us — by refusing our wishes and by fulfilling them. But he who only wills what God wills escapes both catastrophes. 'All things work together for his good.'

14th April 1881. — Frightful night; the fourteenth running, in which I have been consumed by sleeplessness. ...

15th April 1881. — To-morrow is Good Friday, the festival of pain. I know what it is to spend days of anguish and nights of

agony. Let me bear my cross humbly. . . .
I have no more future. My duty is to satisfy the claims of the present, and to leave everything in order. Let me try to end well, seeing that to undertake and even to continue, are closed to me.

19th April 1881. — A terrible sense of oppression. My flesh and my heart fail me.

'Que vivre est difficile, ô mon cœur fatigué!'

. . . .

. . . .

END OF VOL. II.

APPENDIX.

The following short but valuable criticism of Amiel's philosophical thought, in its more technical aspects, has been sent me, at my request, by a friend well qualified to speak in the matter. — M. A. W.

So far as can be judged from the published fragments of the Diary, Amiel was not an adherent of any philosophical system. Ideas, however, which, for brevity's sake, may be called Hegelian, but which may have been derived from the most various sources, were constantly at his command as means of criticism and as aids to imagination; and where these ideas touched him nearly, as in all matters affecting the religious life, he made them his own and founded his life upon them. One remark at least on æsthetics — an analysis of the pleasure produced by so-called imitative art — a distinction between character and disposition, directed against Schopenhauer's view that character is invariable; a doctrine of moral freedom in the same key as that distinction, treating moral freedom as not innate, but acquired; and above all, an ardent conviction of the essential truth of *the true*[*] Christian religion, and a conception of 'immanence' akin, as Amiel expressly says, to the religion of Spinoza;—all these ideas and be-beliefs reveal an æsthetic, a psychology of morals, and a theology drawn in essentials from the spiritual philosophy of which we may take Hegel as the representative. 'Hegel libère tout autrement la pensée,' he says in criticising Havet's *Origines du Christianisme;* and in the first consciousness of failing health (in 1876) he recurred with pleasure to a Hegelian conception that seemed to invest the intellectual life with peculiar dignity and interest.

But Amiel was always repelled by what he considered the Spinozistic and Hegelian tendency to replace religion by philosophy. The *amor intellectualis* can never, he says, take the place of 'amour moral.' He uses Hegelian and Intellectualist as equivalent terms. Goethe, again, is 'Spinozist to the core,' or 'un Grec du bon temps.' Even Schleiermacher, of whose Monologues he speaks with enthusiastic admiration, 'hardly mentions the existence of evil.' The capital fact is not metaphysical, but moral; not even Immanence, but *Sin*. The neo-Hegelians appeal to the intelligence, not to the will, and so 'Ruge et Feuerbach ne peuvent sauver l'humanité.'

---

[*] Cf. 'Quand le christianisme sera mort, la religion de Jésus pourra survivre,'

Amiel had a strong sympathy with mysticism. He quotes from European mystics, and recurs frequently to Oriental ideas, especially to the notions of Nirvâna and of Mâyâ.* It was not only his profound religious instinct, and his curious psychological experiences, but also an innate distrust of apparent reality, that was active in this sympathy. Amiel was well aware of his tendency, 'Mon instinct est d'accord avec le pessimisme de Bouddha et de Schopenhauer.' His references to Mâyâ are in the tone of Schopenhauer, and though he finds the weak point in Schopenhauer's psychology, and rejects the fundamental axiom of his pessimism, yet Schopenhauer's influence can be traced in much of Amiel's meditation.

Perhaps he was the more open to this influence because of a certain affinity with that French intellect which he so subtly criticises. Extremes meet in philosophy, and abstract logical antitheses are apt to favour mysticism. Sometimes — for his thought varied continually — Amiel treats the absolute as 'the zero of all determination,' and so as excluding the relative; the infinite as the unknown, or as

* Cf. Schopenhauer, *World as Will and Idea*, Eng. Tr., vol. i. p. 9, 'The ancient wisdom of the Indian philosopher declares, "It is Mâyâ, the veil of deception, which blinds the eyes of mortals and makes them behold a world of which they cannot say either that it is or that it is not."' This is, Schopenhauer continues, 'the world as idea subject to the principle of sufficient reason.'

the immensity of space or time; and the ideal as nowhere to be found in reality. In as far as these conceptions ruled his mood, Amiel's pessimistic instinct had an intellectual root. But comments of this nature, which some passages of the Diary might seem to invite, would be found nugatory when confronted with others. Among these others is a saying with which I end this note — 'Le devoir a la vertu de nous faire sentir la réalité du monde positif, tout en nous en détachant.'

NOTES.

[*A few of the following notes are translated from the French edition of the Journal.*]

1. P. 10.—*Il Penseroso*, poésies-maximes par H. F. Amiel: Genève, 1858. This little book, which contains 133 maxims, several of which are quoted in the *Journal Intime*, is prefaced by a motto translated from Shelley —'Ce n'est pas la science qui nous manque, à nous modernes; nous l'avons surabondamment. . . . Mais ce que nous avons absorbé nous absorbe. . . . Ce qui nous manque c'est la poésie de la vie.'

2. P. 12.—Charles Secrétan, a Lausanne professor, the friend of Vinet, born 1819. He published *Leçons sur la Philosophie de Leibnitz, Philosophie de la Liberté, La Raison et le Christianisme*, etc.

3. P. 31.—Étienne Vacherot, a French philosophical writer, who owed his first successes in life to the friendship of Cousin, and was later brought very much into notice by his controversy with the Abbé Gratry, by the prosecution brought against him in conse-

quence of his book, *La Démocratie* (1859), and by his rejection at the hands of the Academy of Moral and Political Sciences in 1865, for the same kind of reasons which had brought about the exclusion of Littré in the preceding year. In 1868, however, he became a member of the Institute in succession to Cousin. A Liberal of the old school, he has separated himself from the Republicans since the war, and has made himself felt as a severe critic of Republican blunders in the *Revue des deux Mondes*. *La Religion*, which discusses the psychological origins of the religious sense, was published in 1868.

4. P. 34.—At this period the controversy between the orthodox party and 'Liberal Christianity' was at its height, both in Geneva and throughout Switzerland.

5. P. 37.—Gustave-Adolphe Hirn, a French physicist, born near Colmar, 1815, became a Corresponding Member of the Academy of Sciences in 1867. The book of his to which Amiel refers is no doubt *Conséquences philosophiques et métaphysiques de la thermodynamique, Analyse élémentaire de l'univers* (1869).

6. P. 37.—The name of M. Albert Réville, the French Protestant theologian, is more or less familiar in England, especially since his delivery of the Hibbert Lectures in 1884.

Athanase Coquerel, born 1820, died 1876, the well-known champion of Liberal ideas in the French Protestant Church, was suspended from his pastoral functions by the Consistory of Paris, on account of his review of M. Renan's *Vie de Jésus* in 1864. Ferdinand-Edouard Buisson, a Liberal Protestant, originally a professor at Lausanne, was raised to the important functions of Director of Primary Instruction by M. Ferry in 1879. He was denounced by Bishop Dupanloup, in the National Assembly of 1871, as the author of certain Liberal pamphlets on the dangers connected with Scripture-teaching in schools, and, for the time, lost his employment under the Ministry of Education.

7. P. 56. — This is one of the passages which rouses M. Renan's wonder. 'Voilà la grande différence,' he writes, 'entre l'éducation catholique et l'éducation protestante. Ceux qui comme moi ont reçu une éducation catholique ont en gardé de profonds vestiges. Mais ces vestiges ne sont pas des dogmes, ce sont des rêves. Une fois ce grand rideau de drap d'or, bariolé de soie, d'indienne et de calicot, par lequel le catholicisme nous masque la vue du monde, une fois, dis-je ce rideau déchiré, on voit l'univers en sa splendeur infinie, la nature en sa haute et pleine majesté. Le protestant le plus libre garde souvent quelque chose de triste, un fond

d'austérité intellectuelle analogue au pessimisme slave.' — (*Journal des Débats*, September 30, 1884.)

One is reminded of Mr. Morley's criticism of Emerson. Emerson, he points out, has almost nothing to say of death, and 'little to say of that horrid burden and inpediment on the soul which the churches call sin, and which, by whatever name we call it, is a very real catastrophe in the moral nature of man; — the courses of nature, and the prodigious injustices of man in society affect him with neither horror nor awe. He will see no monster if he can help it.'

Here, then, we have the eternal difference between the two orders of temperament — the men whose overflowing energy forbids them to realise the ever-recurring defeat of the human spirit at the hands of circumstance, like Renan and Emerson, and the men for whom 'horror and awe' are interwoven with experience, like Amiel.

8. P. 102. — Mably, the Abbé Mably, 1709–85, one of the precursors of the Revolution, the professor of a cultivated and classical communism based on a study of antiquity, which Babeuf, and others like him, in the following generation, translated into practical experiment. 'Caius Gracchus' Babeuf, born 1764, and guillotined in 1797 for a conspiracy against the Directory, is sometimes called the

first French Socialist. Perhaps Socialist doctrines, properly so called, may be said to make their first entry into the region of popular debate and practical agitation with his *Manifeste des Égaux*, issued April 1796.

9. P. 109. — '"Persifflez les pharisaïsmes, mais parlez droit aux honnêtes gens" me dit Amiel, avec une certaine aigreur. Mon Dieu, que les honnêtes gens sont souvent exposés a être des pharisiens sans le savoir!' — (M. Renan's article, already quoted.)

10. P. 111. — *Polyeucte*, Act V. Scene v.

'Mon époux en mourant m'a laissé ses lumières;
Son sang dont tes bourreaux viennent de me couvrir
M'a dessillé les yeux et me les vient d'ouvrir
Je vois, je sais, je crois——'

11. P. 121. — A Synod of the Reformed Churches of France was then occupied in determining the constituent conditions of Protestant belief.

12. P. 129. — Louise Siefert, a modern French poetess, died 1879. In addition to *Les Stoïques*, she published *L'Année Républicaine*, Paris, 1869, and other works.

13. P. 134. — 'We all believe in duty,' says M. Renan, 'and in the triumph of righteousness;' but it is possible notwithstanding, 'que tout le contraire soit vrai — et que le monde ne soit qu'une amusante féerie dont aucun

dieu ne se soucie. Il faut donc nous arranger de manière à ceque, dans le cas où le seconde hypothèse serait la vraie, nous n'ayons pas été trop dupés.'

This strain of remark, which is developed at considerable length, is meant as a criticism of Amiel's want of sensitiveness to the irony of things. But in reality, as the passage in the text shows, M. Renan is only expressing a feeling with which Amiel was just as familiar as his critic. Only he is delivered from his last doubt of all by his habitual seriousness; by that sense of 'horror and awe' which M. Renan puts away from him. Conscience saves him 'from the sorceries of Maïa.'

14. P. 160.—Ernest Havet, born 1813, a distinguished French scholar and professor. He became Professor of Latin Oratory at the Collège de France in 1855, and a Member of the Institute in January 1880. His admirable edition of the *Pensées de Pascal* is well known. *Le Christianisme et ses Origines*, an important book, in four volumes, was developed from a series of articles in the *Revue des deux Mondes*, and the *Revue Contemporaine*.

15. P. 171.—Amiel had just received at the hands of his doctor the medical verdict, which was his *arrêt de mort*.

16. P. 191.—Compare this paragraph from the *Pensées* of a new writer, M. Joseph Roux,

a country curé, living in a remote part of the *Bas Limousin*, whose thoughts have been edited and published this year by M. Paul Mariéton (Paris: Alphonse Lemerre) —

'Le verbe ne souffre et ne connait que la volonté qui le dompte, et n'emporte loin sans péril que l'intelligence qui lui ménage avec empire l'éperon et le frein.'

17. P. 207. — Ximénès Doudan, born in 1800, died 1872, the brilliant friend and tutor of the De Broglie family, whose conversation was so much sought after in life, and whose letters have been so eagerly read in France since his death. Compare M. Scherer's two articles on Doudan's *Lettres* and *Pensées* in his last published volume of essays.

18. P. 235. — Compare La Bruyère —

'Entre toutes les differentes expressions qui peuvent rendre une seule de nos pensées il n'y en a qu'une qui soit la bonne; on ne la rencontre pas toujours en parlant ou en écrivant: il est vray néanmoins qu'elle existe, que tout ce qui ne l'est point est foible, et ne satisfait point un homme d'esprit qui veut se faire entendre.'

19. P. 243. — Amiel's expression is *Les Parnassiens*, an old name revived, which nowadays describes the younger school of French poetry represented by such names as Théophile Gautier, Leconte de Lisle, Théodore de Bauville, and Baudelaire. The modern use

of the word dates from the publication of *Le Parnasse Contemporain* (Lemerre, 1866).

20. P. 284.—Victor de Laprade, born 1812, first a disciple and imitator of Edgar Quinet, then the friend of Lamartine, Lamennais, George Sand, Victor Hugo; admitted to the Academy in 1857 in succession to Alfred de Musset. He wrote *Parfums de Madeleine*, 1839; *Odes et Poèmes*, 1843; *Poèmes Evangéliques*, 1852; *Idylles Héroiques*, 1858, etc. etc.

21. P. 293.—Madame Necker de Saussure was the daughter of the famous geologist, De Saussure; she married a nephew of Jacques Necker, and was therefore cousin by marriage of Madame de Staël. She is often supposed to be the original of Madame de Cerlèbe in *Delphine*, and the *Notice sur le Caractère et les Écrits de Mdme. de Staël*, prefixed to the authoritative edition of Madame de Staël's collected works, is by her. Philanthropy and education were her two main interests, but she had also a very large amount of general literary cultivation, as was proved by her translation of Schlegel's *Lectures on Dramatic Literature*.

INDEX.

About's satire and irony, i. 298.
Absolute, Amiel's craving for the, i. 96.
    conception of the, ii. 169, 203.
Absolutism, ii. 70.
Accident, philosophy of, i. 119.
    and Providence, i. 306.
Ackermann, poems of Madame, ii. 167.
Acorn and oak, ii. 315.
Action, Amiel's cross, i. 182.
    = concrete thought, i. 8.
    how to recover courage for, i. 69.
    requisites for, ii. 290.
Activity of the Western Nations, unholy, ii. 279.
Adoration and consolation essential in religion, i. 178.
Advice, giving, ii. 117.
Æschylus's *Prometheus* and *Eumenides*, ii. 136.
Affected poets, ii. 244.
Affirmation and examination, ii. 123.
Age, loss of respect for, i. 230.
    the servitude of, ii. 24.
Alcibiades, ii. 209.
Algebra *v.* life, ii. 95.
All or nothing, ii. 169.
Alps, the, i. 94, 287; ii. 75.
Ambition, Amiel's horror of, i. 189; ii. 200.
    moral, ii. 58.
Americans, the, ii. 279.

Amusement and instruction, ii. 269.
Analysis, extreme, i. 185.
    kills spontaneity, ii. 257.
    of self, Amiel's, i. 279.
    woman's dislike of, i. 304.
Analytic minds, i. 292.
Anger, conquest of, ii. 319.
Animality, the laws of, ii. 214.
Animals, treatment of, i. 274.
Annihilation of Buddha, ii. 29.
Anonymous souls, ii. 37.
Ant v. swallow, i. 142.
A priori speculations, ii. 123.
Arcadia, an expedition into, ii. 182.
Aristotle, ii. 203.
Art, decadence of, ii. 4.
    grand and simple, ii. 245.
    and imagination, ii. 253.
    reveals Nature, i. 186.
Ascension Day, ii. 270.
Atala and *René*, Châteaubriand's, i. 146, 149.
Atheism, effects of, ii. 212.
Atomism, philosophy of, i. 230.
Attila, ii. 287.
Augustine and Lucian contrasted, ii. 217.
Authority v. liberty, ii. 37.
Autumn, melancholy of, ii. 176.
    of life, ii. 12.
    twofold, i. 223.
Azote, woman the social, ii. 135.

BABBLE, ignorant, ii. 240.
Bach's prelude, i. 88.
Bacon on religion, i. 253.
Bahnsen's pessimism, ii. 115.
Balzac, ii. 94.
Bannière Bleue, la, ii. 285.

INDEX.

Banter not humour, ii. 318.
Barbarism, possible triumph of, i. 232.
Basle, ii. 81.
Bayle and Saint Simon, ii. 48.
Beauty, female, i. 301.
    v. goodness, ii. 217.
    and pathos, i. 152, 153.
    and ugliness, ii. 113.
    universal in Paradise, i. 233.
Beauty = the spiritualisation of matter, i. 233.
Beethoven and Mozart contrasted, i. 88, 89.
Being, consciousness of, ii. 308.
    and non-being, ii. 274.
Beranger, ii. 51.
Berkeley, i. 46.
Berlioz, *Romeo and Juliet,* ii. 228.
Bewusstsein, ii. 342.
Biedermann on Strauss, ii. 320.
Biran's Journal, i. 138-140.
Birds in bad weather, i. 278.
Bismarck, i. 306.
Blasés of the world, ii. 298.
Boileau and Fontaine contrasted, ii. 231.
Book, function of the, ii. 235.
Bossuet on charity, ii. 265.
Bourse, movements of the (the beat of the common heart), i. 266.
Brahma, ii. 83.
    his dream, i. 294.
Brahmanic aspirations, ii. 190.
Brahmanising souls, ii. 291.
Brain-decay, Amiel's, ii. 218.
Buddha, ii. 78.
    method of, ii. 330.
Buddhism, ii. 29, 52, 167.
Buddhist tendency of Amiel, i. 273.
Buisson, ii. 37.

INDEX.

CÆSARISM, the counterpoise of equality, i. 229, 230.
Cartesian dualism, ii. 122.
Catholic superstition, ii. 141.
Catholicism, i. 93.
    essence of, i. 214.
    and revolution, ii. 67.
Causeries Athéniennes, Cherbuliez, i. 176.
Cellérier on St. James, i. 53.
Chance and Providence, i. 306.
Change not improvement, i. 251.
    persistence in, ii. 89.
    rules the world, i. 215.
Changeable character, Amiel's, i. 281, 301.
Character, how to judge, ii. 317.
    temperament, and individuality, ii. 47.
    and will, Amiel's lack of, i. 180.
Charity, democratic character of, ii. 269.
Charm, ii. 113.
Châteaubriand, i. 146, 245.
    and Rousseau, i. 148.
Cherbuliez, i. 312.
    Mephistophelian novel, ii. 216.
    on chivalry, etc., i. 175, 218.
Cherry trees and lilacs, i. 3.
Childhood, Amiel's second, i. 219.
    blessings of, i. 296.
    first conversations of, i. 53.
    revived impressions of, ii. 165.
Children, i. 152.
Chivalry, Cherbuliez on, i. 175.
Christendom and Ascension Day, ii. 270.
Christian nations, aspiration of, ii. 526.
    preaching, confusions of, ii. 161.
Christianity a vast ocean, ii. 18.
    different aspects of, ii. 19.
    essence of, i. 82.

INDEX. 369

Christianity from a human point of view, ii. 14.
    historical aspects of, ii. 120.
    liberal, ii. 34.
    of dignity instead of humility, i. 174.
    and reconciliation, ii. 272.
    v. religion, i. 271.
    task of, i, 6, 8, 72, 73.
    true, i. 214.
Church and State, proper aims of, ii. 267.
    separation, rejected by the Genevese people, ii. 297.
Churches (the) and Jesus, ii. 3.
Churchyard, reflections in a, ii. 170.
Cid and *Rodogune*, artificiality of, i. 196.
Circumstances, force of, ii. 197.
    influence of, i. 232.
Civilisation, corrupting tendency of, ii. 287.
    confounded with the inner life, i. 92.
    in the light of religion, ii. 55.
Claparède, Edouard, i. 292.
Classification of men, twofold, ii. 322.
Cleanthus, ii. 31.
Cleons, modern, i. 214.
Clever folk defined, ii. 246.
Cleverness, negative character of, i. 300.
Cohabitation of individuals, man's chief problem, ii. 262.
Cohesion essential to society, i. 277.
Comic poets, *rôle* of the, ii. 215.
Common sense, i. 76.
    v. the ideal, i. 126.
    rebellion against, ii. 168.
    worship, i. 44.
Commune of Paris, ii. 105.
Compliance, good-humoured, ii. 154.
Composition, Amiel's laborious, ii. 191.
    the process of, ii. 244.
Compound character of Amiel, ii. 42.

Condorcet's theory, i. 92.
Conflict, man's perpetual, ii. 225.
Conscience, ii. 134.
    abdication of the, ii. 69.
    appeal of, i. 17, 21.
    v. cleverness, ii. 216.
    corruption of the, i. 240.
    and faith, i. 107, 108.
    and history, i. 36.
    individualised by, i. 254.
    v. reality, ii. 59.
    v. taste, ii. 269.
    the voice of God, ii. 266.
Consciousness compared to a book, ii. 165.
'Consideration,' definition of, ii. 186.
    unsought by Amiel, ii. 186.
Constant, Benjamin, ii. 185.
Contemplation, Amiel's *milieu*, i. 303.
    contrasted with action, i. 303.
    passionate temperament incapable of, i. 291.
Contentment, ii. 311.
    apostolic, ii. 7.
    and submission, ii. 177.
Contradictory aspirations, ii. 213.
Contraries, marriage of, ii. 196.
Coppée François, ii. 195.
Coquerel, ii. 37.
Corinne, I, 141.
Corneille's heroes, *rôles* not men, i. 198.
Courage, Amiel's want of, ii. 145.
Creation, the act of, ii. 194.
Credulity, freedom from, i. 276.
Creed, Amiel's want of a, ii. 157.
Critic, the, i. 76.
    the conscientious, i. 152.
    the true, ii. 40, 51, 245, 248, 255.

INDEX. 371

Critical faculty, abuse of the, i. 114.
    lucidity, ii. 125.
Criticism a gift, ii. 248.
    indifferent, i. 193.
Cross, apotheosis of the, ii. 63, 65.
    (one's) made heavier by repulsion, i. 11.
Crowd (the) and the individual, i. 254.
    instinct and passion of the, ii. 163.
Crowd worship, i. 227.
Crucifixion, the, ii. 63.
Culture, modern, ii. 255.
Cynic, egotism of the, ii. 87.

Dante, i. 81.
    in hell, i. 243.
Darwinism, ii. 237.
    counterpoised by equality, ii. 267.
    inconsistencies of, ii. 213.
Dead and living, the, ii. 171.
    want of respect for the, i. 177.
Death, i. 102.
    Amiel's anticipation of, ii. 335-342.
    anticipation of, ii. 249-253.
    certainty of, i. 168.
    death of, ii. 63.
    speculations respecting, ii. 166.
De Candolle, ii. 5.
Democracy unfavourable to high art, i. 292.
    evil results of, ii. 5.
    fickleness of, ii. 103.
    fiction of, i. 231; ii. 104.
    results of, ii. 294.
    weakness of, ii. 84.
Democratic era, i. 29, 227-232.
Demos, stupidity of, ii. 103.
Dependence and liberty, i. 267.

Depersonalisation, Amiel's, ii. 304.
Descartes on fame, ii. 211.
Desert, the traveller of the, ii. 282.
Desolation and daylight, ii. 138.
Despair, resignation of, ii. 178.
Despotic government and intellectual anarchy, i. 277.
Despotism, i, 267.
    and materialism, i. 60.
    of Russia, i. 122.
Detritus of past eras, ii. 147.
Diderot, i. 311.
'Die unto sin,' i. 158.
Discontentment, i. 151.
Discouragement, Amiel's sin, i. 181.
Discrimen ingeniorum, i. 84.
Disraeli's *Lothair*, ii. 67.
Distilled history, ii. 205.
Divine, glimpses of the, i. 107.
    and human union, ii. 18.
    will, acceptation of the, ii. 220.
Divinity, multiplication of, ii. 308.
Doctor, the model, ii. 153.
Doctors, causes of their mistakes, ii. 152.
Dollar, the almighty, ii. 62.
Double, a characteristic of perfection, i. 224.
Double-faced life, i. 22.
Doubt, i. 158.
    and atheism, ii. 17.
    and obedience, i. 277.
Doudan's *Lettres et Mélanges*, ii. 207-211.
Dragonfly symbol, ii. 283.
Dream-aspect of life, i. 220.
Dreaming, i. 153.
Dreamland and action, ii. 291.
Dreams, ii. 9.
    helpfulness of, i. 178.

INDEX. 373

Duped, fear of being, ii. 16.
Dupes, mental, ii. 198.
Dutchman, twofold aspect of the, ii. 150.
Duty, i. 5, 20, 134, 156; ii. 86, 275.
    double power of, i. 8.
    ignored by both equality and Darwinism, ii. 267.
    negative, ii. 92.
    and pleasure, ii. 190.
    power of the idea of, i. 190.
    the human pole-star, i. 296.
    the sign of nobility, i. 269.
    the *viaticum* of life, ii. 26.
    and trial, i, 260.
    v. the individual, ii. 295.
Dying, words and looks of the, ii. 14, 15.

East and West contrasted, i. 251.
Ecclesiastical struggles, worthlessness of, i. 270, 271.
Education and development, ii. 90.
Effect, the misfortune of Victor Hugo, i. 202.
Effort of modern morality, ii. 91.
Ego, Claparède's view of the, i. 292, 293.
Egotism, i. 30, 36.
Eighteenth century criticism, ii. 160.
Emerson's ideal, i, 37, 46.
English children, ii. 126.
    homes, attractiveness of, ii. 126.
Englishmen, twofold character of, i. 264.
Enthusiasm, cultivation of, i. 212.
    two forms of, ii. 140.
Enthusiastic women, ii. 140.
Epicureanism, intellectual, i. 190.
Epicurism, ii. 53.
Epicurus, ii. 276.
Epigrammatic productions, ii. 318.
Equality a bad principle, i. 215, 229.
    doctrines ii. 104.

Equality of functions, American, ii. 61.
    results of, i. 28–30; ii. 5, 263.
    the counterpoise of Darwinism, ii. 267.
Equilibrium of forces, i. 120.
'Errare, humanum est,' ii. 290.
Error, emancipation from, ii. 125.
Errors, moral and psychological, ii. 161.
E sempre bene, ii. 310.
Esoteric beauty, ii. 113.
Esprit defined, ii. 257.
Essay, function of the, ii. 235.
Etrangères, Amiel's, ii. 199.
Evil, problem of, ii. 29.
    transfiguration of, i. 97.
    ignored by Pelletan, i. 92.
        by V. Hugo, i. 200.
Examination *v.* affirmation, ii. 123.
Example, a good, ii. 105.
    importance of, i. 54.
Existence, submission to the laws of, ii. 154.
Experience, individual and collective, ii. 159.
Extempore preachers, ii. 138.
Extremes, reconciliation of, ii. 129.

FAIR-MINDEDNESS, rarity of, ii. 221.
Fairy tales, their truth, i. 46.
Fais ce que dois, advienne que pourra, ii. 266.
Faith defined, ii. 118.
    has no proofs, ii. 276.
    narrow *v.* enlightened, ii. 120.
    of the present, the, ii. 212.
    and science, ii. 66.
    and truth, ii. 119.
False flag of Christendom, ii. 215.
    originality, ii. 230.
    shame, Amiel's, ii. 145.

INDEX. 375

Fame, achievement of, ii. 211.
Family life, value of, ii. 127.
Fanatics, Indian, ii. 22.
Fastidium, how to avoid, ii. 309.
Faust, i. 157.
Feeling *v.* irony, ii. 217.
    precedes will, i. 88.
    respect for, i. 48.
Feeling, suppression of, ii. 87, 97.
    the bread of angels, i. 238.
    and thought, ii. 139.
Feminine nature, infirmity of the, ii. 139.
Festinat ad eventum, ii. 346.
Feuerbach, i. 25.
Feuille Centrale de Zofingen, ii. 308.
Fiat justitia, pereat mundus, ii. 59.
Fichte, i. 36, 294.
Finite and infinite, ii. 170.
Flânerie, i. 52.
Flattery of the multitude, ii. 162.
Fog, poetry of, i. 260.
Fontaine's defects and beauties, ii. 230.
Fontanès, ii. 37.
Fools, behaviour towards, i. 103.
Force, external, ii. 214.
Forces, opposing, i. 120.
Fragmentary contemplation, ii. 255.
France, Christianity in, ii. 232.
    fundamental error of, ii. 141.
    v. Geneva, ii. 306.
    and Germany, ii. 97.
    philosophic superficiality of, i. 93.
    the centre of the world, i. 289.
Francis of Assisi, i. 274.
Frankness and self-knowledge, women deficient in, ii. 16.

INDEX.

Freethinkers, puerility of the, ii. 68.
Freethought, republic of, ii. 160.
French Academy, eloquence of the, ii. 183.
    drama, an oratorical tournament, i. 199.
    and German literature contrasted, i. 312.
    ignorance of liberty, ii. 74.
    literary method, ii. 75.
    love of æsthetics, ii. 236.
    mind, i. 186; ii. 179.
    philosophy, i. 141.
    poets, modern, ii. 243.
    symbolical authority of the, ii. 75.
    republicanism, ii. 80.
    vivacity of the, i. 199.
Friends, choice of, ii. 324.
Future state, mystery of the, i. 283; ii. 41.

GAIETY and sadness, ii. 245.
Galiani, i. 312.
Gallery, playing to the, ii. 180, 186.
Galley-slaves, modern, ii. 91.
Geneva, appeal to, ii. 297.
    characteristics of, ii. 301.
    v. France, ii. 306.
    oath of old, ii. 331.
Genevese Liberalism, i. 145.
Genghis Khan, ii. 285.
Genius and talent, i. 134.
    writers of, ii. 48.
Gentleman defined, i. 262, 265.
    the Shibboleth of England, i. 262.
German and French literature contrasted, i. 312.
    novels, ii. 97.
    society, vulgarity of, ii. 97.
    thinkers, their repugnance to public life, i. 68.
Germanic mind, tendency of the, ii. 239.

INDEX.

Germans, artistic devotion of the, ii. 239.
    the, masters of the philosophy of life, i. 119.
Germany and France, ii. 95.
Germs of good and bad in every heart, i. 226.
Gethsemane, ii. 338.
Ghost, Amiel a living, ii. 314.
Gifts considered acquisitions, i. 57.
Gioberti on the French mind, ii. 178.
Gioconda, la, ii. 196, 256.
Glory of God, ii. 220.
Glow-worm, i. 58.
God, communion with, i. 1.
    conquest of, i. 98; 115.
    harmony with, i. 286; ii. 7.
    life in, i. 214.
'God and my right,' i. 262; ii. 127.
    and Nature contrasted, i. 250.
    recognition of, ii. 69.
    submission to, i. 258; ii. 178, 334, 335, 347, 350.
    will of, ii. 173.
God's love and chastisement, ii. 272.
    omnipresence, ii. 198.
    perfection, ii. 90.
Goethe, i. 45.
    contrasted with Rousseau, i. 248.
    on fame, ii. 211.
    on self-obscurity, i. 185.
Goethe's want of soul, ii. 107.
    complex nature, ii. 108.
'Good news' of Christianity, ii. 17.
'Good society,' ii. 97.
Good, sum of, perhaps always the same, ii. 6.
    victory of, i. 241; ii. 29.
Goodness and beauty, ii. 217.
    character of, ii. 263.
    conquests of, ii. 238.

Goodness, philosophy of, ii. 168.
    the truest judge, ii. 317.
Gospel, Amiel's belief in the, ii. 157.
    blessings of the, ii. 2.
    the *Eternal*, ii. 19.
    why successful, ii. 109.
Great men, i. 249.
    and small things, ii. 197.
Greeks, changes in character of the, i. 245.
    lessons from the, i. 71.
Grief, luxury of, ii. 117.
    results of, i. 104.
Griefs which cannot be shared, ii. 334.
Growing old, ii. 310.

Habere non haberi, i. 85.
Habit, Amiel a creature of, i. 257.
Habits, life a tissue of, i. 11.
Happiness, Amiel's thirst for, ii. 137.
    contagious, ii. 53.
    cumulative, i. 97.
    defined, ii. 275.
    dreams about, i. 126.
    enjoyment of, i. 58.
    impossible, i. 258.
    pursuit of, ii. 26.
    the best, ii. 223.
    universal yearning for, ii. 272.
Harmony, ii. 57.
    blessings of, ii. 92.
    longing for, ii. 268.
Hartmann, ii. 115.
    his *Philosophy of the Unconscious*, ii. 52.
Havet's *Origines du Christianisme*, ii. 160.
Head and heart, i. 23.
Healing power of life, i. 192.

INDEX.

Health, fraility of, i. 167.
    loss of, ii. 173.
    and happiness, ii. 178.
    and the outer world, ii. 100.
Heart and intellect, ii. 247, 309.
    the mainspring of life, i. 232, 260.
    yearnings of the, i. 257.
Heartless books, ii. 318.
Heavenly moments, ii. 111.
Hegel, i. 218; ii. 160, 203.
    and Leibnitz, ii. 101.
Heim, Charles, i. 273; ii. 14.
Heine and Lamennais contrasted, ii. 39.
Heraclitus, saying of, ii. 133.
Herder's *Lichtstrahlen*, ii. 47.
Hermits and the world, ii. 246.
Heroism, i. 8.
Hindoo genius, the, ii. 189.
Hirn's three principles, ii. 37.
Historical justice, tardiness of, ii. 346.
    law of tempests, ii. 287.
History and conscience, i. 36.
    three views of, ii. 22.
    varied views of, i. 307.
Holiness *v.* liberty, i. 303.
    requisites for, ii. 151.
Hope and duty, i. 296.
    influence of, ii. 72.
    and melancholy, ii. 158.
    not forbidden, ii. 171.
Hora est benefaciendi, ii. 182.
Horace, ii. 232.
Hugo, Victor, a Gallicised Spaniard, i. 204.
    his exaggerations, ii. 226.
    his *Contemplations*, i. 189.
    his literary and Titanic power, i. 202–205.

Hugo, his *Misérables*, i. 199.
    Paris, ii. 225.
Human and Divine union, ii. 18.
    life, the three modes of (action, thought, speech), i. 216.
    personality ignored, i. 138.
    solidarity, i. 267.
Humanism and religion, i. 22–25.
    of Cherbuliez, i. 219.
Humanity, a higher standard of, i. 276.
    benefactors and masters of, ii. 54.
    candidates for, ii. 241.
    ideal of, i. 30.
    slow development of, ii. 214, 261, 326.
    toughness of, ii. 105.
Humboldt, ii. 106.
Humility precedes repentance, i. 117.
    (true) = contentment, i. 103.
Humorist, the true, i. 299.
Hyacinthe, Père, ii. 138.
Hypocrisy and deception, i. 196.

IDEAL conceptions, ii. 261.
Ideal, diminution of the, ii. 36.
    malady of the, i. 126.
    v. material, i. 228.
    v. real, i. 46, 60–62, 234.
    thirst for the, ii. 274.
Ideals, hypocritical, ii. 316.
Ideas, anarchy of, ii. 221.
    formation of, ii. 195.
Ill-health, Amiel's, ii. 177, 201.
Ill-nature, conquest of, ii. 319.
Illness, summonses of, i. 167.
Illusion, benefit of, ii. 73.
Illusions, human, i. 308; ii. 26, 289.
Illustrious men, disappearance of, i. 16.

Imagination *v.* character, i. 18.
    enfranchised, ii. 130-132.
    influence of, ii. 48.
    of Rousseau, i. 245.
Immortality, belief in, i. 295.
    consolations of, ii. 155.
    and annihilation, i. 160.
Impersonality, ii. 49.
    temptations of, ii. 259.
Indecision, i. 135.
    Amiel's, ii. 233.
Independence, Amiel's, ii. 330.
    twofold aspect of, ii. 55.
Independent thought of Geneva, ii. 306.
Indifference of cultivated classes, ii. 87.
Indignation, incapacity for, ii. 117.
Individual and society, ii. 290.
    (the) *v.* duty, ii. 295.
Individualism an absurdity, i. 310.
    epoch of, i. 266.
    and equality, i. 28.
    evils of, ii. 266.
Individuality = character and temperament, ii. 46, 47.
    rarity of, ii. 241.
Inevitable, Amiel's resignation to the, ii. 219.
    acceptance of the, ii. 289.
    the, ii. 206.
Infallibility of judgment rare, ii. 51.
Infinite, communion with the, i. 46-48.
    penetration of the, ii. 291.
    thirst for the, ii. 297.
Infinites, infinity of, ii. 89.
Influence of men of action, ii. 290.
Injustice, Amiel too sensitive to, ii. 332.
Inner life essential, i. 253.
Instinct precedes feeling, i. 88.

Institutions, capacity of, ii. 84.
Instruction and amusement, ii. 269.
Insubordination, increase of, i. 229.
Intellect, aristocratic character of the, ii. 264.
    and heart, ii. 247, 309.
    religion of, i. 23.
    and stupidity, ii. 218.
Intellectualism, ii. 134.
Interests, want of, i. 289.
International influences, ii. 97.
Internationale, the, ii. 102.
Introspection, ii. 101.
Intuition, ii. 317.
Invalid, individuality of every, ii. 152.
Invisible, the universal witness to the, ii. **271**.
Involution, ii. 220.
Irony, law of, ii. 213.
Irreparable, thought of the, i. 285; ii. 23.
Isms, the modern, ii. 302.
Italy, Christianity in, ii. 233.

JANSENISTS *v.* Jesuits, ii. 276.
Jesuits *v.* Jansenists, ii. 276.
Jesus and the churches, ii. 3.
    and Socrates, i. 23.
    comprehension of, i. 6–8.
    faith of, ii. 19.
Job's murmurings, i. 117; trials, ii. 348.
Jocelyn and *Paul et Virginie*, **tenderness and purity** of, i. 191.
John Halifax, Gentleman, i. 261.
Joubert, i. 11–14.
    Doudan's resemblance to, ii. 208.
Journal, Amiel's estimate of his, ii. 204.
    function of the private, i. 41, 42; ii. 235.
Joy expressed by tears, i. 242.
Judaism of nineteenth century, i. 6.

INDEX.

Judgment, impersonality of, i. 134.
    of character, ii. 317.
    self-interested, ii. 88.
    and understanding, ii. 110.
Justice defined, ii. 237.
    forgetfulness of, ii. 88.
    v. love, i. 200; ii. 60.
    will ultimately prevail, ii. 344, 345.

KANT'S *radicale Böse*, ii. 55.
Kindness and wariness incompatible, ii. 264.
    the principle of tact, i. 35.
Krause's religious serenity, i. 44.

Laboremus, ii. 50.
Laborious lives, ii. 85.
Labour question unsolved, i. 73.
La Bruyère, ii. 232.
La Fontaine, ii. 209.
Lamartine, ii. 51.
    his *Préludes*, ii. 181.
    his dislike of Fontaine, ii. 232.
Lamennais, i. 245.
    contrasted with Heine, ii. 39.
Laprade, Victor de, affectation of, ii. 284.
Last words and looks of the dying, ii. 14, 15.
Latent genius, i. 156.
Latin world, the, ii. 122, 240.
Laveleye's *L'Avenir Religieux*, ii. 212.
Law, eternity of, ii. 261.
Lectures, Amiel's, ii. 272.
Legal fictions and institutions, ii. 38.
Legouvé's *Nos fils et nos filles*, ii. 268.
Leibnitz, ii. 29.
    v. Hegel, ii. 101.
    and Spinoza, ii. 343.
Lessing's principle, i. 101.

Letter and spirit, i. 60.
Letters, studied, ii. 257.
Leveller, the modern, i. 214.
Levelling down, ii. 5.
Liberalism, political, ii. 35.
Liberty and religion, ii. 67.
    and revolution, ii. 81.
    diminished by democracy, i. 230.
    in God, i. 82.
    possible suppression of, ii. 70.
    the true friends of, ii. 70.
    true, ii. 326.
    v. authority, ii. 37.
    v. holiness, i. 303.
Life, aim of, i. 98.
    a calvary, i. 158.
    a dream, i. 293.
    a perpetual combat, ii. 213.
    brevity of, i. 216, 249, 256, 283; ii. 24, 78, 82, 201.
    definition of, ii. 205.
    different aspects of, ii. 25.
    drama, a monologue, i. 129.
    frailty of, ii. 283.
    matter to be spiritualised, ii. 313.
    melancholy aspect of, i. 208.
    ocean of, i. 87.
    proper treatment of, ii. 289.
Life, the Divine, ii. 61.
    the true, ii. 327.
    tenacity of, ii. 333.
    v. logic, ii. 146.
Light and beauty, i. 205, 206.
    without warmth, i. 24.
Link of humanity, the, ii. 271.
Literary ambition, Amiel's, ii. 237.
    career, Amiel's impediments to a, i. 91.
    gentlemen, ii. 183.

INDEX.

Literature and science, ii. 94, 95.
Little things, influence of, i. 305.
Logic *v.* life, ii. 146.
'Lorelei,' ii. 238.
Lotze, i. 311.
Lovable, Amiel's taste for the, ii. 310.
Love, i. 41, 156.
    a young girl's, ii. 176.
    and contemplation, i. 180.
    and knowledge, i. 24.
    and holiness, power of, ii. 35.
    eminently religious, i. 209, 284.
    tendency to postpone, ii. 15.
    v. justice, i. 200; ii. 60.
    woman's supreme authority, ii. 60.
Lucian and Augustine contrasted, ii. 217.
Luck, good, i. 306.
Luther on humanity, ii. 103.

MADNESS defined, ii. 133, 305.
Maïa, ii. 83, 131, 134.
Malignity of the world, ii. 331.
Man and woman contrasted, ii. 60, 61.
'Man,' in essence and principle, ii. 190.
    the true, i. 60.
Mannerisms, ii. 233.
Manou on Woman, ii. 33.
Many, the, and the few, i. 267.
Marcus Aurelius, aim of, ii. 213.
Martyrdom, nobility of, ii. 328.
Martyrs, ii. 22.
Masses, frivolity of the, i. 252.
    impetuosity of the, ii. 163.
    the, and demagogues, ii. 104.
Material results, ii. 327.
Materialism, i. 30, 60, 237.

Mathematical and historical intelligence, i. 84.
 v. sensuous minds, i. 120.
May, caprices of, ii. 32.
Mediocrity, era of, i. 28.
 the result of equality, ii. 5.
Meditation, joys of silent, ii. 277.
Melancholy, Amiel's tendency to, i. 279, 285; ii. 8, 77, 82, 92, 171, 172, 188, 189.
 and hope, ii. 158.
 below the surface, i. 102.
 universality of, i. 227.
Memories, painful, ii. 247.
Memory a catacomb, Amiel's, ii. 303.
 deficient, i. 115.
Men and things, Amiel's relation to, i. 187.
Mephistopheles, weakness of, ii. 87.
Mérimée's letters to Panizzi, ii. 345.
Method in religion, secondary, ii. 271.
Michelet, i. 93.
Milieu, a wholesome, ii. 223.
Millennium, the, ii. 345.
Mind and soul, ii. 199.
 and the infinite, ii. 260.
 described, ii. 308, 315.
 forms and metamorphoses of (the one subject of study), i. 2.
 not phenomenal, ii. 199.
 science of, ii. 168.
 the march of, ii. 343.
Minds, abstract and concrete, i. 83.
 well-governed, i. 292.
Minors in perpetuity, ii. 69.
Miracles, ii. 121.
Misérables, Victor Hugo's, i. 199.
Misspent time, ii. 184.
Mist and sunshine, i. 260, 261.

INDEX. 387

Misunderstandings, i. 4, 280.
Modern man, character of the, ii. 251.
'Modern spirit,' the, ii. 107.
Modesty, i. 76.
'Moi,' the central consciousness, ii, 201.
Molière, ii. 232.
    on reasoning, ii. 92.
Monad, the human, ii. 144.
Monads, conscious, ii. 206.
Mongol invasion, ii. 286.
Monod, Adolphe, i. 31.
Montaigne, ii. 232.
Montesquieu, ii. 142.
    saying of, ii. 162.
Moonlight reflections, ii. 157.
Moralists, sugar, ii. 269.
Moral law, reconciliation of faith and science by the, ii. 156.
    philosophy of Geneva, ii. 305.
    v. natural, ii. 59.
    v. physical science, ii. 168.
Morals, psychology and system of, i. 80.
Morning and evening conditions, i. 78.
Mortification, ii. 65.
Mozart and Beethoven contrasted, i. 88, 89.
'Much ado about nothing,' ii. 200.
Mulock, Miss, i. 261.
Multitude, flattery of the, ii. 161, 162.
Music, Wagner's, depersonalised, i. 136-138.
    effects of, ii. 57.
Musician, the modern, ii. 229.
Musset on De Laprade, ii. 285.
Mystery of Providence, ii. 307.
Mysticism, so-called, i. 99.

NAPOLEON, i. 306.
National competitions, ii. 6.

388   INDEX.

National, types, i. 265.
    preferences unknown to Amiel, ii. 227.
Nationalities, ancient and modern, i. 95.
    imply prejudice, i. 194.
    Quinet's studies of, i. 171.
Nationality and the State, i. 134.
Nations, destinies of (Æschylus), ii. 136.
Natural man, the, ii. 55-57.
    v. moral, ii. 58, 59.
Naturalist thinkers (φυσικοί), ii. 167.
Nature, Amiel's enjoyment of, i. 287; ii. 1, 11, 27, 75, 110, 174, 181, 182, 235, 247, 270, 280, 306, 316.
    enjoyment of, i. 5, 26, 42, 43, 50-52, 64-66, 73, 74, 100, 102, 140, 182, 183, 186, 188-190, 223, 224, 237, 238.
    continuity of, ii. 309.
    v. conventions, ii. 239.
    and God contrasted, i. 250.
    the kindly voice of, ii. 316.
    the law of, ii. 58.
    without man, i. 137.
    worship of, ii. 107.
Naville, Ernest, i. 142.
    on *The Eternal Life*, i. 161-165.
Neckar, the river, i. 183.
Necker de Saussure, Madame, ii. 293, 305.
Negative minds, danger of, i. 194.
Neo-Hegelians, i. 22.
New birth, the, i. 159.
Nicole and Pascal, ii. 48.
Nihilism, Russian, ii. 102.
Nirvana, ii. 279.
Nobility, true, i. 261.
    and vulgarity, i. 227.
Normal, the, to be chosen, ii. 159.
North, poetry of the, i. 74.

INDEX.

Nostalgia of happiness, i. 153.
Nothing is lost, i. 217.
Nothingness, ii. 73.
    man's, ii. 78, 82.
    realisation of, i. 128.

OBEDIENCE the chief mark of religion, ii. 176.
Obermann, ii. 52.
Oblivion man's portion, ii. 282.
Obscure self, the, i. 130.
Obstinacy, i. 165.
Odyssey, the divine, i. 61.
Old age, ii. 247.
    our views clearest in, ii. 277.
Old, the art of growing, ii. 177.
Olivier's *Chansons du Soir*, ii. 92.
Opinion, i. 39.
    and belief, ii. 322.
    too much despised by Amiel, ii. 332.
Optimism and pessimism, ii. 29, 155.
Orators, ii. 140.
Order, i. 166.
    attempts at, ii. 262.
    harmony with universal, ii. 224.
    and law, ii. 80.
    the only positive good, ii. 275.
Oriental element, benefit of the, i. 252.
    happiness, ii. 278.
Originality, modern lack of, ii. 241.
    ridicule the result of, ii. 164.
Origins all secret, ii. 194.
Outside and inside, i. 25, 60, 101; ii. 180.
Overrating, result of, ii. 117.
Oxygen and azote, human, ii. 218.

PAIN, i. 111, 118.
    and comfort, i. 32.

Pantheism, i. 261.
    of Krause, ii. 122.
Pantheistic disinterestedness, ii. 190.
Paradise, echoes of, ii. 57.
Paradox, i. 246.
Paris, the French townsman's axis, i. 290.
Pascal, ii. 217.
    and Nicole, ii. 48.
    on development, i. 229.
Passion and reason, ii. 84.
Passionless man, the, i. 135.
Passions, life of the, i. 109.
    conquest of the, i. 184.
Past, poetry of the, i. 255.
    Reminiscences of the, i. 235–237.
    the interpreter of the present, ii. 143.
    woman, the priestess of the, ii. 135.
Pathos and beauty, i. 153.
Patience, the test of virtue, i. 259.
Peace, ii. 225.
    true, i. 285.
    twofold aspect of, ii. 152.
Pedantic books, i. 311.
Pelletan's *Profession de foi*, i. 92.
Pensée writers, i. 16.
Penseroso, Amiel's, ii. 10.
People, emotion of the, ii. 298.
Perfection as an end, i. 272.
    attainment of, ii. 203.
    of God, ii. 90.
    search for, i. 114.
Persiflage, ii. 318.
Pessimism, ii. 115.
    and optimism, ii. 29, 155.
    Amiel's tendency to, i. 285.
    helplessness of, ii. 49.

INDEX.

Petöfi's poems, ii. 285.
Pharisaical people, ii. 299.
Philistinism, increase of, ii. 4, 5.
Philosopher, ambition of the, ii. 268.
Philosophy defined, ii. 124.
    and religion, ii. 66.
Physical *v.* moral science, ii. 168.
Piety defined, ii. 265.
    and religion contrasted, i. 227.
Pity, exhibition of, ii. 243.
    and contempt, i. 309.
Plaid, the *chivalrous*, i. 235.
Plato *v.* Saint Paul, ii. 101.
Plato's *Dialogues*, i. 89.
Playthings of the world, i. 268.
Pleasure and duty, ii. 190.
Plotinus and Proclus, ii. 279.
Plutolatry, ii. 62.
Poet and philosophy contrasted, i. 82.
Poetry flayed by science, ii. 95.
    of childhood and mature age, i. 175.
    the expression of a soul, ii. 254.
Points, straining after, ii. 193.
Political liberty of England, i. 277.
    windbags, ii. 266.
Politician, aim of the honest, ii. 162.
Popular harangues, ii. 140.
Portraits and wax figures contrasted, ii. 253.
Poverty a *crime* in England, i. 263.
Practical life, Amiel unsuited for, ii. 43.
Prayer, blessings of, ii. 265.
Prejudice essential to nationalities, i. 194.
    better than doubt, i. 195.
Prestige, French worship of, ii. 95.
Pride and discouragement, i. 11.
    moral and religious, ii. 317.

Pride, two conditions of, i. 99.
Priesthood, domination of the, ii. 69.
Prince Vitale, Cherbuliez, i. 217.
Principiis obsta, ii. 56.
Privilege only temporary, ii. 323.
Professor, obligations of a, ii. 187.
Professorial lectures, ii. 272-274.
Progress, absolute and relative, ii. 159.
    results of, ii. 325.
    Victor Hugo's religion of, i. 200, 201.
Protestant *v*. Catholic countries, ii. 67.
Protestantism defined, i. 270.
    advance guard of, ii. 38.
    historical, ii. 37.
Protestants, liberal, ii. 37-39.
Proudhon, i. 245.
    his axiom, ii. 116.
Providence, ii. 172.
Province defined, ii. 302.
Psychological study, Amiel's aptitude for, ii. 43.
Psychologist, the, ii. 99.
Psychology, applied, ii. 200, 203.
Punctum saliens, ii. 315.
Punishment softened by faith, i. 117.

QUANTITATIVE and qualitative, i. 92, 93.
Quinet, i. 93.
Quintilian, saying of, ii. 140.

RABELAIS, ii. 232.
Racine, i. 197, 202.
Radical jugglery, ii. 162.
Rain, the country in, ii. 112.
Rationalism, i. 174.
Ready-made ideas, i. 101.
Real and ideal, i. 234; ii. 274.

INDEX. 393

Realism in painting, ii. 253.
    suppression of, ii. 98.
Reality and appearance, ii. 180.
    character with no sense of, i. 289.
Reason and passion, ii. 84.
Reconciliation and Christianity, ii. 272.
Redeemed, motive power of the, ii. 18.
Regenerate man, ii. 57.
Reinvolution, psychological, ii. 315.
Religion and liberty, ii. 67.
    and philosophy, ii. 32, 38, 66.
    and piety contrasted, i. 227.
    indestructible, i. 278.
    life in God, ii. 31.
    phases of, ii. 265.
    refreshing power of, i. 252.
    and Utilitarianism, ii. 212.
    without mysticism, i. 178.
Religions, multitude of, i. 308.
    effect of political, ii. 233.
Religious man, the (an intermediary), ii. 224.
    views, Amiel's, ii. 336.
Reminiscences, vague, i. 207.
Renaissance, the, Fontaine's horizon, ii. 232.
Renan, i. 312.
    his object, style, ii. 236.
Renan's *Les Evangiles*, ii. 236.
    Vie de Jesus, ii. 108.
    St. Paul, ii. 40.
René and *Atala*, Châteaubriand's, i. 146-151.
Renunciation, benefit of, ii. 328.
Repentance and sanctification too exclusively preached, i. 178.
    simple, ii. 64.
Republic, the normal, ii. 303.
Repugnance, Amiel's twofold, ii. 299.

Resignation, manly, i. 45.
Responsibility, i. 20.
    dread of, i. 67.
Restlessness, Amiel's, i. 123-126.
Reveries, i. 48-52.
Réville, ii. 37.
Revolt instinctive, ii. 55.
Revolution and Catholicism, ii. 67.
    v. liberty, ii. 81.
Ridicule, fear of, ii. 164.
Right apart from duty, a compass with one leg, ii. 266.
Rights, abstract, ii. 266.
River, a beautiful life compared to a, ii. 311.
Roads, high and cross, ii. 158, 159.
Rôle, our twofold, ii. 340.
Romance peoples, the, i, 119.
Rosenkrantz's *History of Poetry*, i. 118.
    on Hegel's logic, i. 186.
Rousseau and Châteaubriand, i. 146-151.
    an ancestor in all things, i. 247.
    his letter to Archbishop Beaumont, i. 244.
    his regard for style, ii. 236.
    on savage life, ii. 196,
Ruge's *Die Academie*, i. 22, 25.
Russian national character, i. 121.

SACERDOTAL dogmatism, i. 174.
Sadness and gaiety, ii. 245.
St. Evremond, ii. 232.
    James's Epistle, i. 52.
    John's Gospel, i. 6.
    Martin's summer, i. 73.
    Paul and St. John, i. 31.
    Paul and Plato, ii. 101.
    Simon and Bayle, ii. 48.
Sainte-Beuve, i. 312; ii. 50, 185, 208.

INDEX. 395

Saintly alchemy, ii. 17.
Sanctification implies martyrdom, i. 156.
Sarcasm, repulsiveness of, ii. 319.
Satan, possible conversion of, i. 241.
    the father of lies, i. 240.
    his territory, i. 174.
Satiety, preservative against, ii. 309.
Satirist, the, i. 299.
Savoir vivre, ii. 98.
Scepticism and intellectual independence, i. 276.
Schelling, i. 293.
Schellingian speculation, ii. 13.
Scherer, i. 44, 273, 312; ii. 57, 80.
Scheveningen, ii. 146.
Schiller on superiority and perfection, i. 175.
Schleiermacher, i. 174; ii. 106.
    his *Monologues*, i. 36.
Scholasticism, ii. 123.
Schopenhauer, ii. 29, 45, 46, 47, 53.
    his pessimism, ii. 155.
Science and faith, ii. 66, 117, 156.
    and literature, ii. 94.
    and religion. ii. 167.
    and wisdom, i. 232.
    march of, ii. 221.
    weakness of, i. 47.
Sea, the, ii. 147.
    conversation of the, i. 291.
Secrétan's philosophy, ii. 12.
Secrets, hidden, i. 103.
Seed-sowing, i. 53.
Self-abandonment, i. 180.
    -annihilation of, ii. 224.
    -approval and self-contempt, i. 99.
    -conquest, i. 155.
    -contempt, excessive, ii. 91.

Self-abandonment, conversation with, ii. 234.
— -criticism, i. 184.
— -distrust, Amiel's, i. 110, 114, 173, 272.
— -education, hatred of, ii. 222.
— -glorification, i. 143.
— -government misunderstood, ii. 302.
— -ignorance, cause of, i. 279.
— -interest *v.* truth, ii. 20, 21.
— -love, i. 103, 111.
— -preservation a duty, ii. 250.
— -renewal, ii. 106.
— -renunciation, i. 4, 112, 128; ii. 9.
— -rule the essence of gentlemanliness, i. 263.
— -sacrifice, ii. 86, 173.
Selfishness and individual rights, ii. 266.
Seneca, ii. 37.
Sensation, nature of, i. 292.
Sensorium commune of nature, ii. 308.
Separation of modern society, ii. 87.
Separatism, ii. 302.
Septimius Severus, motto of, ii. 50.
Sex, the virtue of, ii. 61.
Shadow and substance, ii. 178.
Shakespeare, i. 197.
Siefert's Louise, *Les Stoïques*, ii. 129.
Silence and repose, i. 291.
— effect of, i. 45.
— of nature, ii. 312.
Sin, definition of, ii. 56.
— frivolous idea of, ii. 135.
— pardon of, ii. 18.
— the cardinal question, i. 23.
Singing, rustic, i. 143.
Sismondi, i. 144.
Sivaism, ii. 115.
Slavery, i. 73.

Sleep, i. 85.
Soap-bubble symbol, ii. 283.
Social charity and harsh justice, i. 201.
Socialism, international, ii. 102.
Society, ii. 97.
    and the individual, ii. 224.
Socii Dei sumus (Seneca), ii. 31.
Socrates and Jesus, i. 23.
Solitariness of life, i. 128.
Solitary life, Amiel's, i. 152.
Solitude, human, ii. 335.
Soul, abyss of the, ii. 88.
    and mind, ii. 199.
Soul, dominical state of the, ii. 278.
    ghosts of the, i. 208.
    history of a, ii. 205.
    three powers of the (counsel, judgment, and action), i. 113.
Soul's wants ignored by the Church, i. 177.
Southern Europe, statesmen of, ii. 70.
    theatre, masks of the, i. 197.
Sparrenhorn, ascent of the, ii. 76.
Speech, mystery of, i. 53.
Spinoza, i. 109.
    and Leibnitz, ii. 343.
Spirit, voice of the Holy, ii. 224.
Spiritual existence, ii. 260.
Spontaneity, the question of, ii. 101.
Staël, Madame de, ii. 185, 191.
    on nationalities, ii. 228.
    her *L'Allemagne*, ii. 305.
Stahl's *Les histoires de mon Parrain*, ii. 268.
State, the model, ii. 96.
    true foundations of a, ii. 86.
Statistical progress and moral decline, i. 29.
Stendhal, ii. 94.

Stoicism, ii. 167.
    and suicide, i. 295.
Stoics, the, i. 109.
Strauss, ii. 320.
Struggle of opposing forces, ii. 268.
Stupidity and intellect, ii. 218.
Style, Renan's main object, ii. 236.
Sub-Alpine history, i. 95.
Subjectivity and objectivity, i. 33, 72, 139, 187.
    of experience, i. 292.
Submission, ii. 285, 290.
    not defeat, i. 269.
Subtleties not helpful, ii. 289.
Subtlety and taste, ii. 209.
Success, i. 306.
Suffering, way of, ii. 91.
    produces depth, ii. 53.
    triumph of, ii. 63.
    result of, ii. 173.
    universality of, ii. 272.
Sunshine and mist contrasted, i. 260, 261.
Supernatural, the, i. 271; ii. 121.
Swiss critics, i. 142.
    ungracefulness of the, ii. 4.
Sybarites, modern, ii. 269.
Symbols, decay of, ii. 321.
Sympathy, i. 25.
    and criticism, ii. 256.
    moral, ii. 113.
    of Amiel, i. 274.
    with our fellows, i. 309-311.
Symphonic pictures, Berlioz's, ii. 229.
Synonyms, passion for, ii. 233.
Systems defined, i. 249.

TACITUS *v.* the chroniclers, ii. 237.
Tact, measure, and occasion, ii. 246.

INDEX.

Taine on the *Ancien Régime*, ii. 193.
Taine's *English Literature*, ii. 94.
Talent and genius, i. 134.
    triumphs of, i. 246.
Tamerlane, ii. 287.
Taste ignored in German æsthetics, ii. 97.
    v. conscience, ii. 269.
Teaching, successful, ii. 90.
    the art of, i. 226.
Tears and joy, ii. 64.
    origin of, i. 241.
Temperament, character, and individuality, ii. 47.
Temptation our natural state, ii. 55.
Temptations, etc., never ending, i. 259.
Tenderness towards our neighbours, ii. 243.
Thales, hylozoism of, ii. 194.
Theism, Christian, i. 270.
Theory and practice, i. 33, 130.
Thought and feeling, ii. 139.
    a kind of opium, i. 135.
Time, flight of, i. 192; ii. 24.
Timidity, Amiel's, ii. 44, 192.
    and pride, Amiel's, i. 180.
Tocqueville, i. 27, 28.
    on obedience, i. 277.
'To every man his turn,' ii. 310.
Too late, i. 237.
Töpffer, i. 52.
    his tourist class, i. 289.
Totality, Amiel's tendency to, ii. 43.
Tradition *v.* force, i. 231.
Trial and duty, i. 260.
Trials, i. 117.
True love defined, ii. 325.
Truth and error, i. 75.
    and faith, ii. 118–120.

INDEX.

Truth, common fear of, ii. 21.
    identification with, i. 99.
    rarely sought for, ii. 222.
    the test of religion, ii. 212.
Truthfulness, i. 103.
Truths, philosophic, ii. 195.
Turin, i. 94.
Twentieth century, newspaper of the, ii. 344.

UGLINESS and beauty, ii. 113, 114.
    disappearance of, i. 232.
Unconscious nature of life, i. 179, 193.
Understanding and judgment, ii. 110.
    the art of, i. 265.
    things, requisites for, ii. 256.
Unexpected, the, i. 116.
Unfinished, the, i. 249.
Unions, a mystery in all, ii. 217.
Unity of action, Amiel's want of, ii. 258.
    of everything, i. 108.
Universal suffrage, ii. 163.
Universe, different relations of the, i. 81.
Unknown, domain of the, ii. 276.
Unselfishness implies love, i. 309.
Usefulness, Amiel's doubts as to his, ii. 188, 189.
Utilitarian materialism, i. 30.

VACHEROT'S *La Religion*, ii. 31.
Vae victis, ii. 281.
Vanity, the last sign of, ii. 252.
Vesta and Beelzebub, i. 22.
Via dolorosa, i. 158.
Vinet, i. 69.
    his praise of weak things, ii. 264.
Virtue a *sine qua non*, ii. 85.
Visionaries, good and bad, i. 80.

Voltaire, i. 309; ii. 232.
Voltairianism, ii. 160.
Vulgarisation, causes of modern, ii. 241.
Vulgarity and nobility, i. 227.

WAGNER, i. 136.
Want, sense of, i. 125.
War, ii. 213, 214.
War rumours, lessons of, ii. 287.
Wariness and kindness incompatible, ii. 264.
Wasted life, i. 237.
Watchwords of the people, ii. 298.
'We' always right, ii. 164.
Weak, charity towards the, ii. 264.
Weather, caprices of the, i. 215.
Weber, Dr. George, i. 183.
Weltgeist, the, ii. 345.
Weltmüde, the, i. 285.
West and East contrasted, i. 251-253.
Whole, sense of the, i. 187.
Whole-natured men, disappearance of, ii. 91.
'Whom the gods love die young,' i. 259.
Wickedness, fascination of, i. 239.
Will, England the country of, i. 263.
    feebleness of the, i. 107.
    preceded by feeling and instinct, i. 88.
    the, i. 139.
Winter in Switzerland, ii. 280, 281.
Wisdom, i. 213.
    the heritage of the few, ii. 84.
Wisdom's two halves, ii. 132.
Wit, Doudan's, ii. 207.
Woman a '*monstre incompréhensible*,' ii. 16.
    and man contrasted, ii. 60-62.
Woman's faithful heart, i. 210.
    family influence, ii. 135.

Women, austere, ii. 325.
    emancipation of, ii. 34.
    Manou's views of, ii. 33.
    never orators, ii. 138-141.
Women's love, i. 304.
Words, careless use of, ii. 240.
Work the flavour of life, ii. 348.
World, meanness of the, ii. 282.
Worship, humanity needs a, ii. 2.
Worth, i. 165.
    individual, i. 271.
Writing, the art of, ii. 192.

YOUNG, secret of remaining, i. 212.
Youth and manhood, i. 50.
    renewal of, ii. 27.
    revival of, ii. 106.
Youthful impressions, i. 100.
    presumption, ii. 159.

ZENO, i. 37; ii. 276.

THE USE OF LIFE

BY

The Right Hon. Sir JOHN LUBBOCK, Bart.,
M.P., F.R.S., D.C.L., LL.D.

Cloth, gilt top. 12mo. $1.25.

CONTENTS.

CHAPTER I.
The Great Question.

CHAPTER II.
Tact.

CHAPTER III.
On Money Matters.

CHAPTER IV.
Recreation.

CHAPTER V.
Health.

CHAPTER VI.
National Education.

CHAPTER VII.
Self-education.

CHAPTER VIII.
On Libraries.

CHAPTER IX.
On Reading.

CHAPTER X.
Patriotism.

CHAPTER XI.
Citizenship.

CHAPTER XII.
Social Life.

CHAPTER XIII.
Industry.

CHAPTER XIV.
Faith.

CHAPTER XV.
Hope.

CHAPTER XVI.
Charity.

CHAPTER XVII.
Character.

CHAPTER XVIII.
On Peace and Happiness.

CHAPTER XIX. Religion.

THE MACMILLAN COMPANY,

66 FIFTH AVENUE,   NEW YORK.

BY THE SAME AUTHOR.

THE BEAUTIES OF NATURE

AND

THE WONDERS OF THE WORLD WE LIVE IN.

Cloth, gilt top. 12mo. $1.50.

"We know of none other better fitted to present 'the beauties of nature and the wonders of the world we live in,' to the popular understanding and appreciation than Sir John Lubbock, who is at once a master of his chosen topic and of a diction unsurpassed for clearness and simplicity of statement. It is a volume which the reading public will recognize and hail immediately as among the most delightfully instructive of the year's production in books. There is matter in it for the young and mature mind.... One cannot rise from the perusal of this volume, without a consciousness of a mind invigorated and permanently enriched by an acquaintance with it." — *Oswego Daily Times.*

"It is a charming book.... Few writers succeed in making natural history, and indeed scientific subjects, more than interesting. In the hands of most authors they are intolerably dull to the general reader and especially to children. Sir John Lubbock makes his theme as entrancing as a novel.... The book is magnificently illustrated, and discusses the wonders of the animal, mineral, and vegetable kingdoms, the marvels of earth, sea, and the vaulted heavens. In the compass of its pages an immense amount of knowledge which all should know is given in a manner that will compel the child who commences it to pursue it to the end. It is a work which cannot be too highly recommended to parents who have at heart the proper education of their children." — *The Arena.*

THE MACMILLAN COMPANY,

66 FIFTH AVENUE, NEW YORK.

BY THE SAME AUTHOR.

ON BRITISH WILD FLOWERS.

With Illustrations. Cloth. 12mo. $1.25.

"All lovers of Nature must feel grateful to Sir John Lubbock for his learned and suggestive little book, which cannot fail to draw attention to a field of study so new and fascinating." — *Pall Mall Gazette.*

FLOWERS, FRUITS, AND LEAVES.

With Illustrations. Cloth. 12mo. $1.25.

SCIENTIFIC LECTURES.

With Illustrations. Cloth. 8vo. $2.50.

CONTENTS: On Flowers and Insects. — On Plants and Insects. — On the Habits of Ants. — Introduction to the Study of Prehistoric Archæology, etc.

"We can heartily commend this volume, as a whole, to every one who wishes to obtain a condensed account of its subjects, set forth in the most simple, easy, and lively manner." — *Athenæum.*

THE ORIGIN AND METAMOR= PHOSES OF INSECTS.

With Illustrations. Cloth. 12mo. $1.00.

POLITICAL AND EDUCATIONAL ADDRESSES.

Cloth. 8vo. $2.50.

"Will repay the careful attention of readers who desire to be acquainted with the best thoughts of a practical and sagacious mind on the most important topics of public and national interest." — *Daily News.*

FIFTY YEARS OF SCIENCE.

Cloth. 16mo. 75 cents.

THE MACMILLAN COMPANY,

66 FIFTH AVENUE,   NEW YORK.